HERITAGE OF
THE WEST

HERITAGE OF
THE WEST

CHARLES PHILLIPS

CRESCENT BOOKS
NEW YORK

Text
Charles Phillips

Captions
Candace Floyd

Research
Leora Kahn
Meredith Greenfield

Photography
Bettman Archives
State Historical Society
of Iowa
National Archives,
Washington, D.C.
Library of Congress

Design
Dick Richardson

Editorial
David Gibbon
Pauline Graham

Commissioning
Andrew Preston
Laura Potts

Production
Ruth Arthur
David Proffit
Sally Connolly
Andrew Whitelaw

Director of Production
Gerald Hughes

CLB 2325
© 1992 Colour Library
Books Ltd, Godalming,
Surrey, England.
All rights reserved.
This 1992 edition
published by Crescent
Books, distributed by
Outlet Book Company,
Inc., a Random House
Company, 225 Park
Avenue South, New York,
New York 10003.
Printed and bound in Italy.
ISBN 0 517 68907 3
8 7 6 5 4 3 2 1

CONTENTS

INTRODUCTION
Page 10

1 PIONEERS
Page 14

2 THE RIVER
Page 34

3 FUR
Page 58

4 LAND
Page 72

5 GOLD
Page 90

6 INDIANS
Page 106

7 CATTLE
Page 140

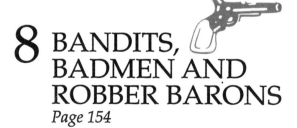

8 BANDITS, BADMEN AND ROBBER BARONS
Page 154

9 WATER
Page 174

10 MYTH
Page 190

INTRODUCTION

From at least the time of the French and Indian War, the American West haunted the imagination of European immigrants to the North American continent. They dreamed of freedom, of cheap land and quick fortunes, of escape and renewal, and they moved relentlessly, generation after generation, from the foothills of the Appalachians to the shores of the Pacific, transforming everything they touched and in turn being transformed.

The story of that centuries-long migration has often been told, usually as a series of colorful, violent, and romantic adventures that came more or less to an end with the "closing" of the frontier in the 1890s. But the Frontier was mostly an intellectual construct: an imaginary line on a map beyond which the topography was vague and enticing, turned into a metaphor for organizing Western history. Unfortunately, some also used it as the foundation for a racist ideology celebrating base greed as a religious calling and social violence as moral regeneration.

Since the night Frederick Jackson Turner first advanced his "frontier thesis" to a group of bored academics in *fin de siecle* Chicago, writing about the West has itself been a rich vein for exploration by American scholars. Long before Turner, a legion of romanticists – Western publicists, dime-novelists, and newspapermen – had prospected in Western history the way '49ers had scratched at the placer fields of California, looking for nuggets, for tales of desperation and of derring-do. But with the coming of what the Frankfurt School called the "culture industry" to the West, the motherlode was discovered. By mining its history, scholars believed they were striking the core of the American character.

Turner's great insight came from his reading of the 1890 census, which concluded that a "frontier line" could no longer merely be defined demographically, so the frontier was more than a figment of his imagination. As a metaphor for the migration of Anglo-Europeans across the American subcontinent, the frontier proved a very powerful creation indeed, one that dominated western history and historiography for more than half a century. There were regionalists, Prescott Webb comes to mind, who insisted on seeing the West as a geographical area first, and here and there a historian interested in Native Americans might point out that the Indians tended to see the migration not as the "opening" of "virgin" land, but as an occupation. For the most part, however, the important works of Western history had as their ideological and intellectual underpinning Turner's Frontier Thesis.

Recently Turner's thesis has come under attack by a number of historians, including Patricia Limerick, whose work seeks to define the West strictly as a region (a semi-arid land – to use Webb's phrase – "with the heart of a desert"), to include in that history the groups (Native Americans, Hispanics, Blacks, and women) traditionally ignored, and to explore certain constants (the belief in absolute innocence, the profit motive as a passion, the quick turn to violence, racial scapegoating, environmental brutality) in the history of the Western region.

As a result, the West has become an ideological battleground, and Western history is currently a "hot topic" for the culture industry. And the struggle is more than academic. For, unlike any other region of the United States, the American West continues to matter. New England Puritans and Southern Planters had their day, of course, but they no longer provide the image Americans see when they look into their

American Frontier Life, an 1852 painting by A.F. Tait. White settlement extended as far as Kentucky in the 1770s, but the frontier line was mutable as colonial troops laid claim to an area, then retreated to more established forts, and Indian tribes returned to their territory.

mirror of cultural myths. The Westerner does. Strong and silent, essentially innocent, slow to anger but decisive in battle, the mythological Westerner valued freedom above stability, believed in himself instead of institutions, and saw the West as a place to escape to and grow rich in, often overnight. He inhabited the Old West, now vanished, where rugged individuals lived by a strict moral code and a quick gun. That code – and a belief in the gun – is his legacy to modern Americans.

As an idea, then, the American West continues to attract the adventuresome and the desperate; continues to rule the American imagination. This is the story of that idea, and of those who were its emblem, the Daniel Boones and Kit Carsons, the Wyatt Earps and John Wesley Hardins, the Crazy Horses and Geronimos. But it is also the story of the reality behind that idea, of the soldiers and merchants and farm wives and sodbusters and hidalgos and peasants and mineworkers and real estate promoters who settled a continent staking their claim to the future.

As a region, the American West also continues to flourish, with its expansive politics, its entrepreneurial verve, its attempts to remake nature. This, then, is also the story of that region, of its native inhabitants and those who stole their lands, of its industries and their environmental degradations, of its desperate dependence on natural resources – water as well as gold – and their exploitation and depletion.

In short, what follows is a popular history of the American West, and it pretends to be nothing more. That does not mean, however, that it is simply a collection of colorful anecdotes, punctuated here and there by violence, and rounded off with character sketches of a few famous western eccentrics.

To meet the challenge of telling the history of the American West in a brief compass, I have opted for an organization that overlaps geographical areas and chronological periods. Chapter One, for example, begins with the pioneers, led by men like Daniel Boone, crossing the Allegheny Mountains through the Cumberland Gap in 1775, and runs through the Louisiana Purchase in 1805. Chapter Two drops back to the late 17th century with the coming of the French down the Mississippi, takes us through the War of 1812 and continues with the history of riverboat trade well into the 1840s. Chapter Three drops back again to the Lewis and Clark Expedition, covers the machinations of speculators and entrepreneurs in exploiting the new land and its native inhabitants, and ends with the Mexican War.

While the progression throughout the book is generally chronological, reflecting the way the various geographical regions of the American West were in fact settled by the descendants of Europeans who called themselves Americans, in addition certain themes – dreams of cheap land and quick fortunes, frontier violence, the Indian "problem," the ideal of individual freedom – that characterized the psyche of the westerner and helped form the myth of the Wild West, run throughout the entire text. Finally, for me, the various tellings of the story of the West are as much a part of its history as the events and personalities, which results in some emphasis throughout on the activities of Western ideologues of whatever stripe.

As for my own bias, I should warn the reader that the idea of "progress," which still dominates the American political agenda on both the Left and Right, has lost the promise it held for me in my youth. While, like most Americans, I have long been fascinated by the American West, have lived there, have written about it, have dreamed Western dreams, the banner of progress under which the West has traditionally marched seems a tattered and shabby thing waving over an unnecessary genocide and a land desiccated by the greed that progress sought to gussy up. In short, I love the West – and despair for it.

None of which should be allowed to get in the way of telling a good story. For my ability to do that I have several surrogate fathers to thank, among them George P. Elliott and Sherman Paul, the former who taught me to write, the latter who taught me to think. I could not have written a word, however, without the aid and support of my partners at Zenda, Inc. – Patricia Hogan, L. Edward Purcell, and especially Alan Axelrod, two of whom are themselves Western historians. In addition, I owe much to my collaborator, Candace Floyd.

Finally, I must thank my father, Charles Lamar Phillips, Sr. Especially, I would like to recall for him an afternoon in Iowa City when the gunslingers of the Writers' Workshop were looking to put another notch on their sixshooters and there was no way out of town. Stick with it, he advised. Nothing happens overnight. As a boy, who, like all true Westerners, was in flight from his ancestors, it was a revelation for me to hear that one of them had planned it that way, had worked all his life to provide for the luxury of latter-day fortune hunting. To my father, then, heading West, I dedicate this book.

Charles Phillips, Nashville, Tennessee

An attack on an emigrant train bound for California, based on a painting by Wimar.

1

PIONEERS

The American West was born in the European struggle for empire, its creation shaped especially by the conflict between England and France. During the early seventeenth century both countries began inching their way onto the North American continent, and by the mid-1600s both were in a position to challenge the New World monopoly that Spain had built during a century of exploration and conquest.

By then, English immigrants had established compact little settlements along the Atlantic coast, while the more adventuresome French – hard-boiled *coureurs de bois* and black-robed Jesuit missionaries – had spread westward down the St. Lawrence and into the expanses of the interior. Their approaches to the bands of native hunters and gatherers already occupying this "new" world were quite different. Instead of displacing the Indian from his land, as the Englishman was wont to do by forced eviction or legal chicanery, the Frenchman more often moved into his wigwams, married his daughter, and introduced him to the Mother Church.

The century-long contest between the two nations for colonial possessions throughout the world began in earnest around 1689 with the War of the League of Augsburg, called King William's War by the British colonials. When war broke out, the French *coureurs* were ready to lead their Indian friends in raids on the outlying English settlements in New England and New York. They did so for the duration of the intermittent conflicts – Queen Anne's War, King George's War, and the like – that followed.

The British settlers had their Indian allies, too. They could supply more cheaply than the French the textiles and hardware the Indians, grown quickly dependent on European technology, demanded in exchange for fur. In general, trading partners made less reliable comrades-in-arms than blood relatives: nevertheless, during the incessant warfare, when the French sent "their" Indians to raid the thinly populated British villages, the English protected themselves by an uneasy alliance with the Iroquois, who controlled the Mohawk Valley and the St. Lawrence River, the two major approaches to the interior of the subcontinent.

By the treaties that followed the various wars, sovereignty shifted back and forth with the signing of each new soon-to-be-violated peace. Not only the power politics of nations an ocean away, but also local colonial developments contributed to the conflict. Land speculators in the several sea-board colonies formed rival companies to lay fanciful claim to western lands beyond the Appalachian Mountains. The French began building a string of forts on those same lands in the Upper Ohio River valley to protect their own and their Indian allies' interests. And the Iroquois Confederacy made an attempt to establish itself as the clearing house for all the native American tribes trading with the French and the English.

Just as the long-term struggle between France and England was heating up in the aftermath of the Treaty of Utrecht, the Iroquois bid for hegemony collapsed at a huge powwow in Logstown, Pennsylvania. At that same moment, in May of 1754, Lieutenant Colonel George Washington from Virginia, in effect the twenty-three-year-old hireling of a land-speculation corporation called the Ohio Company, arrived at Fort Duquesne, near what would one day become Pittsburgh, to teach certain French "interlopers" a lesson.

An engraving of a pioneer family from a wagon train building a log cabin in the frontier wildernes.

THE BEGINNING.

Washington's appearance in the Ohio valley and his inglorious defeat by combined French and Indian forces sparked a conflict that would spread from the American wilderness over vast stretches of Europe and across the high seas to the edge of the Near East. By the time it was over, France, Austria, Sweden, a number of small German states, and Spain, took up arms against England and Frederick the Great's Prussia. In Europe the fighting came to be known as the Great War for the Empire. The English called it the Seven Years War. Typically, the myopic American colonists dubbed this first truly world-wide conflict the French and Indian War.

The Seven Years War brought France's New World ambitions to a decisive and abrupt halt. France surrendered Canada in 1760, and by the terms of the Peace of Paris three years later ceded all her claims east of the Mississippi to England, and those west of the river to Spain. For Europe, the matter was settled, but not so for the native Indians and the American settlers.

As Francis Jennings has often pointed out, the French and Indian War was, from the point of view of the Indians themselves, merely the first in a series of wars waged by the various Algonquin tribes of the Old Northwest originally against Britain and then against the United States. From their great victory over Major General Edward Braddock on the meadowlands of Fort Duquesne in 1755 through the vicious border skirmishes of Pontiac's Rebellion and the American Revolution, to their final defeat by Mad Anthony Wayne at Fallen Timbers in 1795, the Algonquins' objective was to force the English-speaking aliens to withdraw. The great world-wide conflagrations in which France lost Canada and England was soon to lose its thirteen seaboard colonies were minor concerns in the Algonquin's forty-year struggle to liberate themselves and their lands.

From the settlers point of view, however, the ouster of the French from North America confirmed England's domination of the continent as far west as the Mississippi, and thus changed the goal of the

A Currier and Ives print of frontiersmen defending themselves against Indians. The frontier was pushed farther and farther West as more and more people left to seek adventure in the land of new opportunities.

A frontier woman wields an axe to defend herself and her child against an attack by a bear. Stories of the extreme conditions out West filtered back to the East, deterring all but the most brave from moving to the frontier.

French and Indian War from establishing control of the Upper Ohio to the opening of the trans-Appalachian West. To understand the American Westerner, Patricia Limerick has argued, one must understand the profit motive not as a rational goal but as an all-encompassing passion. And it is certainly true that during the late seventeenth century in Britain's American colonies a voracious land hunger unlike anything the world had yet seen filled the breasts of the white settlers we would come to call Pioneers.

The passionate and mutual hatred that sprang up between native Indian and American Pioneer had its roots in the French and Indian War.

The Indians almost always bore the brunt of the fighting, and almost always did most of the dying,

The Louisiana Purchase, March 9, 1804, a painting by Alfred Russell. By this deal, President Thomas Jefferson nearly doubled the size of the United States by purchasing land from the French for about $15 million.

but next to them, white settlers along what would become known as the frontier suffered the greatest number of casualties. Indeed, for several years, the Delawares – France's most important Indian allies – raided freely the settlements along the frontier, pushing back the western borders of Pennsylvania, Maryland, and Virginia by a hundred miles. The Delaware were brought to a tenuous peace through the auspices of the Iroquois and the promise of hunting rights in Western Pennsylvania, which would remain free of white settlement.

The Treaty of Easton (Pennsylvania) lasted a month, right up until the British managed, on November 25, 1758, to take Fort Duquesne, no longer defended by the Delawares, and rename it Fort Pitt. Ensconced in Fort Pitt, the British built the first of three roads that would traverse western Pennsylvania, and the settlers, blithely ignoring the treaty, pushed west once again.

The pattern of White/Indian promise and betrayal on the frontier was established. Even after the French defeat at Quebec a year later and the surrender of Canada, the war in the Ohio Valley dragged on for another four years, with considerable loss of life and a horrid cruelty and ferocity on all sides. Nothing seemed to daunt the settlers. Despite continued Indian attacks and an official proclamation on October 13, 1761, reiterating the terms of the Treaty of Easton, would-be pioneers poured into the troubled West.

Not surprisingly, hard on the heels of the Treaty of Paris, which officially ended the war on February 10, 1763, came colonial petitions to King George to allow settlement in Illinois and West Virginia. The colony of Virginia calmly asserted claims to the territory covered by present-day West Virginia, Kentucky, Ohio, Indiana, Illinois, Michigan, Wisconsin, and parts of Minnesota. In September of 1763, the land-speculation firm called the Mississippi Company, led by who else but George Washington, received a royal grant of two-and-a-half-million acres between the Ohio and Wisconsin rivers for settlement by Virginia soldiers who fought in the war.

Since the earliest royal charters – when an ignorant Crown had blandly granted to Massachusetts, Connecticut, Virginia, both Carolinas, and Georgia all the land from their Atlantic frontage west to the Pacific, subject to extinguishing of the Indians' title – land speculation had been a favorite American pastime. It had even taken on a patriotic hue in the decades preceding the French and Indian War when the competing claims of the colonies were at least levelled against the onerous French.

A group of men formed a company, obtained a reasonably sound title to a tract of wilderness from the Colonial government or from the king, hired a few agents, printed a few advertisements, and lured the gullible and the greedy onto small plots of land that sold at amazingly inflated prices. All the settlers had to do was clear their lands, build their cabins, and kill off the nearby Indians, to see their real estate rise in value as the wilderness receded further west. To them, "uninhabited" land was worthless, and they – speculators and settlers alike – deserved whatever they made for "opening" the land, for their foresight and for the risks they took.

And now that the official border was with Spain along the Mississippi, all the land between the Appalachian Mountains and that border appeared "unimproved" – land ripe for "opening."

The Delawares had seen it all before, on the other side of the mountains, where their people had been disenfranchised and made "women" to the clever and powerful Iroquois while the whites chopped up their hunting ground into disgusting little homesteads. Among them there arose a soothsayer, the "Delaware Prophet" Neolin, who urged a total break with the whites. They blocked the Indians' path to heaven, he argued, calling them "dogs clothed in red" who came only to troubled land. "Drive them out," he demanded. "Make war upon them."

As his words – and those of other Indian revivalists – spread through the Ohio Valley and westward, they found a hearing among many Indians, who were not at all pleased with the Peace of Paris. The Algonquins in particular felt betrayed by the French, who had deserted them, and challenged by the English, who continually ignored the treaty-established boundary of the Appalachians. The result became known as "Pontiac's Conspiracy," though Pontiac himself was only a local Ottawa war chief in a huge resistance movement that included any number of tribes spread over the vast regions of the old northwest – mostly Algonquin tribes like the Ottawa, Chippewa, Potawatami, Shawnee, Delaware, even the Sauk, but also at least one of the Iroquois "nations," the Seneca, as well as bands of Hurons and a few Erie warriors.

If the border skirmishes of the French and Indian War had been harsh, the frenzy of Pontiac's "rebellion" was horrifying. This time, civilians did indeed suffer the greatest number of casualties. Rampaging warriors slaughtered some 2,000 settlers, but killed only about 400 soldiers. Though the victims were generally those who violated the bans against invading Indian territory, the exuberantly brutal Indians nevertheless inflicted incredible tortures, mutilating the captured, and practicing ritual cannibalism on the fallen. White survivors were forced to flee, seeking refuge in towns and forts.

The savagery, however, was not confined to one side of the conflict. The British commander in chief, Lord Amherst, responded to news of the Indian uprising with orders to extirpate the belligerents, taking no prisoners, and putting "to death all that fall into your hands." He even requested one of his colonels "to send the small pox among disaffected tribes of Indians." The plan was abandoned for fear of infecting his own people, but revived later during the siege of Fort Pitt.

Parleys were a common practice in backwoods warfare, and during one such sitdown with the besieging Delaware chiefs, the fort's acting commander – a Swiss mercenary named Simon Ecuyer – presented the Indians, as a token of his personal esteem, with two blankets and a handkerchief infected with the pox from the fort's hospital. Captain William Trent, who provided the blankets, gloated: "I hope they will have the desired effect." The Delawares understood the hidden message behind his taunt and withdrew immediately. But they were already infected from handling the blankets, evidently, for an epidemic swept through the tribe, killing off the Great Chief Shingas, and his brother Pisquetomen, among hundreds of others.

A brutal vigilantism sprang up among the white settlers as well in response to the Indian attacks. A mob from Paxton and Donegal, Pennsylvania, massacred a group of peaceful Conestoga Indians in Lancaster County two months after Pontiac had sued for peace and Lord Amherst had reluctantly accepted. The rage with which they stabbed, hacked, and mutilated the defenseless tribe, innocent of any participation in the uprising, was a measure of how far the border skirmishing had traveled toward racial warfare. That warfare would be marked by a lack of mercy on both sides over ever-disputed lands, in which atrocity became the rule.

King George used Pontiac's rebellion as an excuse for reasserting his control over the American colonies. By the Royal Proclamation of 1763 he declared the hostilities over and limited white settlement by and large to the territory east of the Appalachians. He argued that an army of occupation was necessary for colonial security, and sent more troops to patrol the forts built along the border he had marked off between the colonials and the Indians.

The proclamation's boundary line was the reality behind the great American myth of the Frontier. The Proclamation Line was not a frontier in the usual,

Emigrants float down the Ohio River on a flatboat. The route from Pennsylvania, where land was becoming scarce, to the West began at Pittsburgh, followed the Monongahela River and continued southwest along the Ohio River. Once in the Northwest Territory, new emigrants found land aplenty, and a rough-and-tumble atmosphere in the few settlements and forts.

European sense of a border between two sovereign powers. For political reasons, the King had defined the frontier as a demarcation behind which the he would allow "civilization" to flourish and beyond which "savagery" would be contained. The native Americans – the savages – he in effect claimed as his private wards, who had the use of his land as a hunting ground as long as his "Royal Will and Pleasure" decreed. Colonials could not trespass on that land without his blessing.

The army of occupation did not stay long on the frontier. Once the French were gone and the Indians pacified for the moment by treaty, it marched from the western forts to the coastal towns, where it could enforce the king's "Will and Pleasure" on the colonists more effectively. Consequently, the boundary did not hold. With the Indians defeated and the Royal troops back east enforcing the various new taxations and trade restrictions, the new American "frontiersmen" continued the advance of "civilization" into "savage" territory.

By the 1770s white settlement had reached Kentucky, and the Shawnees had moved to the attack again. Lord Dunmore, Virginia's governor, who had granted veterans of the French and Indian War the land in the first place, called out the militia. The Shawnee appealed for help to the Iroquois. The Five Nations had for centuries brilliantly manipulated European rivalries to their own advantage and had made the turning of their backs on other tribes into a political art form. It was not yet clear that their subtleties would be wasted with the backwoodsmen of the American Frontier, and they typically refused to get involved. The Shawnee were defeated, after killing some fifty whites and wounding a hundred more.

"Lord Dunmore's War," a brief and ugly affair, was fought not just against the Shawnee, but also to spite a king who wanted to halt the westward course of the colonials' empire. A year later, the American Revolution would begin, fought in large measure for the same purpose. When it was over, the Proclamation Line faded into history. But the idea of a frontier between civilization, created by white men, and wilderness, inhabited by savages, would become the major justification for the extermination of proud and diverse cultures in the search for cheap land and quick fortunes, a search that for Westerners defined freedom itself.

The invasion of the West by white settlers was triggered by the massive immigration of the Scotch-Irish in the decades just prior to the Revolution. They were fleeing the bad harvests, high rents and the suppression of Presbyterianism among Lowland Scots and Englishmen who had settled a century before in Northern Ireland's Ulster plantations. By

1770 more than 400,000 of them, joined by a few Germans escaping the poverty of the Rhine's Palatine, some Huguenots and Scandinavians, and here and there a Highlander, had spread through Pennsylvania and on into the forests as the better land disappeared.

Fed by the great land hunger of the American Frontier, some then turned north into New England, but most trekked south down the Appalachian trench until they reached the foothills and wooded valleys of the Carolinas. And finally, of course, they began heading north and west again, across the eastern mountains into the wilderness beyond.

In the early eighteenth century, except for the settled seacoast, the entire American subcontinent west to the Mississippi was one gigantic forest, broken occasionally and dramatically by a marsh or prairie and outlined by stretches of laurel and rhododendron along the high ridges of the Appalachian. Huge spruce trees, hemlocks and firs stretched along the high ground from New England to Tennessee. Oaks and chestnuts ranged from New Jersey and Pennsylvania to northern Virginia. Pine and oak ruled the southern forest. And all of them rose from underbrush that in places made a man invisible at a few yards.

It was into this forest that the pioneers plunged, hacking out the clearings where they settled their wives, children, cattle and pigs, warily eying the forest that surrounded them and threatened to swallow them. In those woods they knew there was abundant game: buffalo and deer, squirrels and rabbits, but also bear and wildcats, cougars and wolves – and Indians who could slide in and out of sight like ghosts.

When they arrived the forest was so thick and vast that the only paths or traces – trails did not yet exist in fact or in the language – they could find were those trampled down by the buffalo that meandered aimlessly, beginning nowhere really and going there, too. The footpaths of the Indians were invisible to the untrained eye. Even so obvious a gateway through the mountain as the Cumberland Gap, which was an ancient Indian passage, escaped their notice till a Virginia speculator found and named it at mid-century.

The Germans weren't much for traveling. They found their land, squared up their timbers, built solid houses and went into farming or manufacturing. They and the Swiss began to arm the frontier with the long-barreled flintlock, first called the Pennsylvania, then the Kentucky, rifle. It was evolved from principles they had learned in Central Europe, where for two centuries armorers had understood the advantages of spiral grooved barrels while the rest of Europe limped along with smoothbore guns. Along with the ax, the flintlock became standard

A frontier woman defends herself against a surprise attack by Indians. Misunderstandings, distrust, and outright hostility plagued relations between white pioneers and the Indian tribes who had inhabited America for centuries, not helped by an evolving pattern of political promise and betrayal that began to dog their dealings with Indians.

frontier equipment, shaping the very nature of the men who used it.

And these men were mostly the Ulster Scots, a peripatetic lot who formed the advance guard of western expansion through the end of the century and beyond. For housing, they notched a few logs and slung them together into crude cabins. They killed trees by girdling them, leaving them standing while they farmed the sun-drenched spots between them till the soil gave out or they got the itch to move on.

By the time the tide of immigrants, led and dominated by the Scotch-Irish, began flowing through the Cumberland Gap into the West, the pioneer character had taken shape. These Westerners had seen Indians torture their friends and slit the bellies of their pregnant wives. They had hidden in the woods, watching as their loved ones were captured, raped and killed, and they were forced to choose

between suicide and a chance to seek revenge. Their hatred of the Indian was implacable, and the ambushing, murdering, and scalping they had done in turn was justified in their eyes and the eyes of their righteous and vengeful Old Testament God.

To a man they hated the East – Eastern politics, Eastern taxes, Eastern elitism and Eastern capital. They knew the frontier was not heaven; it was a hunting ground not only for savage Indians but for a race of low-life land speculators who cheated them out of house and home at every opportunity; it was filled with outlaws and renegades and killers and braggarts and ne'er-do-wells of all kinds. But the West was also the place to start over, the place where everyone got a second chance. Westerners did not judge a man on his past too quickly. Most of them had been in debt or in trouble, too, at one time.

In short, Westerners thought of themselves as a new breed, and perhaps they were. Hardship had made them stern, violent, clannish, hard-bitten, and fiercely independent. The constant danger of the frontier tended to produce stoic, suspicious, die-hard realists who were also brave, upright, and bold. Though semi-literate, overly proud, and excessively cantankerous, they were also honest and direct, often rudely so.

Their greatest resources were their endurance and their prolific reproduction. They lived by their own labor and ingenuity, producing – at least at first – with their own hands every stick of furniture, every piece of clothing, every meal, every drink of liquor they had in the deep, foreboding forests of the American interior. A slice of land represented to them not wealth so much as dignity: here, in the wilderness, a poor man could subdue and replenish the earth, and by doing so achieve a certain integrity in his life.

The obsession with land, and what it represented, had brought them to the wilderness. But, as David Lavender points out, the insatiable lust for it created, too, the paradox of the frontier character. Having fought for their plot of ground, and secured it with incredible toil, many became immediately dissatisfied and went looking for something else, something more, further on. The restlessness of the pioneers, in Lavener's felicitous words, was "so bone deep it seemed like a new human instinct."

From the ranks of these pioneers there would appear the first of many Western heroes, a deerslayer and Indian-fighter named Daniel Boone, whom his wilderness brethren were proud to consider a first among equals, so emblematic of life on the frontier did his story become. Boone was the archetypal frontiersman, the uncrowned king of the wilderness.

Along with George Washington, Boone had been among General Braddock's troops at Fort Duquesne when a huge Delaware war party, some Canadian militiamen and a few French regulars killed or wounded 977 out of 1450 men in the opening battle of the French and Indian War. Indeed, it was there that Boone first heard from a fellow volunteer about a place called Kentucky.

Born of a lapsed Quaker in 1734 in southern Pennsylvania, where the frontier land-hunger was especially strong, Boone became one of the earliest of the "long-hunters" who crossed the Appalachians in the 1760s. From his home base in Yadkin County, North Carolina, where his father had moved the family when Boone was nineteen, he roamed the game-rich wilds of Kentucky for months, sometimes years, at a time, seeking enough deerskin to allow him to make ends meet.

Plagued by debt like most pioneers, uneasy with the growing number of new neighbors he found each time he returned home, Boone developed the burning conviction that there was a fortune to be made beyond the mountains. Financed by the flamboyant North Carolina promoter, Judge Richard Henderson, he hacked the first rude road over the Cumberland Gap and founded Boonesborough, where he settled his wife and eight children along with five other Yadkin County families. He became the captain of the permanent settlers who began laboring westward to occupy the Bluegrass in 1775,

An 1830s woodcut of a pioneer family captured by Indians. Despite King George's Proclamation of 1763 to limit settlement, pioneers pushed Westward, confronting Indian tribes struggling to preserve their centuries-old way of life.

and Boonesborough became an enduring bastion of the American frontier.

Boone had been fighting Indians since he was a teenager, during the fierce Yadkin Valley raids from 1758 to 1760, again in the French and Indian War, and in sporadic wilderness encounters. A Shawnee siege of Boonesborough at the beginning of the American Revolution, however, became the most important of his many battles. Henry Hamilton, Britain's brilliant liaison with the Indian, and perhaps the most hated man in the West, hoped to wipe out the Kentucky settlements on his way to capturing Fort Pitt, which lay on the fork of the Ohio River and was the key to the entire frontier.

Once Hamilton controlled Fort Pitt, he could force the Americans east of the Appalachians for good, and restore the Northwest to the Crown's tribal allies, who would be free to embrace English

The Sac and the Fox, after a drawing by Charles Bodmer. The bellicose nature of the Sac and Fox tribes made them much feared by white settlers.

trade. Boone foiled the plan in a complicated delaying tactic that involved his surrender to the Shawnees and the pretence that he had turned traitor. As their captive, he delayed an attack for three days until his settlement could be reinforced, after which he escaped to mount a successful resistance.

Some found his behavior outrageous and accused him of cowardice and collaboration, but a court-martial called by the Virginia Militia at Logan's Station, Kentucky, completely exonerated the crafty backwoodsman. The general consensus had become that Boone's purchase of time was central to the salvation of the frontier during the American Revolution, the high water mark of his adventuresome life.

Ultimately, though, Boone's military career was to end in personal tragedy. During the last major conflict of the Revolution, the Battle of Blue Licks on August 19, 1782, the militia Boone marched with chose to ignore his warnings and plunged headlong into an Indian ambush. Among the many mowed down desperately trying to wade back across the Licking River to safety was Boone's own beloved son, Israel.

Though Boone was a great hunter and a mighty warrior, he was not much of a businessman.

Some of it was bad luck. Boone shared his fellow westerners' prejudices against all things Eastern, and especially against Eastern speculators. Determined to beat them to the Bluegrass, Boone took off to Virginia in 1780 with $20,000 of his and $30,000 from his friends to buy the warrants they needed for undisputed title to Kentucky's open acreage. On the way to the land office in Richmond, he stopped for the night at a tavern in James City. When he woke up the next morning, his saddlebags – and the money – was gone. Though most of his friends did not hold the loss against him, the whiff of scandal remained.

And bad luck aside, Boone's very nature was against him in matters of finance. After the Revolution, Boone's fame began to grow in a fashion that would become standard for many a Western legend: he became a hero in the popular literature read primarily by Easterners. His press agent was a Pennsylvania schoolteacher named John Filson, who traveled to Kentucky in 1782 and wrote a laughably inaccurate and romantic piece of Western propaganda called

The Discovery, Settlement, and present State of Kentucke, which included a section subtitled "The Adventures of Col. Daniel Boone."

Boone's fortune at last seemed secure. Eastern readers with a little capital could think of no better way to dabble in Kentucky real estate than to call upon the famous woodsman to serve as their proxy. By this time, Boone knew opportunity when it came a'knockin', and for every track of land he surveyed and staked a claim to, he demanded half be deeded over to him as his fee. Yankee investors, even newcomers to the West, gladly paid the fare.

Soon, Boone moved to the south bank of the Ohio, where he opened a tavern and traded in goods of all kinds – skins, furs, horses, flour, tobacco, whiskey, and the occasional slave. And he was at last able to pursue with gusto the passion of every pioneer: the land business. By 1788, he owned better than 50,000 acres.

Boone was a knowledgeable, competent, and honest surveyor, but in Kentucky that was not enough. Wilderness surveying itself was an inexact science: given the vastness of the areas involved, conflicting claims were the rule instead of the exception, and there were plenty of hard-nosed speculators willing to take advantage of these Kentucky "shingles." Unable to shake his sense of the woods as untouched and virgin land, Boone often staked claims to land already deeded to others. And once he had located and surveyed an area, he often put off establishing clear title to it while he went off hunting, never imagining there were those who might use the delay to their advantage.

As his correspondence grew increasing acrid in the 1790s, Boone's innate dislike of those who employed him only made matters worse. He dismissed their legalistic squabbles, which he detested, and swore he would never live within a hundred miles of a "damned Yankee." But times had changed, and to his chagrin Boone found himself regarded as a fraud by many Kentuckians, who accused him of being a "chimney corner" surveyor, a man who stayed at home by his fire and took wild guesses at the boundaries he recorded. Because Kentucky was still the West, rumors that he was to be assassinated began to circulate. Then came the lawsuits, and with them the mounting debt. When he went to sell off his land, he discovered that he, too, was a victim of his frontier ways – someone else *legally* owned much of it.

Civilization had come to Kentucky, and with it courts and lawyers. Men like Daniel Boone, thousands of them, who thought that hacking out a clearing in the woods and chasing off a bunch of savages was enough, suddenly found themselves deprived of the one thing that they prized most, their plot of dignified earth. And just like Daniel Boone, they too would now load up their wagons and pack off with their families toward the new boundary between civilization and wilderness: the Mississippi.

Daniel Boone was, of course, not the only well-known pioneer to lead the exodus from the East. James Harrod, a hot-tempered Pennsylvanian, established an enclave a few miles west of Boone's settlement on the Kentucky River, and so did Benjamin Logan, who would become a Virginia legislator. And during the Revolution, the most famous Indian fighter was George Rogers Clark. Clark led his backwoods troops in defense of Western outposts against the Northwest Algonquins and the Appalachia confederacies, urged on by the sly and ruthless Henry Hamilton.

For the most part, the quarrel between the American Colonies and the English King had little interest for the Indians of the Old Northwest. It was instead the horde of land-hungry pioneers grinding remorselessly forward every year that worried them, and they pursued their own general policy of raiding across the Ohio, as they had been doing for years. After all, once the Revolution was over, the new government of the United States sounded much like the old English Crown, talking of the "introduction of the arts of civilization" that would "ultimately destroy all distinction between Savages and civilized people."

Such talk had little meaning in the face of the race hatred of the pioneers. Regardless of what the paternalistic, leisured ruling class had to say, these Westerners clearly intended to destroy them. No Algonquin could forget, for example, the fate of a band of Pennsylvania Delawares, converted to Christianity by Moravian missionaries, during the Revolutionary War.

Spurred by the British, the Iroquois – threatening to "make broth" of the now meek Moravian Indians – raided again and again their quaint, neat little villages, where they raised livestock, cultivated orchards, tilled the soil, and worshipped God daily. At the same time, the American backwoodsmen decided against all evidence that the Moravian villagers were harboring hostile Indians and descended upon them. As the erstwhile Delawares – men, women, and children – were being herded into their church, they asked only for a few minutes in

George Rogers Clark (1752 - 1818), born to a wealthy family in Virginia, gained control of the old Northwest Territory from the British during the Revolutionary War. He seized from the redcoats their forts at Kaskaskia and Vincennes, and in so doing crushed British hopes of dominating the land west of the Appalachians.

which to kiss one another goodbye and sing "the most High." The Americans granted their request, and when the song was done, slaughtered them.

In response, the Algonquin tribes along the upper Ohio swept into the valley, captured a militia colonel named William Crawford, tied him to a stake by a long leash, and cooked him alive.

After the war, the Algonquins would meet the westward movement of the white settlers with just such determination, and the area north of the Ohio became a hotbed of frontier violence and atrocity. The Indians resisted the new Congress's attempts to persuade them to cede land to the government by treaty. In fact, some tribes, such as the Shawnee, refused to take part in any peace process at all.

The British made things worse by continuing to meddle in Indian affairs even after the 1783 Treaty of Paris supposedly brought the Revolution to a close. Hoping to weaken the already uneasy American confederation of states, they adamantly refused to abandon the posts from which they had controlled the waterways along the Canadian border since the French and Indian Wars, citing as an excuse the former colonists refusal to pay war debts to loyalists and Tory merchants.

From the disputed posts, the British supplied the Algonquins with goods and, most likely, with weapons, as they sent out agents to urge the tribes to form a confederation like the Iroquois in order better to resist U.S. encroachment. Encouraged by British

George Rogers Clark leading his band of frontier soldiers through freezing water toward Vincennes in February 1779. These cold, hungry men followed Clark to victory against the British in the Northwest Territory, opening the way for thousands of settlers to move into the area.

support, the Shawnee, Kickapoo, and Miami tribes vowed to hold the line at the Ohio River. But the Delaware, Wyandot, and Seneca demurred, realizing that such a demand would lead to out-and-out war with the Americans.

But raid and counterraid kept the frontier seething with unrest. As the pioneer migration continued apace despite the government's effort to check it, the Indian position hardened. In the face of the uncontrolled squatting, the Algonquins rebuffed all attempts to negotiate treaties for their land. When the Americans sent two expeditions into Ohio in 1790 and 1791, the first led by General Josiah Harmer, the second by the Territorial Governor, they were completely destroyed by the Miami, the Shawnee,

and the Wyandot, under the able leadership of a chief named Little Turtle.

More American were killed than had fallen in any battle of the Revolution. The 630 casualties was the largest body count since the massacre of Braddock's troops at Fort Duquesne back in the Seven Years' War. President Washington responded by appointing "Mad Anthony" Wayne commander in chief of the new American army, now called the Legion of the United States. The curtain had risen on the final act of the Algonquin's forty-year war of liberation.

The fighting lasted till 1795, when General Wayne's victory at the Battle of Fallen Timbers forced the Indians to sue for peace. A few months later,

Wayne met with a thousand representatives of the Delawares, Potowatomis, Wyandots, Shawnees, Miamis, Chippewas, Ottawas, Weas, Piankashaws, Kickapoos and Kakaskias for fifty days of feasting and barter. Wayne alternately threatened and entertained his recent foes, and ultimately the combination of intimidation and hospitality led to the Treaty of Greenville.

The long resistance movement was over. As the white hordes poured into Ohio and Illinois, the Algonquin retreated to the far corners of their former domains and passed over into the strange country west of the great Father of Rivers, where those who had managed to survive the ravages of the last forty years found waiting for them the fierce Plains Indians whom they knew by the name Sioux, or "enemy." And as the frontiersman themselves pressed close against the eastern banks of the Mississippi, they began to stir up trouble with the Spanish authorities controlling the river.

For the native Americans the fertile hunting ground west of the Mississippi was home, either by virtue of centuries of use or by recent conquest of enemy tribes. The French crown had never cared much for the area, thinking it an expensive colony with disappointingly little in the way of mercantile treasure to exploit, and the king gave it away, at the first opportunity, to the Spanish. Spain wanted the trans-Mississippi as a buffer, first against Britain and then against the United States. The British treated the native inhabitants as pawns in their international games of intrigue and empire.

But the new American president, Thomas Jefferson, saw in this "Louisiana" the answer to his Indian problems. Like King George half a century before, he hoped to fill the lands beyond the boundary line formed by the Mississippi River with Indians and check the rapid westward expansion of his rapacious and troublesome pioneers. Most of them, however, unlike their president, saw in Louisiana the promise of cheap land, low taxes, and a better life.

The westerners were thrilled when Jefferson created a new frontier by the simple expedient of purchasing the entire wilderness beyond for a mere $15 million cash in 1805.

It was the greatest land deal yet in the history of the West.

Davy Crockett (1786-1836) campaigns in Tennessee for a seat in the U.S. House of Representatives. Crockett entered politics in 1820 as a member of the Tennessee State Legislature. Losing a bid for re-election to Congress in 1835, he decided to explore Texas, and on March 6, 1836, he was killed while fighting at the Alamo.

2
THE RIVER

In prehistoric times the ancestors of such Native American tribes as the Yuchi, Creek, Chickasaw, Natchez, Quapaw, and Osage built low mounds in which they buried their dead all over the wilderness that Thomas Jefferson would one day buy from Napoleon. Other tribes, even more ancient, made their homes in the caves and rock shelters along the shores of the Mississippi and the Missouri. But by the time the first Europeans arrived, these primitive bluff dwellers had long disappeared, as had the mound-building Woodland and Mississippi cultures.

Throughout the Colonial period, two main linguistic groups occupied the Louisiana heartland. To the north, the land belonged to the Algonquin tribes – the Indians of the Old Northwest. South and west of the river, their hereditary foes, the Sioux – tribes like the Iowa, Kansa, Missouri, Oto, Quapaw, and Osage – held sway. Both groups, unlike the confederated Iroquois and the southern "civilized" tribes, with their long houses and stockaded towns, inhabited for the most part flimsier tipis and tipi-like structures, with outer shells of hide, matting or bark.

All tribes felt the impact of the white invasion long before the Louisiana Purchase. A century before, for example, the French had driven the Sac and the Fox into the part of Louisiana that would become known as Missouri. Originally, the home of the Sauk and the Mesquakie (as the Sac and the Fox called themselves) had been much further north: the former in the Upper Michigan peninsula and the latter along the southern shores of Lake Superior. Early in the seventeenth century, the Mesquakie had been eased off their lands by the Chippewas and moved gradually southward until they occupied the area

around Lake Winnebago and along the Fox River, where the French found and named them. Similarly, in the mid-1600s the Iroquois and the French chased the Sauk south to Green Bay, where the two tribes forged their close alliance. When the French tried to punish the Fox for attacking French fur traders, the tribe sought refuge with the Sac. And when the Sac – at that point on good terms with the French – refused to give up their new allies, the Europeans vented their wrath on both tribes, forcing them to migrate south yet again.

They arrived in the Mississippi Valley implacably bellicose, and they remained that way to the bitter end. They attacked and displaced another Algonquin tribe, the Illinois, whose land they coveted, then undertook wars of extermination against the Missouri and the Peoria. After smallpox finished what the Sac and the Fox started, the Missouri simply disappeared as a "nation": a few survivors joined the Osage, others the Kansa tribe. The Peoria, their ranks greatly depleted, established villages near St. Louis and sought the protection of the whites from their relentless enemies. But long before that, in fact by the beginning of the eighteenth century, the Sac and the Fox held in undisputed possession all the territory north of the Missouri River and east of the Grand River to the Mississippi.

To the whites – the French, the Spanish and the Americans in turn – the Sac and the Fox appeared

Pioneers on the banks of the Mississippi River prepare for the next stage in their journey West. Thomas Pinckney's Treaty, signed in 1796 by the United States and England, allowed the Americans free navigation of the River.

intensely savage, rude, untrustworthy, and disposed to wander, and each group of whites in turn both hated and feared the two tribes' fighting prowess while admiring the freedom and efficiency of the Sac and Fox political administration.

From Algonquin stock, mixing the culture of their Woodland ancestors with practices adopted from the Plains tribes, The Sac and the Fox made combat the center of their existence. Though tribal authority rested nominally with a civil chief, backed by a council of adult males, much depended on personality. Any brave who could attract sufficient followers for a war party became a war chief and wielded influence with the tribe and on the council so long as his exploits succeeded, or his dreams and visions remained vivid and inspiring. Proud, vain, and intemperate, they were constantly at war with their Indian neighbors and with the French, severely hindering colonial trade on the upper Mississippi throughout the early eighteenth century.

Three times, Louis XIV sent expeditions against them, the last in 1734 – a dispirited campaign that ended in an indecisive peace the following year. Afterward, the Sac and the Fox pretty much went their own way, beginning their winter hunt each year after a fall harvest and continuing on through March or April, when they returned to their villages to plant crops. Their agriculture was rather more extensive than that of the Sioux tribes. Cultivating land along the Mississippi, they raised as much as 8,000 bushels of corn a year and smelted 5,000 pounds of lead a season at mines belonging to the tribe. The surplus in corn, lead and furs they sold to white traders.

Given their history, the Sac and Fox not surprisingly much preferred to do business with the British when they could. It was a habit that did little to endear them to the French, or later the Americans, reinforcing their image as the archetypal "bad" Indians.

Much more to the white settlers' tastes was a tribe like the Osage. In fact, of all the Indian tribes living along this new frontier, it was the Osage who excited the interest and admiration of the Europeans.

When the first French explorers reached the region late in the seventeenth century, the tribe lived near the mouth of the Osage River, but by 1718 the Great or Big Osage, who called themselves Pa-he'tsi (or "campers on the mountains"), had moved upstream

Westward ho! – a romanticized picture of pioneers struggling across the mountains of the Western United States. The white settlement pattern of America has been one of Westward movements. Since the seventeenth century, settlers from New England and Virginia set out West to find new, more abundant lands.

and established villages at the river's headwaters. The rest of the tribe, the Little Osage, moved – along with their defeated cousins, the Missouri – westward up the Missouri River and called themselves U-teshta, "campers in the low land."

Subsisting chiefly through hunting, the Osage often traveled sixty miles a day; their war parties trekked even greater distances. Osage braves hunted from March to August, returning to the cone-shaped huts of their irregular villages to harvest the modest crops of corn, beans, and pumpkins they left unfenced all summer. Late in September, the fall hunt began, ending around our Christmastime. They then stayed in camp till the spring came, and the hunt for bear and beaver began again.

Those families fortunate in the hunt provided for

Running Fox, Chief of the Sac Indians, in a drawing by George Catlin.

the destitute, sending provisions to the homes of the poor, the widowed and the fatherless. Osage politics operated with the same spirit of consideration. Without a regular code of laws, the Osage governed instead by a tacit understanding of the right to command. Though they vested nominal authority in a small number of usually hereditary chiefs, those chiefs never made important decisions without consulting the warriors' council.

Early on, the Osage established a reputation among the whites for general sobriety that made them, to white eyes, conspicuous among the various Indian tribes. Constantly forced to defend their hunting grounds against encroachments by admiring whites and enemy Indians alike, they developed a reputation for being warlike and hostile, but not, like the Sac and Fox, treacherous. They grew especially close to the prominent St. Louis family, the Chouteaus, who maintained exclusive trading privileges with the tribe throughout the eighteenth century.

The other tribes hated the Osage for the special treatment accorded them by the white settlers, but they had their pride. As one old chief told the Chouteaus: "You are surrounded by slaves. Everything about you is in chains, and you are in chains yourself. I fear if I should change my pursuit for yours, I too should become a slave."

But the sad truth was that over the course of two centuries, the tribes – both Sioux and Algonquin – that lived along the Mississippi and hunted in the vast interior had become all but financial slaves to the Europeans. For the Indian trade was carried on by credit, within the infamous "factor" system whose workings made the Indians dependent for vital goods on the individual traders. And however much an Osage or a Sac and Fox leader might hotly deny it, they were essentially hirelings for the fur companies, and as such pawns in the economic game of chess played by foreign mercantile powers.

The process had started innocently enough. From the time Champlain founded Quebec in 1608, *coureurs de bois* – as casual with their lives as the most ferocious warriors and almost as skilled at woodcraft – chased furs ever deeper into the wilderness. In their wake came French Catholic missionaries, hunting for souls and undaunted by the dangers of the forest. The hardy explorers and the Jesuits, the latter dubbed "Black Robes" by the Indians, built forts all along the far reaches of the Great Lakes. To these remote outposts came the Indians, with animal hides for sale and strange tales about a great "father" of rivers they called the "Mesippi."

In 1763, the French intendant in Canada, Jean Talon, commissioned a fur trader named Louis Jolliet to explore the unknown river described by the Indians. Talon hoped this father of waters might prove to be the fabled passageway to the Pacific. He had reason, however, to worry that the new governor, on his way over from France, might not approve his plan. Louis XIV did not appreciate the exploits of his wandering subjects and wanted his New France, which he had taken over from a trading company, populated by hardworking and docile farmers. Two years before he had rejected another scheme by two *coureurs* to create a trading company that would service the northern fur supply by sea, using the yet-to-be-discovered Northwest Passage, and forbidden all but a privileged few from engaging in the fur trade at all. He sent women to entice the wild trappers into a more settled life, placed a bounty on large families, and urged the Church to excommunicate men who left their farms without permission.

Spurned by their king, two fur traders – Pierre Radisson and Medart Chouart – turned to the English and established the Hudson's Bay Company in 1672. Arriving to take over the governor's chair the next year, the Comte de Frontenac realized the importance strategically and economically of the nascent international competition, and he approved Talon's commissioned expedition without hesitation. In June, Jolliet and a Jesuit priest named Jacques Marquette lowered their two birchbark canoes into the muddy water of the Mississippi.

Marquette and Jolliet reported many strange sights along the way – fish so large they threatened to rip apart the canoes, huge herds of grazing buffalo, wildly vivid Indian paintings a bit upstream from the mouth of the Missouri – but they never did find the Northwest Passage. Nor did they find any silver or gold (the traditional impetus for European exploration), though not for want of trying. They turned back before they reached modern-day Arkansas, fearful of blundering into Spanish territory and causing an incident that might earn them the ire of their reluctant king.

Marquette lingered behind in the wilderness to convert the natives, while Jolliet dashed back to Quebec to report on their expedition. Scarcely two years later, the Jesuit was dead, broken by the rugged climate. Jolliet, now a former explorer, grew embittered at the lack of the recognition he believed he deserved, and he wandered from one minor government job to another for the rest of his life.

Not deterred by their fate, Rene-Robert Cavelier, Sieur de La Salle, came back a decade later looking for the Northwest Passage Marquette and Jolliet had

Lewis and Clark depicted with one of their expeditionary force while distributing presents to the Mandans as a goodwill gesture.

somehow failed to find. Assured by Indians *en route* that the Missouri ran all the way to the Pacific, La Salle became convinced that the Missouri was the main river, the Mississippi merely its tributary. Nevertheless, he followed the Mississippi to its mouth and laid claim to the river, its branches, and all the land thereabouts, which he called "Louisiana," after a king who couldn't have cared less.

La Salle had great plans of empire, which would become a typical frontier dream, but he was murdered by one of his own men on a second trip to the wilderness. The French king and his all but bankrupt court were heartily sick of the place. The French government tried turning over the development of the colony to a French banker and wealthy merchant named Antoine Crozat, and one Mothe Cadillac, the founder of Detroit and governor of Louisiana, but the one lost his shirt and the other his job looking for silver the Indians had hoodwinked them into believing existed. After that the king tried a stock company, put together by Scottish financier John Law, in what became the first great floating credit scheme. Neither Etienne De Bourgmont, nor Captain Claude Dustine, nor Philip Renault could find the kind of precious metals that eager Frenchmen, clamoring to invest in first the Company of the West and then the Company of the Indies, had counted on to make them rich.

Big capital flocked to Law's speculative venture, and when the great "Mississippi bubble" burst, it wrecked the French economy and killed the development of the Louisiana colony. The company's agents had managed to found what would become a great city, New Orleans, but abandoned it for the time being when the crash came. And the Sac and the Fox never let up. Increasing trouble with the two tribes prompted the company to petition the king to take Louisiana back in 1731, which he did. And still the Indians fought the company's agents, like Renault, well into mid-century. They were with the British, of course, against the Osage and the French at Braddock's defeat outside Fort Duquesne in the French and Indian War.

The French Crown never could decide what to do with Louisiana. Its original plan to create an agricultural kingdom across the sea resulted in a meager scattering of settlements in Nova Scotia, along the St. Lawrence, and here and there in Louisiana. In contrast, the divines and trappers who traveled up and down the Mississippi, filled with

Tchong-Tas-Sáb-Bee ("Black Dog") second chief of the Osage tribe. Settlers in the new Western territory preferred to deal with the Osage above all other tribes.

missionary zeal or searching for precious metals and the non-existent Northwest Passage, explored and mapped one of the greatest river systems in the world, made peace with the majority of the native inhabitants, and came to rule the wilderness. It was a vague sort of rule, resting not on force of arms but on native good will, and it had little need for permanent settlements. Though the king, the court, and French investors had good reason to be unhappy with John Law's company, its activities helped the French pioneers by increasing their trade with the Indians and more firmly establishing their claim to the area. For, unlike the French Crown, they were in Louisiana to stay.

In 1762, a New Orleans firm received from the French government a monopoly on the fur trade along the Mississippi and the Missouri as part of an official attempt to speed the post-Seven-Years-War economic recovery in Louisiana. Two years later, Pierre Laclede – a principal in the firm – and his

The Jolly Flatboat Men, engraved by T. Davey after an 1847 painting by Bingham. In much of the territory east of the Appalachians, a boat was the only efficient mode of transport. Few trails existed, and travelers on those that did were in grave danger of attack by Indians or wild animals.

Despite the arrival of steamboats, flatboats were the cheapest way to ship goods up until the 1870s, but they were sometimes an insurance risk as navigators often spent idle time drinking cheap whiskey.

Tecumseh, Chief of the Shawnee. In 1811, Tecumseh urged all tribes east of the Mississippi to ally against the white settlers. On November 7, 1811, General Harrison routed the gathered tribes in Tecumseh's absence, and they were never to form a credible threat to white settlers again.

precocious fourteen-year-old stepson, Auguste Chouteau, established their headquarters at a little wilderness settlement called St. Louis. By then they knew that their government had lost Canada and her possessions east of the Mississippi to England at the Treaty of Paris. But it was not until they had actually set up business that they heard about the secret treaty with Spain. Two years earlier, long before they had begun their journey upriver, France had ceded all of its colony west of the Mississippi and the city of New Orleans to Spain. The King of France had abandoned them, and the New World, entirely.

Spain was in no hurry to occupy the wilderness in North America. Though Spanish officials moved into relatively civilized New Orleans sooner, it took seven years for them to arrive in the hinterlands and pick up the reins of government. In 1765, the French commander at Fort Chartres, who was serving in the Spaniards stead, surrendered the French capital of Upper Louisiana to the British and removed his garrison to St. Louis, there to await the tardy transfer

of the colony west of the Mississippi to its new Iberian masters in 1770.

Even after the transfer to Spain, the colony continued generally to follow the laws and customs of Paris, not Madrid. Spain invited French settlers east of the river to relocate on good terms, and they did, much preferring to live under the flag of erstwhile allies than that of bitter enemies. Spanish became their official language, of course, but they still spoke French. Many Frenchmen were appointed to office, though the appointments now carried Spanish titles. Spain changed only the laws providing for the acquisition of land and regulating inheritances. Otherwise, it kept its administration of Louisiana simple: a governor general in New Orleans appointed a lieutenant governor, who resided in St. Louis and for the most part ran the territory north of the Arkansas River to Canada.

Spain saw in the wilderness not an empire, but a buffer – against British ambitions and the rapaciousness of its American colonists – and so sent few colonists of its own. Hence Louisiana remained

thoroughly French until its transfer to the United States in 1804. During the forty years of Spanish rule, the frontier was a society dominated by fur traders rather than settlers, and the inhabitants suffered little of the Americans' land hunger. They clustered along the banks of the Mississippi in settlements that were still not much more than trading posts. Spain followed the French lead in Louisiana when it came to the Indians, promoting unity with all tribes and adopting the practice of recognizing all Indian land claims. It did not fortify the French settlements against the Indians, and few if any of Louisiana's "Creoles" fell victim to the tomahawk.

They lived in leisurely manner, these easy-going French pioneers in their sleepy little villages. Their homes doubled as places of business, and they surrounded these with orchards and gardens and barns and stables, fencing everything with cedar-picket stockades or high stone walls. Along the narrow, dusty lanes that ran between the houses and turned to mud with every rain, they allowed their livestock to wander. Most of the villagers worked sporadically in the common fields on the village outskirts. Each had his own strip to cultivate, but the richer residents secured larger tracks and sometimes worked them with slaves.

The wealthy, as they always have the world over, dominated local affairs, but generally they did not

Pioneers from Connecticut on a 600-mile, ninety-day journey to eastern Ohio in 1805. The Treaty of Greenville following General Anthony Wayne's victory at the Battle of Fallen Timbers provided for a payment of $20,000 for Indian lands, which comprised Ohio and a portion of Indiana.

draw class lines too strictly. They loved to gamble, often wagering considerable sums, and they mingled with the poor at cards, around the billiard table, and along muddy race tracks. Gracious and hospitable, they opened their doors to strangers and travelers. French Catholic to a man, they saw no reason for harsh distinctions between religious and social life, so Sundays became not merely a day for worship but also an excuse for celebration. Church holidays featured music and dancing, and everyone – old, young, rich, poor, free and slave – joined in the festivities. Only the Spanish officials and the priests complained about the lax moral standards of the fun-loving Louisianans.

Occasionally a band of Indians might appear, seeking a conference with local leaders. Now and again the return of a party of traders might create some excitement. But mostly the calm was punctuated by frequent and elegant balls and by the normal Saturday night dances. The fur traders were the only ones ever to stray far from the village, trekking expertly into the wilderness along a few poorly marked trails. Except for these traces and the village lanes, roads hardly existed. When folks traveled any distance at all, they used the river.

They plied the Mississippi in *pirogues*, hollowed-out logs shaped like canoes, and for larger loads in the flat-bottomed boats they called *bateaus*. The bateau floated downstream easily enough, but it took strong backs to push it upstream against the current. A trip from St. Louis to New Orleans could easily take three months.

The river traffic was controlled by a few French merchants residing in the principal villages and running the entire economy of Louisiana. They bought, sold, and traded any commodity they believed would turn a profit, and profits could be huge. But frontier ventures were also extremely risky, and most of Louisiana's sharp entrepreneurs hedged their bets by dabbling in several of the major local enterprises – fur trading, farming, leadmining and saltmaking. The St. Louis merchants in particular ruled the fur trade, though many residents in villages all along the river exchanged goods with the local Indian tribe for fur and peltries. A chronic shortage of money led the Spanish authorities to approve the use of pelts as legal tender, and as barter in fur became the medium of exchange, the St. Louis merchants grew even more powerful.

Theirs was an indolent life, and they had no reason to complain of the lackadaisical administration of the Spanish. But the American Revolution would change all that.

At first they were all for it, this revolt of their fellow North Americans. Even before Spain declared war against Britain in 1779, St. Louis authorities unofficially helped George Rogers Clark in his conquests above the Ohio River, and they kept open the Mississippi-Ohio supply route to the American army by taking up arms against the combined British, Sac and Fox force along the river. But soon, they began to have doubts. The French Creoles still living in the Old Northwest saw it first: the harsh and disorganized government the "Americans" established in the land they took from the British. Even before the war ended, the majority of the Creole families moved across the Mississippi. It took Spain a little longer to catch on.

At first, Spain worried about Britain. Even after the revolution ended, the English continued pigheadedly to hold on to their posts in the Old Northwest, poaching on both Spanish and American territory. But, within a decade, they were pushed out by the American settlers pouring over the Alleghenies and cutting a bloody swath right through Algonquin land to the banks of the Mississippi. Suddenly Spain realized there was no longer a vast wilderness between these active, restless, energetic Americans and its tranquil, laconic Creole colonists.

Spain tried various schemes to stem the tide, attempting to make Louisiana a haven for those disgruntled with the United States. It entered into numerous intrigues to separate the western territories from the states, encouraging the grandiose plans of men like Colonel George Morgan, who – disappointed with Congress for refusing to back a land deal – wanted to establish a semi-autonomous colony called New Madrid. It gave asylum to Louis Lorimer, an Indian trader in the pay of the British who had led his Shawnee and Delaware followers on several raids against Kentucky villages. Finally, it hired a famous revolutionary war figure and inveterate intriguer named James Wilkerson to act as its agent in recruiting prominent Americans who would be willing to become obedient Spaniards.

Spain did manage to lure many Americans, among them Daniel Boone, to whom it offered generous land grants and the chance to clear his debts. Wilkerson seemed particularly adept at enticing Kentuckians, and he hoped to tempt Kentucky itself into breaking away and joining the Spanish empire. Spain even began to accept Protestants, if they would subscribe to a loyalty oath. Finally, in 1795, Spain signed a treaty that opened the Mississippi River to American trade, and the American immigration into its colony became a flood.

The immigrants were attracted by Louisiana's two great assets: free land and no taxes. True, they nominally abandoned their new-found nationality, but they no more ceased to be American than the Creoles had stopped being French a generation before. They shied away from the French villages, locating on isolated farms as they always had. Compulsive doers, comfortable with political talk, jury duty, hotly-contested elections, they looked on the French not as charming and relaxed, but as supercilious and lazy. Regardless of the oaths they took, they rejected European values and institutions, especially the Catholic Church. Under the winking eyes of the Spanish authorities, they continued to practice their intensely emotional brand of Christianity. They brought with them their quick tempers, their taciturn manners, and their violent ways, and by the close of the century they were in the majority.

In short, they still spoke the language of the American West. And when Spain, realizing its mistake, belatedly threatened to close the Mississippi and the port of New Orleans to American traffic, its new settlers were as ready as their relatives and friends back in Kentucky and Tennessee to go to war to keep the river trade flowing.

Spain considered taking a stand in Louisiana against its European and New World rivals, but in the end recognized that, despite all the money and

A sketch of the levee at New Orleans by Joseph Horton. The business boom in the South brought with it great prosperity, making the Mississippi a busy waterway and the levee at New Orleans a hive of industry.

effort it had wasted, Spanish Louisiana was no more successful an American Empire than French Louisiana had been. She gave the place back to France, again by secret treaty, in 1800. France in the meantime had changed much more than had the colony, undergoing a bitter and bloody revolution and the rise of Napoleon. For a moment, Napoleon contemplated making Louisiana the footstool of his empire, but then a couple of rich Americans arrived in Paris. Emissaries from a nervous Thomas Jefferson, who unlike his Western citizens did not want to go to war over the river, they were shocked by the deal the Emperor offered them.

The French merchants and settlers who inhabited the vast lands purchased by the United States in 1804 had never made any effort to overthrow their monarch, French or Spanish, and no popular uprising forced Louisiana into the American fold. They had already lived under two flags. Now, as the Stars and Stripes ran up the pole, they characteristically shrugged and went about their business. Before the year was out, the residents of St. Louis, led by the prominent Chouteaus, were enthusiastically entertaining two of their new president's special emissaries – Meriwether Lewis and William Clark.

Jefferson had sent the two young men, after Congress approved his purchase and made Louisiana the United States' newest territory, to discover just how much land he had in fact bought for his $15 million. Lewis and Clark departed on their famous expedition from St. Louis in 1804. Behind them, many of the town's residents fully believed they would find the Northwest Passage at last, and St. Louis would be the point of departure to the Pacific and the marvels of the Orient beyond. They would have no more luck than their predecessors on that score, but they would discover a new natural wealth of indescribable variety and abundance. And they would tell the world.

Lewis, a woodsman and hunter from childhood, who at twenty had helped to suppress the Whiskey Rebellion, had most recently been Thomas Jefferson's secretary. Once he had persuaded the President to let him lead the already-planned expedition, he recruited his former comrade-in-arms, William Clark, younger brother of the famed Indian fighter and Revolutionary War hero, George Rogers Clark. Lewis was twenty-nine, Clark thirty-two, and the adventure of their lives lay ahead of them.

They started out with twenty-nine in their party, including a few Frenchman and a goodly number of

An 1878 photograph of the interior of a Mississippi River steamboat. Passengers could choose between traveling inside in the well-lit and beautifully appointed quarters, or on the decks with their wonderful views.

Kentuckians. Some, like Simon Kenton, were already well-known frontiersmen. Others, like John Colter, would become famous. Along the way they would pick up an interpreter named Toussant Charbonneau and his wife, Sacajewa, a Shoshoni who would prove invaluable as a guide and become an American legend. Only one member of the expedition died en route, Charles Floyd, nephew of one of Kentucky's first explorers, from a burst appendix.

The Missouri, which Lewis and Clark followed into the interior, had been chartered only as far above St. Louis – itself not much more than a trading center of perhaps two hundred houses – as the Mandan villages in the Dakota region where they would make their winter camp. Their trek westward would take them as far as the Columbia River in modern-day Washington, then only chartered at its mouth. The country in between was a blank, populated by myth and imagination with tribes of man-hating Amazons, who amputated their breasts to better draw bow-and-arrow; Welsh-speaking Indians descended from an ancient Celtic wanderer; the lost tribes of Israel, and even eighteen-inch devils at a place named *Les Cotes Bruless*.

They found instead peaceful Otos, whom they befriended and gave medals stamped with the likeness of Thomas Jefferson; hostile Teton Sioux, who demanded tribute from all traders and whom they fought, establishing a lasting enmity; Shoshoni, who welcomed with open arms Sacajewa, their little sister, kidnapped as a child by the Mandans; in all more than fifty tribes, with whom they made for the most part amicable contact. They found an Eden, full of giant, ten-thousand-plus buffalo herds, and elk and antelope so free from human contact that they tamely approached members of their troop. They also found a hell, blighted with mosquitoes so numerous they were forced to breathe them, and winters harsher it seemed than any could reasonably hope to survive. They got desperately lost, then found their way again; catalogued a dazzling array of new plants and animals; even unearthed the bones of a forty-five-foot dinosaur.

When they returned to St. Louis from their expedition in September of 1806, they were eagerly greeted and grandly entertained by Pierre and Auguste Chouteau. They had traveled nearly 8,000 miles. If they had failed to do the impossible and discover the fabled Northwest Passage, nevertheless the glowing descriptions they gave of this vast new West provided impetus to the westward migration now becoming a permanent part of American life, a movement that would soon make St. Louis one of the world's great cities.

The news Lewis and Clark got from the Chouteaus, however, was not nearly as good. The new governor

Death of Tecumseh, *leader of the Indian confederation, a colored woodcut by Davis. In 1813, General William Henry Harrison attacked Tecumseh and his brotheras they retreated with British troops at the Thames River in Ontario, during which Tecumseh died. He was viewed as a genius, not only by his own people but also by his enemies and by his foster brother Daniel Boone. With his death died Indian resistance in the Ohio Valley. He was buried secretly. His grave has never been found.*

Andrew Jackson, elected President of the United States in 1828, took care of the nation's "Indian problem" with great dispatch. Indians in the Southeast were driven along the "Trail of Tears" to a land that was falsely promised always to be theirs. Tribes in Illinois and Florida were subjugated by Federal troops.

of the Louisiana Territory, whom Jefferson had appointed, probably at the urging of Vice President Aaron Burr, had turned out to be a disaster. A natural cloak-and-dagger man and a secret traitor, James R. Wilkerson had gone from being an agent in the pay of the Spanish to a U.S. general and the top-ranked officer in the post-revolutionary army. Not only had he made the rivalries in the territory between old time residents and newly arrived land speculators immeasurably worse, but he had also sent secret messages to the Spanish authorities in Santa Fe suggesting they arrest Lewis and Clark if they could track them down.

From the Chouteaus, the two explorers no doubt had a description of Wilkerson's inauguration: a huge celebration, immensely enjoyed by St. Louis' citizens, at which the Governor revealed his great fondness for the bottle. The Chouteaus would surely have expressed their resentment at Wilkerson's attempts to elbow his way into their fur-trading business. And Lewis and Clark could hardly have missed the dark talk, especially among English-speaking residents, of a Western Conspiracy – a plan gossip said Wilkerson had hatched to detach the West from the United States and make Aaron Burr its president.

Wilkerson was in fact deeply involved with Burr in some sort of scheme. Burr had spent two weeks in the fall of 1805 consulting deep into the night with the Governor. The lawless conditions in the territory, created in large measure by the wide-open speculation resulting from disputed Spanish land-grants and the burgeoning mining business, made Louisiana a perfect spot for nefarious plots. And Burr, who had killed Alexander Hamilton in a duel in New York and was quite popular in the anti-Federalist West, attracted followers from Tennessee, Kentucky, and Ohio, as well as along the river. Among them, at least at first, was a hot-tempered Tennessee politician named Andrew Jackson. A famed Indian fighter and a compulsive duelist, Jackson was well on his way to becoming the West's second great popular hero, after Daniel Boone.

Rumors of the Burr-Wilkerson plot reached the president in 1806. When they got bad enough for Jefferson to be forced to investigate, Wilkerson stayed true to form and blamed the entire conspiracy on Burr, who, fecklessly enough, claimed they had

A midnight race on the Mississippi River. Together with the Ohio and Missouri rivers, the Mississippi was a major route used by pioneers traveling Westward. People from the Middle Atlantic states traveled along the Ohio to the Mississippi, then south to the Missouri, which flows from southwestern Montana through the Dakotas, Nebraska, and Missouri to the Mississippi River at St. Louis.

merely intended to invade Mexico and declare him emperor. Though it was a proper enough dream for a westerner in the Napoleonic Era, Burr found himself on trial for his life for treason. He was acquitted, but there proved to be enough evidence to implicate Wilkerson, and so much bitter opposition to him in St. Louis that Jefferson removed him from office on March 3, 1807. The President replaced Wilkerson with a very popular appointment indeed – his former private secretary, now famous explorer, Meriwether Lewis.

Wilkerson's governorship revealed the unsettled quality of the frontier. The United States had still only a quite tenuous hold on its western lands, and westerners themselves, even the best citizens, had a difficult time with questions of legality. Governor Lewis's term would say much about the unrelenting hardness of frontier life.

Well-educated, sophisticated, but mercurial, Lewis felt deeply the responsibilities of his position. He tried to remain efficient and impartial in his administration of the Louisiana Territory, but he also worried incessantly about his standing in the faraway federal capital, and he assumed personal blame for the troubles he encountered among the area's Indians.

Economic depression in the East had increased the already heavy flow of immigrants into the territory. As white settlement pushed farther and farther into ancient hunting grounds, the cycle of raids, murders, and acts of revenge so common to America's Indian-White relations began yet again. In 1805, Lewis's co-explorer William Clark, now promoted brigadier general and made Superintendent of Indian Affairs, concluded a treaty with a few drunken Sac and Fox warriors that greatly irritated the tribes' true leaders, and time and again led to the spilling of blood. By 1808, even the Osage, Louisiana Territory's most powerful tribe, had launched retaliatory raids and were threatening open war.

From the beginning, Lewis had realized that trouble with the Indians was inevitable. He reorganized the militia to prepare for the coming crisis, and with the help of Clark averted general hostilities with the Osage. The two promised to help fight the tribe's vicious Sac and Fox enemies in

An engraving after a sketch by Charles Bodmer of Massika, a Saki (Sac) Indian, and Wakusasse, a Musquake (Fox) Indian. Bodmer, with his patron Prince Maximilian of Wied, came to St. Louis in 1833 to study the native peoples of the plains. He sketched these members of the Sac and Fox delegation, which sought the release of Black Hawk, a prisoner in Jefferson Barracks. Their "roach" hairstyles were common to Missouri River tribes.

return for a substantial portion of Osage land. But despite his foresight, many in Louisiana found Lewis "unsympathetic," even impatient, with traders, while overly delicate in his concern for Indian rights.

Lewis was simply too thin-skinned to handle the harsh criticisms and wild-eyed attacks typical of Western politics. Accusations that he was misappropriating public funds, a quite common complaint against territorial officeholders whether it was true (as it often was) or not, took their toll on his sensitive soul. Always moody, he began to drink heavily. William Clark tried to help his friend by inviting him to come and live with himself and his new bride, but the governor turned him down, choosing instead to take up residence with Auguste Chouteau.

From there, in 1809, Lewis left St. Louis for Washington, where he hoped to explain the confusion over his personal expenditures to the new administration headed by James Madison. Somewhere along the way his melancholy overwhelmed him. In western Tennessee, he apparently committed suicide.

Two years later, the trouble Lewis had always feared with the Indians finally arrived. For many moons, a Shawnee chief named Tecumseh and his brother, a one-eyed epileptic named Tenskwatawa, and called the Prophet, had been trying to gather together a confederation of Ohio Algonquins and the southern tribes. In 1811, Tecumseh's followers spread terror along the frontier. William Henry Harrison, governor of Illinois Territory since 1800, led the counter-attack, and frustrated Tecumseh's dreams of confederation at the Battle of Tippecanoe. Meanwhile, fighting broke out also with the tribes of the upper Mississippi, and Louisiana's new governor – Kentucky Congressman and soldier Benjamin Howard – called out the militia.

The British, of course, supported the frontier skirmishes, and they served as one more cause for Congress to declare war against Great Britain, which it did in July of 1812. Suddenly the Indian threat seemed serious indeed, though the occasional raids and the murder of isolated families kept settlers on edge mostly because the feverish temper of the war magnified the threat. Captain Nathan Boone, Daniel Boone's son and an Indian fighter for most of his life, patrolled the Missouri River with his band of mounted rangers, and some real fighting occurred at Portage des Sioux, but during the next two years it was more alarm and rumor than actual combat that spread fear and uncertainty throughout the territory.

It was only after the War of 1812 was over that the threat became real. Despite Andrew Jackson's undeniably great victory at the Battle of New Orleans, the war was not much of a success. At the Treaty of Ghent, the British had managed to bargain for the cessation of all military activity on the frontier until the United States had concluded treaties with the "Indian allies of the English." And while many of the tribes felt betrayed by the British as the latter retreated into Canada, they soon realized that they were free to roam the trans-Mississippi west at will because the Americans were hamstrung by an international agreement. William Clark, who had replaced Howard as governor, could not officially fight back as Indian raids grew bolder and bolder in the six months following the treaty, when the Indians launched the most destructive attacks of the entire war.

By 1815, however, the tide had turned, and Clark, Auguste Chouteau, and Ninian Edwards, serving as United States commissioners, opened treaty conferences at Portage des Sioux that ultimately resulted in the signing of a peace agreement by some twenty-nine tribes. The War of 1812, now finally over in the West, had bound the region firmly and forever to the young nation. Clark stayed on as governor for another six years, helping to insure that those treaties and the one which followed removed, on the whole, the Indian danger to western migration. Settlers flocked west, speculation ran wild, credit expanded, land values mushroomed, western boosters began plotting towns and organizing counties, and Andy Jackson – hero of the War, champion of the common man, quintessential Westerner – became president.

All the Indians suffered loss of land and the humiliation of defeat, but perhaps none more than the southern "civilized" tribes. Under Jackson, they were run completely off their land and removed by forced march beyond the great river to a forsaken place called Indian Territory. On the infamous "Trail of Tears," former Cherokee braves approaching the river could hear the strange sounds of a new invention chugging up and down the Mississippi in service of the West's new god, commerce.

The steamboat, invented about the time Tecumseh first came to them with his visions of a native-American empire, did what three great European nations had failed to do in almost three centuries of effort – tamed the river. The Mississippi riverboats were a microcosm of the Louisiana frontier. Devoted to gambling and trade, they were plush and decadent, and required quick wits and strong backs to operate effectively. Paddling along the muddy waters, they were the West's supreme mode of locomotion for about as long as the Spanish had ruled its colony. But in that time, the Americans, with the help of these steam-powered, flat-bottomed vehicles, would transform the Father of Waters from a wet gash separating civilization and savagery into a gateway for the opening of a continent.

A broadside from the Hannibal and St. Joseph Railroad offering land in northern Missouri at various prices per acre. In 1862 the Pacific Railway Act gave railroad companies five square miles of land on either side of every mile of track laid. The companies then sold on much of this land through aggressive advertising.

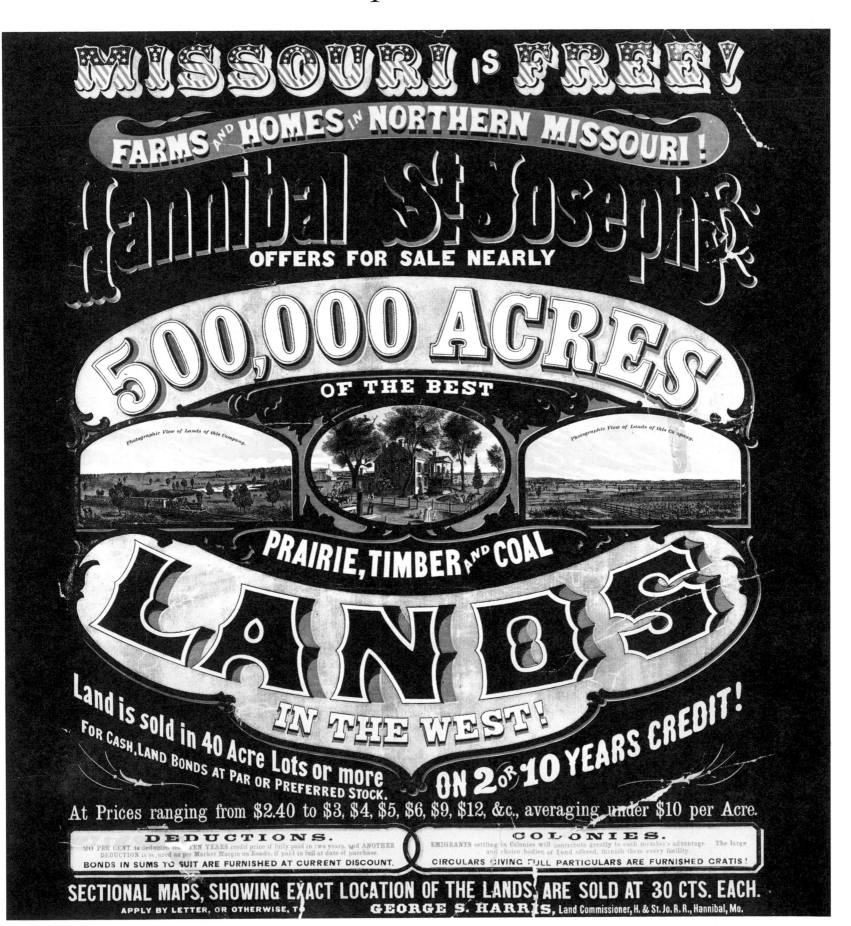

3

FUR

For two centuries, the fur trade had been the only true trade of the North American wilderness, simply because pelts – beaver, fox, mink, martin and otter – were the only items found in the wilderness worth anything at all back in the capitals of Europe and along America's eastern seaboard. Despite much wishful thinking and a good deal of wasted prospecting, the other traditional forms of portable wealth – gold and silver – continued to elude the French *coureurs de bois* and the British trappers who paddled their log canoes into the interior. So they threw up flimsy trading posts, collected pelts from the Indians, moved in with the native women, and settled for servicing the demands of contemporary fashion.

The fashion industry was then fueled by the "absolute necessity" of beaver hats for gentlemen, and fur trim of all kind on collars, cuffs, hems, bonnets, and boots. Alone, or in small groups, or backed by well-financed corporations, the fur traders ranged first the old Northwest, then the wilds of the trans-Mississippi and Rocky Mountains, and finally the Pacific Northwest, looking for easy money off nature's bounty. Unlike the American colonials, they

weren't especially enamored of land; they were businessmen, seeking fortunes.

The Indians, of course, were their proletariat, and the profitable commerce in animal peltry was often simply called by the whites the "Indian trade." After the French and Indian War, that trade was exploited by two British giants: the North West Company and the Hudson's Bay Company. Before the Louisiana Purchase, the Americans – blocked from the trade early on by the French and their Indian allies and later by the Canadian monopolies – trapped only casually and part time. But even before Lewis and Clark had returned from their expedition, Westerners had started forming corporations themselves and cutting each others throats for the incredible profits the fur trade would yield, until silk replaced beaver as the material of choice in the high hats of the city.

St. Louis, located on the west bank of the

A Hudson Bay Trading Store. The Hudson Bay Trading Company was one of two early fur-trading giants, but it did not retain its near monopoly for long. After the Lewis and Clark expedition, independent fur traders started forming their own companies throughout the West.

Mink trappers in the wild. The hatters' choice of beaver for standard top hats made this the favored pelt, but mink, fox, martin, and otter were also plentiful.

A fur trapper's cabin in the wilderness. Beaver pelts got in the fall, winter, and early spring were thicker than those of summer, so trappers had to go to work when the weather was at its worst, hunting in ice-cold streams and rivers.

Mississippi, just below the mouth of the Missouri, was perfectly positioned to become the raucous capital of the fur trade. By the end of the War of 1812, the new steamboats transported men and supplies into the wilderness and brought back peltry by the ton, nearly $4 million in this "brown" gold by 1830. As the shipments passed through the ever growing number of warehouses along the waterfront, taverns and grogshops sprang up to serve the trappers, rivermen, wagoners, old Indian fighters, and drifters who met there to drink, boast, gamble, fight, and generally raise hell. Crime ran wild. Thieves, thugs, troublemakers, even a kidnapper or two, slunk along the muddy, unpaved streets of the city at night, and soon the saying was common in St. Louis that "God would never cross the Mississippi."

Where Angels feared to tread, the fur trappers rushed in, not only across the Father of Waters but on up into the Rocky Mountains, and soon they were known everywhere as "mountain men." The requirements for the profession were not all that different from those of a farm laborer – a strong back, a healthy constitution, the knack for handling tools and weapons. Many, in fact, were ex-farm hands grown bored with the settled life. Perhaps 2,000 mountain men roamed the wilderness, essaying a trapper's life, before fickle fashion took a turn to the Far East.

The job itself called for months, even years, of usually solitary labor in the wilderness, fighting off grizzly bears and unfriendly Indians in for the most part unexplored country. The Blackfeet, especially, were a problem. Hostile since Meriwether Lewis had shot two members of a party attempting to steal his horses and rifles, they killed perhaps 500 mountain men in the thirty years between the time of the

A frontiersman leads his horse downstream through the water to cover their tracks, depicted in a W.M. Cary woodcut. Competition was fierce among the mountain men, who took elaborate steps to guard against sharing the whereabouts of good trapping areas with their comrades.

Fur traders weighing pelts on a steelyard, in a watercolor drawing by Paul Rockwood. When Lewis and Clark returned from their expedition they reported huge populations of beaver along the Missouri and in the Rockies, sending hundreds of hopeful trappers West.

expedition and the decline of the American fur trade in the late 1830s – a twenty-five percent mortality rate.

The trapping itself was no picnic. Universally, trappers used a five-pound steel trap with a five-foot chain, which they buried in streams, covered with twigs, and scented with musk to attract the beaver. Since the pelts were only valuable when they had thickened during the fall, winter, and early spring, trappers for the most part spent their days wading in ice-cold water, with no prospect of bath or change to dry clothes.

As their work took them further afield, the mountain men returned to St. Louis less and less frequently, relying on an annual rendezvous to meet their co-workers and trade in their furs. They came with the pelts they had carefully husbanded out of the wilderness and with the Indian women – following a venerable trapper tradition established in French times – they had taken as wives, or at least bedmates. At the rendezvous, trappers could make fortunes overnight. There, each year, they drank, boasted, gambled, fought, and generally raised hell – just as they used to do in St. Louis. For all its hazards and hard times, the trappers' life was one of manly self-indulgence, of constant hunting and fishing, of absolute freedom from taxes, mortgages, proper

wives, the law – a perfect escape from the demands and constraints of a civilization that, unlike God, had no intention of stopping at the river.

As Washington Irving observed in the 1830s, these mountain men had thrown off "everything that may bear the stamp of civilized life" and put on "the manners, habits, dress, gestures and even the walk of the Indian." And when the trapper, in his knee-length hunting shirt of brightly-dyed, ruffled calico, his leather leggings ornamented with strings and fringe, the finest of moccasins on his feet, a scarlet blanket slung cross his shoulder, his hands resting on the pistols and knives stuck in the red sash round his waist, an Indian pipe clenched in his teeth, strolled into St. Louis, it was not to read one of the city's three newspapers, patronize its bookstore, visit its symphony or attend one of the fancy balls up on the bluff, but to head straight for the brothels and gambling dens and whiskey mills down on the levee. "The reckless mountain boys," wrote another observer during the same period, "who had returned from their summer campaigns were the life and terror of the place."

Up on the bluff lived the men who employed the reckless mountain boys. St. Louis' wealthy fur merchants, many of them descended from the original French settlers, all of them aping their sophisticated

Trappers skinning beavers on the Oregon Trail. The work of a fur trapper was brutal; it required months living away from civilization, fending off attacks from grizzly bears and unfriendly Indians, and carrying out the grueling work of setting traps, skinning and preparing hide; all during the freezing winter months.

ways, rivaled one another in erecting limestone mansions sumptuously appointed with mahogany, crystal, velvet and lace. Auguste Chouteau, for example, who as a young man had cleared the land on which Laclerde founded the city, lived in a residence with black walnut floors that his servants polished each day with a fresh coat of wax. He and his fellow aristocrats called the new American entrepreneurs, like William Clark, "Bostons." Not to be outdone, the Bostons used their recently acquired fortunes to build in the grand style. Clark's house included his council chamber, measuring a huge one hundred by thirty-five feet, in which he exhibited all the Indian artifacts he had "gathered" over the years, under a series of massive, elaborate, European chandeliers.

St. Louis' elite may have dressed in lace rather than leather, drank port instead of rye, and attended plays instead of cockfights, but they, too, were a frontier generation, prone to its temperamental ways. Instead of fistfights, they opted for duels. A challenge would be issued, two principals and their seconds would row calmly out to Bloody Island, the city's "field of honor" located in the middle of the Mississippi, there to coolly, decorously, blast away a life. Not as many died on the field of honor as at the hands of the Blackfeet, but their deaths at least were officially recorded, seven of them, prominent citizens all, between 1810 and 1831.

First among the St. Louis fur merchants were the Chouteaus. They had been dealing with the Indians and in pelts, of course, long before the Americans bought the wilderness. After Lewis and Clark departed on their expedition, Auguste Chouteau and his brother Pierre – who had been appointed agent for the Indians of the Louisiana Territory in 1804 – organized a fur trading party to exploit the wilderness now being explored by the U.S. government. They dreamed no doubt of establishing their own great American monopoly to rival those of the Canadians. But they were not the only ones in St. Louis to give serious thought to the expedition and how it might well open commercial possibilities for those with the right backing and skills.

Manuel Lisa had arrived in St. Louis a dozen years before. Born in New Orleans, a Spaniard of vague South American descent, Lisa was a mercenary spy who had dabbled in government contracts and bribes and smuggled contraband goods deep into Spanish territory. Under contract to supply provisions for the 1804 expedition, he and his partner – perhaps intentionally – had so bungled the job that he earned the enmity of the quick-tempered Meriwether Lewis. A violent and ruthless man, Lisa was also an inspired entrepreneur who could talk almost anybody into almost anything, and by the time the two now famous

Above: a Hudson Bay fur trader. Trappers fed the fashion industry with beaver pelts, which were made into hats and used to trim coats, bonnets, and boots. The trade thrived until the late 1830s, when silk replaced beaver as the chosen fabric for top hats.

Left: intrepid Luther "Yellowstone" Kelly had five years of experience trapping along the Yellowstone River in the Montana Territory when, in 1873, Grant Marsh hired him to guide an expedition up part of the river that had previously been thought to be unnavigable.

explorers returned to the city in 1806, Lisa had already begun preparations to send a party of fur trappers into the mountains.

All this time, James Wilkerson, Louisiana's intrigue-loving territorial governor, was playing his own dark game. He had asked Lisa the year before to put off his plans, and when the latter ignored the dipsomaniacal chief executive, Wilkerson dispatched Zebulon Pike on his own "expedition" to Santa Fe with letters warning New Mexico's authorities of this latest American threat to Spanish holdings in the West. But while Wilkerson plotted with Aaron Burr, and the Chouteaus, hoping to join forces for safety's sake, negotiated with the leaders of three other proposed fur trading parties, Manual Lisa hired several members of the Lewis and Clark exploration party, outfitted sixty men and loaded them onto keelboats, and headed up the Missouri in the early spring of 1807.

Somewhere on the upper river Lisa found John Colter, who had remained behind to do a little trapping of his own when Lewis and Clark had headed back to St. Louis. Lisa hired him on the spot, and together the two made history. Colter persuaded

Lisa to build a combined trading post and fort at the point where the Little Bighorn flows into the Yellowstone River. From there, during the winter of 1807-1808, Colter made the most extraordinary solo exploration any American would ever make in the West, traipsing in a circuit through what is now Wyoming, Montana, and Idaho. Almost constantly in virgin wilderness, Colter discovered such wonders as the hot springs, boiling mud holes and geysers of Yellowstone before returning to Lisa's fort.

Such would become the stuff of the John Colter legend, as would his capture by a band of 500 Blackfeet the coming fall. The Indians came upon Colter and a companion trapping near the Jefferson Fork on the upper Missouri. They killed his partner on the spot, then stripped and casually tortured Colter, finally allowing him to run buck naked for his life. He beat all but one of them to the Jefferson Fork six miles away, turned and killed the swift brave, and then hid in the water under driftwood while the rest of the band scoured the shore looking for him. That night he swam downstream five miles, then took to the shore, running this time for seven days and 200 miles to arrive – half-starved, on rock-flayed feet, his

Jeremiah "Liver-Eating" Johnson, one of the last of the mountain men, first arrived at the Missouri River in 1843. A trapper, hunter, and woodcutter, Johnson was also a ferocious Indian killer. His nickname came to him by way of his reputation for killing and scalping Crow Indians, and then eating their livers.

body blistered, dehydrated, and full of festering thorns – once again at Manuel Lisa's fort on the Little Bighorn.

Colter continued trapping for Lisa, but after another narrow escape from the Blackfeet in 1810, forswore the frontier life and retired to St. Louis, where he told tales of his adventures to the eager ears of his old commander, William Clark. By that time, Clark, too, was working for Manuel Lisa, as president of the latter's Missouri Fur Company.

In fact, Colter's boss had been back in the city since 1808, expanding his business. When he first trekked out of the wilderness with his initial crop of pelts in tow, the frontier town's elite was forced to treat him a bit differently than they were wont. The Chouteau's tardy fur-trapping expedition, led by Lt. Joseph Kimball and Lewis-and-Clark alum Nathaniel Pryor, had run into serious trouble with the Arikara Indians. Refused passage, the group returned in defeat from this first encounter of the U.S. Army and Native Americans west of the Mississippi. Having succeeded where others failed, Lisa commanded respect, however reluctant and uncordial.

Lisa was always something of a scoundrel, and he constantly challenged the tolerance of his fellow St. Louis tycoons. After one of the men in his trading party had threatened to quit, Lisa had him executed. When he was tried for murder, however, he beat the charge by accusing his dead employee of being a deserter who "got what he deserved." And though Lisa had a proper bride in St. Louis, he took a least one Indian wife. In general, Lisa carefully courted the Indians with gaudy gifts and liquid spirits, because he fully intended to cut them out of the fur trade completely.

As Lisa explained to the investors in his new and thriving company, the old French and British methods would never work in the American West. The Plains Indians were equestrians. They hunted buffalo and stole horses for a living. Plodding through a prairie swamp and planting traps was beneath them. Instead of reimbursing the Indians, who after all were never very stable workers, to bring in pelts from their tribal hunting grounds, Lisa argued for hiring his own white trappers, paying them to chase the fur wherever they could find it without respect for traditional tribal boundaries, and having them bring their catch back to a central spot – in this case, Fort Lisa on the Little Bighorn – for shipping to St. Louis. No Indians to curry favor with, no string of fortified trading posts to keep up, fewer opportunities to be double-crossed – that Lisa could create such a system and still maintain for years a workable truce on the frontier explains why he had at least a portion of virtually all the fur business out of St. Louis until his remarkably peaceful death in bed at a health spa in 1820.

But when it came to audacity of vision and the stockpiling of profits, Manuel Lisa was a piker compared to John Jacob Astor. Born in Germany, Astor set sail for America after the Revolution, determined to make a fortune. On the passage over he engaged in long talks with a fellow passenger, a furrier by trade, and within twenty years of his landing in New York he had become the richest man in America through the retailing of wilderness pelts. In the years immediately following the Louisiana Purchase, Astor decided to get into the production end of the business – trapping – as well, and he formed the American Fur Company.

The idea was to beat the Canadian monopolies to the vast raw supply of pelts in the Pacific Northwest. In a plan heartily approved by President Jefferson himself, Astor hoped to establish a fur-trading outpost near the site where Lewis and Clark had wintered in 1805-1806. With a certain disdain for the mountain men Lisa employed, Astor reasoned that he would need seasoned professionals to compete with the

Fur trappers floating their pelts down the Missouri River. In a season's trapping, a typical haul consisted of about 120 pelts, which would bring the mountain man $1,000 – much of which he would spend drinking, gambling, and consorting with Indian women.

North West and Hudson Bay companies, and hired their former employees and some French-Canadians to form two parties, one of which would travel by land, the other by sea, to the far side of the continent and found Fort Astoria.

They left in 1810, thirty-three aboard the brig *Tonquin*, out of New York bound round the Horn for the Oregon coast, sixty-four leaving St. Louis heading across the Rockies to a rendezvous at the mouth of the Columbia River. The ship reached the spot first, losing seven men in the high seas during a hasty landing. Half the rest remained behind to build the fort as the *Tonquin* sailed on upriver to trade with Indians. The bargaining did not go well; the *Tonquin's* arrogant and abrasive captain slapped a Salish chief, and a few days later the Indians returned the sentiment by butchering all aboard but five. Four of the survivors escaped by boat under the cover of darkness, but one – gravely wounded – crawled into the hold to die. When the Indians returned the next morning, he touched off the brig's store of gunpowder, killing hundreds of braves and reducing the ship to 290 pounds of splinters.

Seven months later, the overland crew began straggling into Fort Astoria with few furs but many tales from what had been an epic of suffering. Led by a New Jersey-born St. Louis storekeeper named Wilson Hunt, who knew nothing about the wilderness, the party had started out in a race against Manuel Lisa's employees for the then beleaguered Fort Lisa, only to break off and head across country for fear of the Blackfeet. Trading boats for horses with the Arikara and the Mandan, they were the first Americans to traverse the plains, and all went surprisingly well until they broached the Rockies and reached the Snake River. They tried to take the river in canoes, and soon found themselves swirling beneath sheer, mile-high walls. Those who didn't drown and managed to scale the icy rock walls of Hell's Canyon were faced with a winter march through barren land devoid of game. Forty-five of them made it, some in early 1812, others not until the spring, and seven as late as January of 1813.

A supply ship, the *Beaver*, arrived in May. Finally, the Astorians began trapping, buying furs by the thousands, and sending Robert Stuart off

overland to tell John Jacob Astor that at last it seemed his project might work. Stuart went further south than usual and found more easily traveled routes than had Lewis and Clark; routes that would become the Oregon Trail, the major highway of far western immigration.

Gratified by Stuart's report, Astor declared, "I have hit the nail on the head," but he was soon to discover he had more realistically shot himself in the foot. In the east, the United States and Britain were now at war. Fearing attack by British warships, the Astorians—former Canadian fur company employees and none too loyal to the United States or to Astor—sold their fur to their Canadian competitors at much debased prices and turned the fort over to the first Union Jack that sailed into view. The U.S. got the post back under the Treaty of Ghent, but Astor was thoroughly sick of the place by then. He had lost sixty-one lives and, more importantly as far as he was concerned, had not seen a single penny of profit. In fact, he was out some $400,000, which in 1813 was enough of a fortune to give pause even to a man with pockets as deep as the founder of the American Fur Company.

The War of 1812 not only proved fatal for John Jacob Astor's grandiose Astoria dream, it also crippled

Fur traders on the Missouri being attacked by Indians. Fur trappers were plagued by the animosity of the Blackfoot which was roused when Meriwether Lewis shot two Indians trying to steal horses.

Left: a Currier and Ives lithograph of a trapper and his horse, after a painting by Frederic Remington. A trapper's horse was often his only companion in the wilderness.

Right: an old-time Western mountain man on horseback. The rifles carried by mountain men were their only protection, and they would often give their guns names. Yellowstone Kelly called his "Old Sweetness."

the American fur trade in general. Only the wily Manuel Lisa somehow managed to operate during the hostilities, though the diminished fortunes of the Missouri Fur Company were such that most Westerners simply called it "Manuel Lisa's company."

Immediately following the war, the westward movement surged forward again, and by 1815 some fifty wagons were ferried across the Mississippi into St. Louis every day. Along the Missouri, settlement pushed back the frontier thirty or forty miles a year. Hunters, trappers and squatters flooded into the Arkansas River Valley and the Red River valley, to be followed soon by "legal" settlers. In 1819, Congress commissioned an expedition up the Missouri to establish military forts and impress on the Indians – and any British traders illegally trapping in the region – its might and its sovereignty. That same year, wild land speculation – fast becoming a standard feature of western "expansion" – triggered a severe financial panic, and a move to limit western growth was afoot. In 1825, the proposed limitation became law, when President James Monroe approved yet another frontier line separating civilization and wilderness. This one ran through present-day Kansas and Oklahoma, beyond which settlement was forbidden.

Trappers, as always, were not interested in settling the country they explored, and they were even less interested in legal fictions called boundaries. Once again they would blaze the trails that their land-hungry fellow citizens, ignoring their own government, would follow in search of hope and a home.

Manuel Lisa died long before then, but another St. Louis entrepreneur named William Ashley had taken over where he left off. Ashley had been a munitions maker during the war, then a real-estate speculator before the Panic of 1819, and now he had become Lieutenant Governor of the brand-new state of Missouri. In 1821, using his position to advantage, he teamed up with Lisa's former partner, Andrew Henry, and formed the Rocky Mountain Fur Company. He recruited at $200 per annum an astounding group of men – Jed Smith, Jim Bridger, Tom Fitzpatrick, Hugh Glass, the Sublette brothers, James Clyman, Edward Rose – who would usher in the heyday of the mountain man.

In 1823, after Henry had traveled to the mouth of the Yellowstone and built a fort, Ashley led his band of young toughs up the Missouri into the waiting arms of the angry Arikara. Hostile for decades, the tribe was especially incensed over recent protection afforded their ancient enemies, the Sioux, by white traders, and on June 2 they launched 600 strong against Ashley's post, occupied by seventy men. In reply to Ashley's pleas for help, the U.S. Sixth Infantry, under Col. Henry Leavenworth, responded in force, only to be humiliated by the Indians and lose completely the traditional river routes into the wilderness.

Cut off along the rivers by the Arikara, Ashley could not head north either, unequipped as he was to compete with the Hudson's Bay Company or the now-recovered American Fur Company on their well established trapping grounds. He had no choice but to turn west and set out overland. In the fall of 1823, Ashley sent the survivors of the Arikara debacle deep into the Rockies on horseback and by mule train. In a typically American way, what started out as a makeshift and temporary solution became a new and more effective way of doing business.

Each year, Ashley moved men, supplies, and fur between the mountains and the lower Missouri by pack trains and wagons, and to keep in touch with his wandering brigades established the annual rendezvous, which soon became the major institution of the American fur trade. A good trapper arrived at the rendezvous with three or four hundred pelts, a lucky one sometimes with twice that many, and sold them to Ashley, or his successor Bill Sublette, or whoever in later years happened to hold the concession. Before the trade began its decline, beaver might bring between two and four dollars a pelt, which could be resold in St. Louis at a 200 percent markup.

The mountain men were happy, though, with the $2,000 or so they cleared at a time when skilled labor brought perhaps $1.50 a day. The trappers, however, tended to spend much of what they made during the month-long rendezvous itself, on liquor, on Indian women, on gambling, but most of all on the goods and supplies they needed for the coming year – offered them at outrageous prices by the same merchants who bought their furs. In effect, the trappers worked eleven months for a single debauch at the rendezvous. They not only looked like Indians, and acted like them, but economically they were treated by their bosses essentially as the Native Americans had been treated during the three centuries of the "Indian trade."

But what the hell, they loved adventure, which they courted year-long and paid dearly to brag about at the rendezvous. Hugh Glass told of being mauled nearly to death by a grizzly and being nursed back to health by the Sioux. Jim Bridger boasted that he was the true discoverer of the Great Salt Lake. Jim Beckwourth became a war chief of the Crows, while Jeremiah "liver-eating" Johnson carried on a one-man war with the same tribe. Thirty-four-year-old Joseph Walker chose the rendezvous at Green River in 1833 to announce that he was undertaking an expedition all the way to the coast of California. And

he and forty others, backed by sometimes fur trader and most likely government agent Benjamin Bonneville, did so.

Some, like Walker, became known for exploits far beyond those they bragged about at the rendezvous. Bill Sublette became a partner in the Rocky Mountain Fur Company and ended his days rich and famous. Jim Clyman eventually got out of the trade on one of his many wanderings westward and became a founding father of a new state – California. And around the camp fires, listening to the tall tales of a Bridger or a Glass, could be seen the handsome features of a young Christopher Carson, who would become the greatest and best known scout and Indian fighter in the American West, called always by an adoring public "Kit" Carson.

Out of the rendezvous was born a fresh burst of land exploration, and by the mid 1830s American

A W.J. Lubken photograph of trappers and hunters on Brown's Basin Salt River Project in Arizona in January 1908. When later the gold rush began, prospectors found that the early fur trappers had forged the way to the West.

trappers had explored from the eastern slopes of the Rocky Mountains to the Sierra passes into California, from the Columbia River to Death Valley. These were the first white men to gaze upon the badlands of the Great Basin, marvel upon the wonders of Yosemite, stand in awe of the giant redwoods of California.

And at trails' end they discovered an Eden. There, in California, they found prosperity on a grand scale in the sprawling, 50,000-acre ranches of Mexican territory. These tough, ruthless men were charmed by the graciousness of California's fifty leading families, with their fiestas and dare-devil *vaqueros*, their gardens and their breathtaking *la bamba*. If the Grandees were less taken with the Americans, it might have had as much to do with history as with their roughhewn appearance. For Spanish authorities had seen it all before. First came the American trailblazers, the frontiersmen, trappers, adventurers, who wanted to drink you under the table, sleep with your women, and pick your pocket around a card table. And then came the rest: the squatters and settlers, the real-estate promoters and town-planting lawyers, who wanted something much more essential – your land.

If the *Grandees* of California could have seen what was going on back in St. Louis and Missouri, their blood would have run cold. No longer was fur the only, or even the biggest, of that city's businesses. Instead, transportation – riverboats and wagon making and supplies – fed its ever-growing population. And in western Missouri, entirely new towns were springing up, not to service the fur industry, but to outfit the groups and wagon trains passing through as they headed inexorably westward. It was no accident that the senior U.S. Senator from Missouri, Thomas Hart Benton, had adopted a phrase coined by an Eastern newspaperman justifying the quasi-legal activities of western expansion; he called it: "Manifest Destiny."

A Government surveying party and pack-mule train in Colorado in 1878. The United States Government sent supplies through Colorado, along the Colorado River, to its outposts in the deserts of the Southwest.

4
LAND

The mountain men were the midwives for a new wave of migration to the American West. Their exploits encouraged others to engage in another round of exploration, chief among these latest seekers of glory and fortune being Thomas Hart Benton's son-in-law, John C. Fremont. But the "discovery" of new lands for settlement – and the blazing of paths to those new lands – also gave American pioneers a goal: for even the heartiest of the wishful emigrants did not simply load up their conestogas and head west unless they had someplace to go. Finally, as the fur ran out and fashion changed, the mountain men – looking for new jobs – directly encouraged the westward movement by hiring themselves out as explorers, scouts, and wagon-train masters to groups embarking from the growing new supply towns of western Missouri: St. Joseph, Independence, and modern day Kansas City, then called Westport.

The wandering of the fur trappers of course was not the only development in the 1820s and 1830s that led to the great surge of migration beginning about 1841, not the least of the other factors being United States' land policy. With the pacification of the Old Northwest's Algonquin tribes and the Louisiana Purchase, the U.S. government produced it's "final solution" to the Indian "problem." Setting aside land in modern day Arkansas and Oklahoma as Indian Territory, Congress began to sell former Indian lands to its own citizens at bargain rates in order to assure settlement. When other countries, notably Britain, had suggested similar solutions in the past,

the Americans had rattled their sabers and talked of war, but now – at least in their minds – they owned the place. In the long run, no land was safe from the American pioneer, but for now westward movement split north and south around Indian Territory.

Naturally, no one consulted the Indians. When Sac and Fox chief Black Hawk returned with his warriors from the winter hunt of 1830-31 to discover Saukenuk – the tribe's main village at the mouth of the Rock River in Illinois – overrun by white squatters, he threatened war. A spurious treaty signed a quarter of a century before by a few drunken warriors, and never recognized by Black Hawk or his fellow chiefs, had ceded all the Sac and Fox lands in Illinois to the United States. As a matter of expediency, William Henry Harrison deigned to allow the tribe to remain on those lands until the area was needed for settlement. Now, a rush of miners to the Galena lead fields had brought the illegal farmers in its wake, and they destroyed or appropriated the Indians' homes, harvested for themselves the Indian corn, ripped down fences, trampled unused crops, and beat those Sac and Fox in the village who protested. Quick footwork by government officials helped to avert violence that summer and fall, and Black Hawk reluctantly retired to Iowa. But when winter came,

American troops camped near Tampa Bay, Florida. Florida was annexed to the United States after the War of 1812 upon agreement with Spain, which wanted the U.S./ Mexico border far to the east of the Rio Grande in return.

he lead his starving, homeless "British band" – 400 warriors and their families – back across the Mississippi, looking for food.

The U.S. responded hysterically with a show of force, marching troops off to engage the Indians and calling to colors an excessively huge number of militia.

Black Hawk won the first encounter, but that only incensed the Americans. He was betrayed by the British and the Winnebago, both of whom had promised aid but failed to deliver. And he was also betrayed by a member of his own tribe, an ambitious young chief named Keokuk, who urged a substantial number of Sac and Fox to do nothing in order to curry favor with the whites and establish himself as the true, "peaceful," tribal leader. The band was relentlessly hunted down as they fled north along the Rock River into Wisconsin, and massacred when they tried to recross the Mississippi into Iowa. Black Hawk's fate made it clear to those tribes still located east of the Mississippi that armed resistance to the Americans was hopeless.

The Cherokee, especially, took the lesson to heart. In order to fight off forced removal now that Andy Jackson was president, they had declared themselves a sovereign nation in 1827, adopted a constitution similar to that of the United States, sued in the Supreme Court for protection against white land-theft and aggression, and won. But gold had been discovered on their tribal lands, and Georgia simply ignored the Supreme Court's ruling, continuing blithely to appropriate Indian land and trample Indian rights. Encouraged by President Jackson's refusal to enforce the law of the land, Alabama and Mississippi followed Georgia's lead. With Black Hawk's example fresh in their minds, the Cherokees gave up and joined the Chickasaws, Choctaws and Creeks on the Trail of Tears. Of the "civilized" tribes, only the Seminole put up a fight, retreating deep into the impenetrable swamps of south Georgia and the Florida coast. Their resistance cost the Americans some 1500 lives and $20 million before the Seminoles, too, were eventually defeated and forced to migrate west to Indian Territory.

If armed resistance didn't work, and legal remedies were ineffective, perhaps appeasement would stave off the land-hunger of the Americans – so responded the Spanish authorities in the Southwest. When the first trappers began to arrive in the far west, provincial

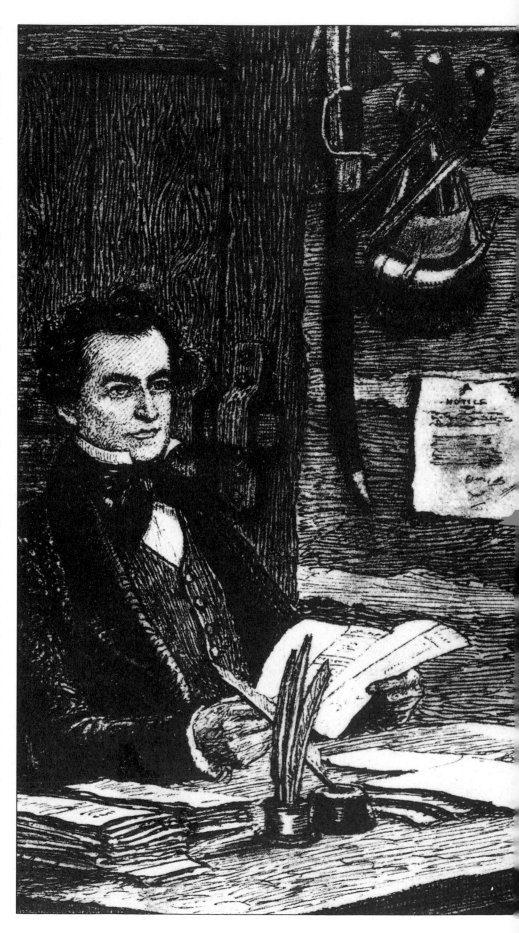

Stephen F. Austin (1793 - 1836) issues a land title to Texas colonists. Austin spent several years encouraging white settlement of Texas, and by 1830, 20,000 people had settled in the region. In an attempt to stem the tide of American expansionism, the Mexican President closed Texas to further colonization by Americans.

governors would occasionally throw them in jail or chase them out of their jurisdiction, but in general Spain continued its age-old habit of conducting business with the fur traders and encouraging those who settled to take out naturalization papers. But the sheer number of settlers eventually made necessary a more official system. Among this latest wave of immigrants there were the bloody-minded adventurers who aimed to displace the legal government and set up one of their own, though these "filibusters" often had in mind joining the United States if they were successful. Spain countered with the *empresario* system, the hiring of agents who swore loyalty to the crown, or soon to the Mexican president, and recruited settlers who also would become loyal citizens of their new country.

Moses Austin was one of the first of the Republic of Mexico's *empresarios*. The old man had made his mark in Missouri mining, but had fallen on hard

General Antonio Lopez de Santa Anna, "Napoleon of the West," fought Sam Houston's rebel Texas army in 1836. The Battle of San Jacinto resulted in Texas becoming independent of Spain, and in Santa Anna being exiled in Cuba. Painting by Paul L'Ouvrier.

times in the economic upheavals of the early 1820s. When he died, his son Stephan carried on the work of creating a Texas colony under the newly independent republic. But Mexico was even more suspicious of the *Norte Americanos* than Spain had been – and with good reason. In December of 1826, the Edwards brothers – Haden and Benjamen – engineered a revolt and proclaimed the Republic of Fredonia. With the help of Austin's militia, the *federales* put down the rebellion by spring of 1827, but it was clear which way the wind was blowing. The next year, Andrew Jackson – avowed expansionist and long-time scourge of the Spanish-speaking peoples of the Americas – became President of the United States. By 1830 there were 20,000 land-hungry Americans in Texas and Jackson was trying to buy the place. That April, Mexico's president closed Texas to any more American "colonists."

But it was too late. The Americans in place had no intention of leaving, and Mexico herself was seething with revolutionary unrest. Soon, it would be apparent that appeasement had gone the way of armed resistance and legal action into the maws of "Manifest Destiny."

For 300 years the land north of modern-day Mexico had been part of a vast Spanish empire, ever since 1536, when Cabeza de Vaca had wandered out of the wilderness in which he had been lost for eight long years. The territory he had explored during his journey was itself an empire worthy of the interest of his fellow *conquistadors*, he felt, albeit a desert empire.

De Vaca had roamed thousands of miles of badlands, where plants were sparse, animals never seemed to drink, and it took a practiced eye to see anything but emptiness stretching to the far horizon. He himself grew to recognize the different kinds of cactus – saguaro, fishhooks, pincushions, hedgehogs, prickly pears (though he called them by other names) – and to appreciate the subtle hues lent the landscape by the sage, mesquite, primrose, four-o'clocks and other wild flowers among which kangaroo rats, ground squirrels, scorpions, peccaries, kit foxes, mule and white-tailed deer, Gila monsters, and rattlesnakes played nature's cruel game of survival. In a region soon to be called Texas, he had climbed the Guadalupe Mountains, a sharp, stratified escarpment that was the remnant of an ancient tropical reef, made up of sedimentary plant and animal remains crystallized into something like limestone, which culminated in the rugged Capitan Reef. From this massive Cap Rock, the half-starved, half-naked wanderer overlooked the plains of Texas and New Mexico. The mile after mile of flatlands, shot through with veins of gypsum and blue-salt crystals, and broken only by brush, arroyos and low hills, reminded him of a limitless sea.

In New Mexico, he found the huge caves that ran under the Cap Rock, filled with eighteen species of bats, as well as stalactites and stalagmites to rival the great cathedrals of Spain itself. From the Carlsbad caverns, Cabeza de Vaca headed south toward the Rio Grande and beyond to the Big Bend country. There the river turned ninety degrees to the north and cut remote canyons through the looming Chisos Mountains. He made his way through this realm of juniper and giant dagger cactus, and, at the higher reaches, of pine and Douglas fir, past dinosaur bones, petrified trees, and fossils embedded in limestone, till he reached a nightmare landscape of striated canyons and blowing sand where the rock was mostly red and so were the rivers. And from there, having seen every type of land the west had to offer but the

The Battle of the Alamo, March 6, 1836. When the Mexican Government attempted to restrict the colonization of Texas by Americans, skirmishes erupted, the most serious of which was the Alamo.

James Bowie (1795-1836). Born in Tennessee, Bowie moved to Louisiana at a young age, and from there to Texas. On March 6, 1836, he fought to the death at the Alamo using his famed bowie knife, and despite suffering from typhoid pneumonia.

for gold and silver. Francisco de Coronado and Juan de Onante forged as far north as the Kansas River in search of a country the Indians called *Quiviria*, but all their cities of gold turned out to be mirages. Their expeditions, however, paved the way for further settlement, and left in their wake a handful of isolated outposts in New Mexico and Texas to assert Spain's title to the West. Throughout the seventeenth century Spain backtracked from these posts to colonize the tremendous stretches of hitherto neglected land. Much of the work was carried out by missionaries, first among them being Father Eusebio Kino, who relentlessly expanded Spain's time-tested mission system into Arizona and Baja California. Kino's activities set the stage for Gaspar de Portila, who in 1769 moved up the Pacific Coast as far north as San Francisco Bay, where he was joined five years later by Juan Baptista de Anza. All that remained was for Anza, the last of the *conquistadors*, to carve a route overland to Arizona to complete Spain's New World colonizing.

Spain's missionaries made effective empire builders. By persuasion or force, they convinced the Indians of the Southwest to help build missions across a frontier – in the more commonplace, Old World sense of the word – that ultimately stretched from the Pacific Ocean to the Red River Valley. These missions reached their apotheosis under the Franciscans in California, who at their peak numbered only thirty-eight souls all told. The padres were patient colonizers, however, assuming from the start that it would take a decade from the time they arrived in an area until they had pacified the local Indians and got the mission functioning properly.

The Church provided each new mission with seed money from a special fund to buy beads, vestments, tools, the necessities of life, and – of course – seeds. Older, established missions were expected to contribute as well, offering whatever they could spare in the way of grain, cuttings, breeding stock, chickens, wine. A couple of padres would arrive on a spot, throw up a temporary chapel and a few rude log cabins, and launch immediately into proselytizing. They purchased the Indians faith with a few glass beads, clothing, blankets, but most especially with food, and they enforced that faith with a detachment of musket-armed soldiers. Once converted, the Indians were not allowed to leave the mission grounds without permission of the clergy. They spent their days tilling the fields and replacing temporary structures with the distinctive architecture of the Spanish West. Not exactly slaves, the Indians nevertheless provided a stable source of labor and were the economic heart of the mission. Over the years, they expanded and developed the compound, and by stages the mission grew into a thriving

immense prairie further north, he turned south again toward Mexico City, the major outpost of an empire that now covered half the known world.

On his long journey Cabeza de Vaca had been a slave, a healer, a hunter, and an itinerant merchant to the thirty different tribes of Indians, some not much more than small bands, he had encountered over nearly a decade. But now he proved himself to be something else, the world's first Westerner, as he announced with willfully blind optimism in his writings: "We concluded that our destiny lay toward the sunset …. It [the country that would become the American West] is, no doubt, the best land in all the Indias. Indeed, the land needs no circumstance to make it blessed."

Inspired by Cabeza de Vaca's accounts, Spanish *conquistadors* ventured back into the region looking

complex, part multiple dwelling, part workshop, part grain bin, all dominated by the church, which sometimes took half a century to complete.

In California alone, six decades after the first padre had arrived, the missions boasted of 17,000 Indian converts, neophytes who not only labored for the church but also displayed considerable talents, for example in music, forming choirs and orchestras that performed at the weddings and fiestas of the *rancheros* and farmers who followed on the heels of the missionaries. Spanish ranches, with their huge land requirements and grand lifestyles, tended to disrupt the mission system, but it was really the harsh authoritarianism and greediness of Spanish officialdom that hampered the Franciscans and other orders in their attempts to assimilate the Indians into Spanish culture. Long before the Mexican government

secularized the missions in the mid-1830s and began breaking them up into ranches, the Iberian Crown had earned the implacable enmity of the Navajos, Comanches, and Apaches, who would continue to fight whites – regardless of national origin – into the late nineteenth and early twentieth centuries.

The Spaniards who trekked north, first into Texas, then New Mexico, Arizona and California, hoped to recreate the good life as defined by Mexico's great *haciendas*. Back there, the gigantic, white-washed houses of the landowner dominated the villages of Indian huts, and the entire estate sprawled over many miles that were roamed by huge herds of cattle and other livestock. The *Grandees* hunted and danced and ate sumptuous meals on their elegant terraces with a host of fellow aristocrats, lawyers, officers and priests, while their managers ran the estates.

The death of Davy Crockett at the Battle of the Alamo. When Mexican troops stormed the mission walls, they killed everyone in sight, including those men who lay wounded on the ground; then they soaked the bodies with oil and burned them.

Reading the Texas Declaration of Independence. On March 2, 1936, Texas formally declared its independence. Sam Houston, shouting the battle cry, "Remember the Alamo," led the rebel army in its successful attempt to rid Texas of General Santa Anna's troops.

It was a life difficult to replicate in the wilderness of Texas, infested with hostile Indians and a thousand miles from the Mexican capital. Instead, most occupied rude cabins and concentrated in the eastern half of the sprawling province, where they lived as pioneers and were required by law to bear arms when they ventured away from home. Like the *Grandees* they loved dancing and raced horses and attended cockfights, but they also understood quite clearly that they could not count much on help from home. In New Mexico, the very towns themselves that sprang up in the nineteenth century would owe their general layout – and their existence in the first place – to fear of marauding Apaches and Comanches.

Only in California, where the mission system had been most successful, did the *rancheros* manage to recapture the grandeur of the homeland and live like princes.

It was no accident then that Texas would prove a hotbed of unrest, even before the Americans began arriving in significant numbers in the 1820s. Since the War of 1812, Galveston Island off the coast of Texas had been occupied by the notorious pirate Jean Laffite, who seized hundreds of Spanish galleons, virtually sweeping Spain from the Gulf of Mexico. And in 1810, a village priest named Miguel Hidalgo had rallied 80,000 peasants into Mexico's first revolutionary army and led them to glorious defeat shouting, "Death to the Spaniards." Such was the territory that proved irresistible to thousands of Americans in the coming decades, lured by the promise of land.

In the aftermath of the Mexican Revolution, the new republic's most famous *empresario* Stephan Austin promised to "redeem" the Texas wilderness by filling it with wholesome, straitlaced colonials who neither drank, cursed, nor gambled, and who were never idle. He was a dreamer, of course, but even if the North Americans had been as he imagined them, the fun-loving Hispanics would not have taken to them any better, for American pioneers, drunk or sober, were racists and had little respect or use for "spics." They came in droves from the hardscrabble farms of Kentucky, the cotton plantations of Georgia, the swampy battlefields of Florida, the mean streets of New York, and while Austin was off in Mexico City in pursuit of land grants, they fed the growing unrest of the Texas frontier with their great propensity for hair-trigger violence.

Among the horde of newcomers were men like Sam Houston. Once he had been governor of Tennessee and married to the beautiful daughter of a prominent family near Nashville. At thirty-five, fleeing rumors surrounding his estrangement from his eighteen-year-old bride, he had resigned his post and moved to Indian Territory, where he lived among the Cherokees and inside a bottle. By the time he had married Tiana Rogers, her tribesmen had changed their name for him from Raven to Big Drunk. Representing the Cherokee in Washington, he lost his temper when a congressman accused him of fraud and beat the elected official with a cane through the streets of the nation's capital. The subsequent trial shook him into sobriety, and he took off for a new start in the West. He rode alone into Texas in 1832, and six months later he was drafting the constitution for an independent Republic of Texas, which Stephan Austin planned to deliver to President Santa Anna in Mexico City.

Santa Anna, a brutal military strongman who had fought his way to power in a civil war, would have none of it. Austin was put under arrest, and before long Houston was in New Orleans looking for volunteers to help steal a nation. Any number of rowdies were willing to answer the call, including a former slave trader named James Bowie, inventor of the infamous Bowie knife, and ex-Tennessee congressman Davey Crockett. Such men, led by hotheads like William B. Travis, made for an unruly army, and only Houston's tactical cleverness saved them from disaster.

Both of the major battles of Texas' war for independence were over in the blink of an eye. Santa Anna's slaughter of the motley crew senselessly

defending a battered old mission in San Antonio called the Alamo took all of ninety minutes. Sam Houston's revenge six weeks later and 225 miles to the east at San Jacinto lasted only 18 minutes. Though the Americans had forcibly separated Texas from Mexico, and the Republic of Texas was recognized by the United States and the international community, especially Britain, its fight with Mexico continued, if sporadically.

The Byzantine maneuverings of America's sectional politics kept the Texas Republic from immediately becoming one of the United States, and meanwhile Texans flirted with the idea of becoming a British ally, and continued to assert sovereignty

Sam Houston (1793 - 1863) served as a congressman and as Governor of Tennessee. A noted Indian fighter, Houston was named commander of the Texan army after the Battle of the Alamo, and, in October 1836, he was elected President of the new Republic of Texas.

south of the Rio Grande against a Mexico that refused to accept the obvious: it had lost its former colony. While Texas raiding parties and Texas Rangers carried on their border warfare against Mexican river towns, settlers elsewhere in the Lone Star Republic began to harvest the fruits of victory.

Really, land was the only apparent asset the infant republic had to offer, but Texas could offer it abundantly. As the new steel plows turned over soil in the thickly-carpeted grasslands of East Texas the land proved fertile beyond imagination, and produced incredible harvests that had Texas farmers spinning tales of twelve-foot-high cotton that renewed itself each season. And with Texas unofficially under its belt, the American West stretched beckoningly toward the Pacific.

Land clearly became the central concept in the ideology of the West. The leaders of the American republic had been from the beginning determined to avoid the fate of Europe, with its small elites, addicted to luxury, and its huge, murderously miserable majorities of people without property. Not just Thomas Jefferson, who idealized the independent and hardworking farmer and became the patron saint of the West, but also John Adams, who declared bluntly that "power always followed property," understood what happened when populations grew, as in the Old World, out of balance with the supply of land.

Cheap credit and a small plot of land somewhere was ever the dream of the West's common man and his political party, Mr. Jefferson's Democracy. And even the privileged class in America, at least before the Civil War, argued that its "experiment" in government depended on the prosperity of individual property holders and thought widely distributed land ownership the best safeguard against dangerous concentrations of power.

It is hardly surprising then that Americans developed what Drew McCoy has called "a vision of expansion across space – the American continent – as a necessary alternative to the development through time that was generally thought to bring both political corruption and social decay." It was a vision of innocence as well as of manifest destiny, and one could hear the romantic longing for the lost purity of Eden in Horace Greely's battle cry of expansion: "Go West, young man, and grow up with the land."

There was something of the missionary's zeal for domination as well as the settler's longing for security

President Anson Jones at the Annexation of Texas on February 19, 1846, after which Federal troops began building a fort above the Rio Grande on land claimed by Mexico. Further fighting broke out on April 25, 1946, and on May 13 President James K. Polk declared war.

wrapped up in this vision of the West as a potential social Eden, and it drew men like Jason Lee, Marcus Whitman and John Spalding – talking about converting the Indians while dreaming of founding a great new state – to Oregon territory in the 1830s. Lee came first, after he had read a letter by a Protestant merchant in the *Methodist Christian Advocate* about three Nez Percé Indians and one Flathead who had appeared in St. Louis in 1831 seeking religious instruction.

Lee persuaded a Massachusetts schoolteacher named Cyrus Shepard to join him, and the two applied to Boston merchant Nathaniel Wyeth, who had recently become a major supplier to the western fur trade, for help in establishing a mission in the Pacific Northwest. Wyeth, an atheist, got them there aboard one of his ships in 1834. His competitors in the British-owned Hudson's Bay Company helped the party establish its mission in the Williamette Valley, among the crude farms of old French *voyageurs* and their Indian wives, partly to prevent the Methodists from moving further into the interior and upsetting the Indian suppliers.

The next year, the Hudson's Bay Company also helped two other missionaries to establish stations in the area, one east of the Cascades at Waiilatpu, on the Walla Walla River, and the other at the Clearwater Fork of the Snake River, deep in the heart of Nez Percé country. Actually, the two groups – Marcus Whitman and his wife Narcissa, and Henry Spalding and his wife Eliza – had arrived together, but could not get along.

Narcissa and Eliza were the first two white women to cross the American continent, and they created quite a stir among Indian and trapper alike. Marcus and Henry were the envy of Jason Lee and Cyrus Shepard until a ship bearing five women reached the Methodist mission on the Columbia that same winter of 1836, and a quick ceremony in a grove of fir trees gave two of the women new last names.

As the fur trade fell into deep decline with the introduction of silk from the East and cheap nutria fur from South America, these missions become the outposts of western migration. Lee's settlement, at least, was quite cognizant of its role. Its fifty-one souls petitioned Congress in 1838 to establish jurisdiction over the territory, flattering themselves that they were "the germ of a great state." All of which was looked at askance by the Hudson's Bay Company, which fancied that the area might well belong to England.

It was about then that the first of the wagon-trains began leaving in 1841. A group of young hardcases under the leadership of twenty-one-year-old John Bidwell set out from Sapling Grove in eastern Kansas for the coast. Each year the number of Prairie Schooners increased, sailing on wild rumors about the golden valleys of California and the black soil of Oregon, and following madly inaccurate maps that made the trip seem easy.

They came by steamboat to the little Missouri towns, jamming the holds and decks with cows and chickens, farm implements and household goods, half of which they would abandon in some God forsaken wasteland on the way. When enough of them had arrived to make a group feel safe, they hired a mountain man, a Tom Fitzpatrick or a Kit Carson, to guide them, and took off in their ordinary farm wagons when the prairie grass was high enough to feed their oxen or their mules.

They waited to pick a captain till they had traveled together for a while, quarreling about firewood, butting in line, carrying on scheming, backbiting, bargain-hunting elections that left the losers disgruntled and bitter. It hardly mattered, however, since most of them paid little attention to their elected leaders anyway, often deposing them, sometimes breaking away from the main train entirely to travel on their own. And for two thousand miles they lumbered along on the Santa Fe and Oregon trails, shouting and bellowing and braying through swirls of dust at the breakneck speed of twelve to twenty miles a day. A train of fifty wagons stretched a mile or so, and when the terrain permitted, the individual wagons traveled side by side.

Occasionally a band of Kansas or Pawnees would ride alongside or hang around the camp at night, begging, sometimes stealing, here and there killing a poor straggler. But for the most part during that first decade, the pioneers were safe enough from everything but an early winter and their own stupidity. Shooting accidents killed more of them than the Indians. Bored children often fell from the wagons and were run over. Some groups got lost. Some starved. A few, like the ill-fated Donner party trapped in the frozen Rockies, turned to cannibalism.

For twenty years, Mexico had dreaded this. Mexican newspapers decried the "fanatical intolerance" of the American pioneers for non whites, and called their country a parasite that "devour[ed] Mexico's entrails." The Texas revolution had proved their point, and now the wagon trains threatened what was left of their land in North America. With Texas now about to join the union, Mexicans were certain that the expansionist colossus hungered for New Mexico and California.

In the mid-1840s, Mexican newspapers began to call for a preventive war against the United States, and the cry was music to the ears of American Westerners who wanted nothing more than an excuse to gobble up the rest of the continent. The brushfire combat along the border flamed into war in 1846.

Antonio Lopez de Santa Anna (1794-1876) fleeing after the battle of Cerro Gordo.

The Mexicans had been right: at the moment Congress drafted the declaration of war on May 9, John C. Fremont was rushing into California; a man name Lansford Hastings was headed east to lure immigrants to the West Coast; a party of Mormons was making its way across Iowa toward the Missouri River and the desert beyond; another Mormon group under Sam Brennan was on the high seas bound for San Francisco, and General Zachery Taylor was already trying to teach a lesson to the Mexicans along the Rio Grande.

The Mexican War made a number of American reputations, including those of generals Taylor and Winfield Scott, Brigadier General Stephan Kearny, commodores Stockton and Perry, Army Scout Kit Carson, Colonel Alexander Doniphan, even Captain Fremont, though he faced a court-martial for his undisciplined glory-hunting. The Americans threatened to make short work of the matter before President James Polk made the mistake of listening to Santa Anna in exile in Cuba when the old autocrat began talking peace. Once he returned to power, Santa Anna immediately revitalized the army. As Taylor and Scott launched the attack on Mexico proper, Kearny marched out of Fort Leavenworth, Kansas, to secure New Mexico and head for California. Led by Kit Carson, Kearny arrived near San Diego to find Commodore Stockton and Fremont already engaged with the hard-riding *vaqueros*, who charged armed with no more than a lance and a lariat, lassoing

their enemies at full gallop, jerking them from their mounts, and stabbing them through with their spears. Meanwhile, Doniphan led his troop of Missouri regulars, after splitting with Kearny in Santa Fe, on an incredible march through the desert to reinforce U.S. troops south of the border, and Commodore Perry took Vera Cruz by sea. In the long run, Mexico had neither the means nor the will to win, and despite some grumbling on the home front it was quite a splendid little affair for the aggressive empire builders of the American West.

By the terms of the treaty ending hostilities, the victors acquired, at a price of $15 million and the assumption of claims by Westerners against the Mexican government, all of modern California, Nevada, Utah, most of New Mexico and Arizona, and a good deal of Colorado. Five years later, the Americans would buy the rest of the present-day continental United States from Mexico in the $10 million Gadsden Purchase.

By then, of course, the troops had long ago returned home to heroes' welcomes and parades were everywhere. But after the giant barbecues thrown by cities like Nashville, and the grand, torch-lit marches of a Charleston, South Carolina, the excitement died down, and many of the men who had marched with Taylor and Scott, Fremont and Doniphan, themselves headed west to the land they had helped conquer. The war with Mexico settled the matter of who owned Oregon officially, but afterward Congress seemed to lose interest in it. It appointed no territorial governor, sent no instructions for establishing a legislature, even though the settlers themselves – some ten thousand strong – had formed a provisional government in 1843. The economy was in shambles. The Hudson's Bay Company which, despite its declining fortunes, had for years absorbed the settler's entire harvest, could not make a dent in the surplus created by the rash of new immigrants farming Oregon's rich soil. So little cash existed that most business was transacted by barter or warehouse receipts, and as stockpiles grew and prices fell, newcomers felt even more destitute than they had back East.

Above: Captain Charles A. May depicted during the Mexican War, May 9, 1846. May falsely boasted that he had captured a Mexican general during the battle at Resaca de la Palma and was later promoted to the rank of lieutenant colonel.

Right: War News From Mexico, a painting by Richard Caton Woodville. Many Americans disapproved of the Mexican War, and it was hotly debated by politicians. In the 1848 election, President James K. Polk's handling of the war was his political undoing.

Even the massacre, in 1847, at the Whitman mission failed to move the federal government to action. One suspects the Whitman's had never been great missionaries. Though Narcissa Prentiss had married Marcus Whitman in order to serve the cause, the thing seemed hastily done, since Henry Spalding, who traveled with them, had been her former suitor back in New York. The four, including Eliza, had the strong-willed contentiousness – and one suspects the sexual repressions – of self-appointed agents of God. Bickering all the way across country, when they arrived in Oregon they divided up Indian tribes and locations like traveling salesmen staking out merchandise and sales territories.

Narcissa's letters to friends and family in the East reveal a lonely, frustrated, overworked woman, severely tested by the daily trials of cooking three meals a day for twenty people, including the eleven orphans duty demanded she adopt, as well as anyone who might wander in, exhausted and half-starved, off the Oregon Trail, which ran past her front doorstep. She quarrelled with the other missionary wives and despaired over the death of her only naturally born child by drowning at age two. Caught up in the tangled race relations of missionary work, ministering

to the spiritual needs her church had invented for those she considered savages, it probably never really occurred to her how God's work might appear to the Indians of the Northwest.

For what they saw was an ever growing stream of white settlers passing through the mission onto their lands east of the Cascades. And what they – the Nez Percé and the Cayuse – heard, from a firebrand Delaware named Tom Hill, was how his tribe had suffered under just such a tide of immigration in the East, ultimately losing their freedom and their homes as a result. There, just as here, angry clashes had resulted when whites trampled crops or poached game; there, just as here, sporadic fighting had broken out when braves stole horses or pilfered camps.

Then came the measles.

In 1847, an epidemic – brought by the immigrants – struck the Cayuses. Half of them died. Marcus Whitman, the missionary doctor, did what he could to alleviate their suffering in unspeakable conditions, but he also continued to engross himself in establishing a new mission on the Dalles River and in building a sawmill and gristmill. When the deaths continued, many of the Indians began to suspect that he was deliberately poisoning them to get their

Zachary Taylor's camp at Walnut Springs, near Monterrey, Mexico, after the Battle of Buena Vista on February 22, 1847. The battle had been unique in being fought almost entirely by volunteers, and it was nearly lost. Taylor returned to Washington shortly after the battle and, basing his campaign on his successes in the Mexican War, won the presidential election of 1848.

lands, especially when most of the sick whites, gathered at the mission after a long summer's trip, recovered.

The Indians sprang from the early morning fog on November 29 to kill Marcus, Narcissa, and twelve white workers, taking five men, eight women, and thirty-four children captive, and leaving two small girls, suffering from measles, to die of neglect. One man fled for help. He drowned in the Columbia River.

Oregon's provisional governor raised a small army, paying it with promises and a few in-kind contributions, but everyone realized the territory was incapable of supporting a large campaign. The mission on the Dalles was fortified, the ringleader arrested, and the captives ransomed for $500 worth of tobacco, shirts, blankets, and bullets. Finally, desperate Oregon officials yet again petitioned Congress for territorial status, but with no more luck than they had had before.

Congress had its hands full trying to govern a country besieged once more by the sectional strife that had sporadically plagued the United States from its foundation. The battle lines were just beginning to be drawn around the issue of slavery, an issue greatly exacerbated by the clamoring of a number of new Western territories for admission into the union. And no mere Indian massacre in some backwater valley on the other side of the country was going to upset the delicate balancing act be played out by the republics elected and appointed officials.

The truth was, however, that Congress could not long do without the West. True, out of twenty million Americans, only some tens of thousands had moved to the entire Pacific coast during the last five years, from 1841 to 1846. But during the same period, fifty times that many had immigrated from overseas, five million mostly German and Irish immigrants packing into the Eastern cities and creating just the kinds of problems the founding fathers had feared.

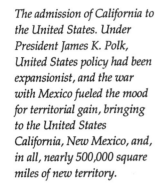

The admission of California to the United States. Under President James K. Polk, United States policy had been expansionist, and the war with Mexico fueled the mood for territorial gain, bringing to the United States California, New Mexico, and, in all, nearly 500,000 square miles of new territory.

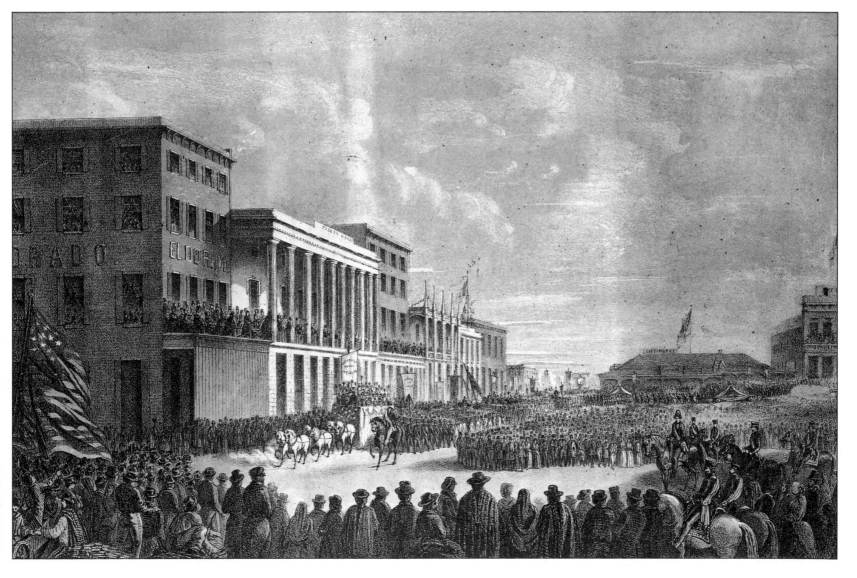

5

GOLD

Depending on how one looked at it, the California gold rush could not have come at a better or a worse time.

Depressed since the end of the Mexican War, the American economy was desperately in need of some relief. The millions of dollars in gold dust that poured into the national income provided just the right jolt. An important group of American historians has always claimed that the Frontier provided a safety valve for the socio-economic pressure cooker of the American East. And while migration westward was steady, it could in no way keep pace with the millions of overseas immigrants to eastern and midwestern cities. It was perhaps more the *idea* of the West than actual immigration that kept the urban nightmares of poverty and despair from boiling over in the 19th century.

By mid-century even the idea was threatened by the growing restlessness of the Plains Indians, who posed more of an ideological than an actual threat. The discovery of gold revived the idea of the West; of starting over, of trading space for time in order to make it big overnight. In the language of America's historical ideologues, the gold rush rekindled the expansionist longings of a young nation to realize its manifest destiny.

On the other hand, the rash of fortune hunters and paradise seekers heading to the far West did have a real impact on the sectional wrangling of the established states. As immigrants to the West, which in general was unfit for slavery, began to demand entry into the union, they destabilized the already precarious regional balance between North and South. The nationalist boom created in part by the gold rush speeded up the country's inexorable march toward civil war.

For centuries Spain had looked for gold in the American West, but it fell to a bankrupt German merchant fleeing his creditors in the Fatherland to at last realize the dreams of the *conquistadors*. Johann August Sutter arrived in Missouri in 1834 determined, like all Westerners, to start over and get rich. As with many, perhaps most, of them he failed, twice trying his luck with the Santa Fe trade, and twice going bust.

Sutter may have been a terrible businessman, but he was a master dissembler, and though he was

San Francisco's waterfront during the gold rush. Nearly $250,000 worth of gold was found in 1848, and much of it was shipped out through the busy port of San Francisco.

bankrupt yet again when he arrived at Jason Lee's mission in 1838 en route to California via Hawaii and Canada, he carried with him letters of introduction from a number of prominent people, including the commander of the Hudson's Bay Company at Vancouver, and the American consul in Honolulu. He used the letters to gain an audience with California's governor, Juan Baptista Alvarado; he used his natural charm, his Old-World polish, and his infectious enthusiasm to con the Mexican official into awarding him a grant of 50,000 acres in the future's state's as yet unsettled but incredibly fertile central valley.

Hot and dry, the valley was a four-hundred-mile long depression walled in by mountains except where the Sacramento from the north, and the San Joaquin from the south, joined into a delta and crashed through the hills into the San Francisco Bay. Settling here, Sutter was far from the population centers of Hispanic California, but – like Lee's mission and the Williamette Valley settlements – his operation was in a perfect position to become a target for westward migration, which fed his dreams of establishing a western empire.

Passing himself off as *Captain* Sutter (for some imaginary military service in the Swiss Guard), he built a fort and stockade and dubbed it New Helvetia, though the locals called it simply Sutter's Fort. He employed Indians in the main, treated them kindly by community standards, established cordial relationships with the area's paltry collection of Mexican farmers, and proffered genuine hospitality to travelers, especially American immigrants. Beloved by everybody but his creditors, Sutter was constantly in debt despite the apparent prosperity of his many projects.

To run one of those projects, a sawmill to produce much-needed lumber, Sutter hired a gentle and melancholy man named Marshall. Even Sutter considered James Marshall, a thirty-five-year-old jack-of-all-trades from New Jersey, strange, but not enough to deny Marshall ten domestic Indians to accompany the ten Mormons who had signed on to dig a millrace at the south fork of the American River. When Marshall showed up at Sutter's Fort in the middle of a thunderstorm late one night at the end of January, 1848, and demanded a secret conference in a locked room, Sutter assumed that the

A Currier cartoon of the rush to get to California. Some argonauts drove farm wagons West over the plains and through the mountains. Others took ships to Mexico or to the Isthmus of Panama, then traveled overland, finally boarding another ship to sail up the coast of Mexico to California. Some forty-niners took an even longer journey, starting in New York Harbor and sailing 13,000 miles around the coast of South America and northward.

John Augustus Sutter (1803 - 1880) came to California in July 1839 to found New Helvetia. When, in 1948, gold was found, his colony was overrun by gold hunters.

young man was simply being his usual "odd" self.

When the two were alone, Marshall carefully and melodramatically unrolled a length of cotton cloth to show his boss a glittering piece of metal he had found four days before, on the morning of January 24, 1848, as he was inspecting the watercourse at Sutter's Mill. Before Sutter leaped to the obvious conclusion, the two looked up precious metals in his encyclopedia. They tested Marshall's sample with nitric acid. They weighed it against silver they had on hand. They dropped both samples in water. Marshall's sank. They boiled it for a day in a kettle of lye. It survived. Then they knew: Marshall had discovered gold.

Sutter's Indians told him that the stuff was cursed, belonging to a demon that lived in a mountain lake lined with golden shores. And when Sutter rode out to inspect the site himself a few days later, he was already worried that gold might indeed prove bad medicine. At least so he said later, when his own dreams of empire had been destroyed by the gold rush that left him an embittered and impoverished man.

Even before he arrived at the mill, another young boy had found more gold and announced it to the other mill hands, whom Sutter and Marshall persuaded to keep quiet until they could get clear title to the area. Sutter traded some clothes and a bit of food with the local Indians for a lease on the land around the mill. The outcome of the Mexican War in California was still unknown, but guessing right

Emigrants Crossing the Plains, *an engraving by F.O.C. Darley. For many would-be gold-seekers, the best way to travel to California was by land, although the unmapped journey held many dangers: Indians, bad weather, and lack of water among them.*

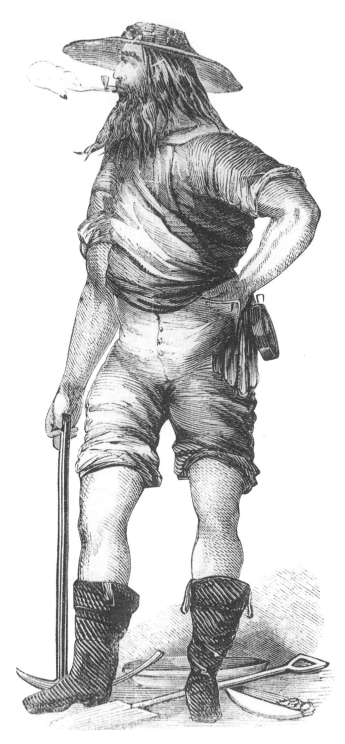

Above: a California forty-niner. In 1849, thousands of gold-seekers left their homes and families to strike it rich.

Right: gold washers at work. In 1848, about 3,000 men already living out West in Oregon Territory, pulled up stakes and rushed south.

Far top right: George W. Northrup of Minnesota with the basic tools of a gold miner: pan, pick, shovel, food, and supplies to last a few months.

Far right: San Francisco on a rainy night in 1858. Walkers not only had to deal with muddy streets, but also rats.

A pioneer caravan bound for California. Many argonauts traveled across the plains so heavily laden that wagon wheels broke or became mired in the sand, and along their routes, nonessential belongings lay abandoned.

San Francisco in 1853, by William Henry Bartlett. The city's population grew from 459 in 1847 to 55,000 in 1855. Facilities included public baths where dusty miners could clean up before a night of revelry.

Above: washing for gold. Miners undertook back-breaking work attempting to separate dirt, sand, and rock from gold. A pan was his most essential piece of equipment; by sloshing water and dirt around in the pan, he became adept at separating gold from lighter debris.

Below: a miner with a cradle in Tuolumne County. The cradle and long tom helped miners sift the earth more quickly and efficiently.

that the territory would be ceded to the U.S., Sutter sent one of his employees to the American authorities in Monterey, asking them to confirm his new lease.

But it was already too late to keep a lid on the find. Henry Bigler, the Mormon diary keeper at the mill, had written to his old pals in the Mormon Battalion who fought together in the war. Some of the children at the mill had shown sample's to a teamster in Sutter's employ. And the messenger to Monterey, Charles Bennett, reacted to the new government's response that "the United States does not recognize the rights of Indians to sell or lease land" by getting drunk and bragging about the bag of gold he brought with him. Even Sutter himself could not keep his mouth shut, telling leaders of the local Mexican community about his new-found riches.

Within six weeks, Sutter's entire staff had abandoned his stores, farms, ranches and mills to join every local inhabitant except the sick and the lame to look for gold in the waters off the south fork of the American River. But that was as far as it went. Though rumors about Sutter's gold floated about the cities of California, and a new San Francisco newspaper called the *Californian* announced the discovery on March 15, 1848, few seemed especially interested. The Spanish West had been built on rumors of gold, and most people discounted them. By May, of California's 14,000 whites, including some 7,500 Hispanic *californios*, only a few hundred were trying their hand at prospecting.

Then a loud-mouthed, big and burly Mormon elder named Sam Brannan visited Sutter's Mill. During the Mexican War, Brannan had sailed a shipload of Mormons around Cape Horn up to a little North California seaport named Yerba Buena, "good herb," hoping to establish a colony in the town that the following year would be renamed San Francisco. He fell foul of Brigham Young, however, who had his own plans for a Mormon empire in the Great Salt Lake Valley of the American Desert, plans he made quite clear when Brannan visited Utah in 1848.

Excommunicated by Young, Brannan returned to California to become one of the first of its famous boosters. He had already established San Francisco's first newspaper, *The California Star*, using a printing press he had brought with him on the boat. Now, in partnership with C.C. Smith, he set up store at Sutter's Fort, which among other things furnished supplies to the sawmill on the American River.

When Brannan reached San Francisco, the rival *Californian* had already announced the discovery of gold on the American River, and his own paper was playing the story down as unsubstantiated rumor. Brannan put an immediate end to that kind of coverage. His clothes still dirty from the trip, his

Top: Across the Plains with the Donner Party, *by Charles Nahl. The eighty-seven members of this caravan were trapped by snow in the Sierra Nevadas. Nearly half of them starved to death, and some resorted to cannibalism.*

Above: Pike's Peak or Bust. *Word of ever more lucrative claims lured Easterners across the country Westward.*

Even the climate cooperated as the annual draught shrank streams and exposed deposits of gold-bearing gravel the miners called "bars." At first, Sutter tried to collect royalties from the trespassers, but the miners simply ignored him, and since Mexican land titles did not transfer mineral rights, he had no recourse in law from the new American government.

Perhaps as much as a quarter of a million dollars in gold was taken from the California soil in 1848. It arrived in San Francisco in bottles and buckskin bags, old tins and beat up shoes, and much of it was shipped out to the East around the tip of South America in ships that stopped along the way at ports of call in Hawaii, Mexico, Peru and Chile.

That summer experienced South American miners set sail up the coast. Crowds began to clog the docks of Hawaii, filling to the brim every ship bound for San Francisco—some nineteen vessels in three weeks. Mexicans by the thousands poured overland from the mining fields of Sonora or shipped out of Mazatlan. Prices skyrocketed. Flour that sold for twenty dollars a pound at the beginning of the summer, could reach $800 a pound in the mountains by year's end.

By the time news of the discovery reached the rest of the United States in 1849, the rush was on. The '49ers poured out of Atlantic seaboard cities, Midwestern villages, and Southern plantations, between some sixty and a hundred thousand of them, abysmally ignorant of the geography they were to traverse and the actual conditions they would encounter at journey's end. Maybe a fifth arrived by ship from the Far East and Down Under, from Latin America and Western Europe, but the rest came from virtually every U.S. eastern county.

Some simply hitched up their farm wagons and headed west. Others, aiming for speed, made complicated travel plans by sea and land across lower Mexico or the Isthmus of Panama. Those on the Eastern Seaboard clambered aboard sleek clippers, jerry-rigged hulks, coastal freighters, fishing smacks, even river steamers for the 13,000-mile voyage around the Horn.

Some fifty of them left New York Harbor for San Francisco in 1849 alone, on trips that could take twelve and frequently took six months. Accommodations were awful. Owners fitted their boats with little staterooms, took on inexperienced crews, loaded them up far beyond capacity, and set sail on one of the world's worst ocean courses, where one could encounter everything from windless weeks to hurricanes and even snowstorms. If the tempests or the doldrums did not get to them, the rotten food and the boredom was sure to.

Surprisingly few of the vessels actually sank, however, and when they reached San Francisco, the

mane of black hair still unwashed, he rushed through the streets of San Francisco waving a quinine bottle full of gold dust and bellowing "Gold! Gold! Gold from the American River!"

Within a fortnight, San Francisco's population had dropped from several hundred to a few dozen. Stores and shops were closed as workmen and clerks simply dropped what they were doing and left for the south fork. Houses sat empty and locked next to deserted fields.

By midsummer, Brannan was supplying some 4,000 miners with picks, shovels, and pans from a brand-new store he had built right next to Sutter's Mill. By the end of the year, the number of miners had swelled to as many as 10,000.

crew as well as the passengers were likely to abandon ship and head for the hills. Within a year of the discovery in the Sierra, 'Frisco had burgeoned into a major seaport, with more ships ashore than were anchored in most of the world's other harbors. Deserted boats were run aground and leased as stores and hotels, or quickly disappeared under the ambitious land-fill programs of rapacious real-estate promoters. Each day, thirty new houses sprang up to meet the needs of a population that would exceed 50,000 by the time the rush began to sputter.

They were mostly young men, and a few whores, all heavily armed, hard drinking, hopeless gamblers, who filled the city's more than 500 bars and 1,000 dens, where two of them were murdered on the

average every day. San Francisco was a wide-open town, where life was cheap and eggs went for six dollars a dozen, which was still better than the three dollars.apiece eggs brought at the diggings. Landlords made a killing on the rental of the abandoned ships, canvas shanties and wooden tinderboxes. One whore retired after only a year with $50,000 that lonely miners had stuffed in her garters after losing hundreds of thousands of dollars each day in the local gambling halls. Arsonists, looking for an opportunity to loot local establishments, set on the average a fire a day, and San Francisco was razed six times in 18 months. Before it was all over, the local population would turn to vigilante justice and public hangings to bring its wild and woolly citizens to heel.

Bruin Not Bunny, by Charles M. Russell. In the late nineteenth century, travel through the West was still perilous, but with rich strikes being made in California, Nevada, Colorado, and Arizona, the trip seemed worth the risk. By the turn of the century, thousands of mining districts dotted the Western landscape.

The execution of Brace and Hetherington by the Vigilance Committee of San Francisco. In the rough atmosphere of boom-town San Francisco its permanent citizens feared violence and arson – six fires had caused massive damage between 1849 and 1851 – so they decided to take the law into their own hands. The vigilante groups they formed became models for others that flourished on the frontier.

Meanwhile, the men who were making the purveyors of vice and greed rich worked hard for the gold they squandered in the city. Rumors of eight-pound nuggets, and a single pan that produced $5,000 in dust, remained popular around the diggings even after the first big finds of '48 and '49, but after a year or so it became clear that even an ounce a day was good digging. The basic equipment in the gold fields consisted of a shovel and a wash pan, but almost everyone eventually worked a claim by more sophisticated methods. Some used a cradle and a long tom for the sifting of earth, but most wound up working on a crew, shoveling up to a hundred cubic yards of gold-bearing gravel into a sluice fed by water.

From the beginning, the miners insisted on a rough kind of equity in the dispersal and working of claims. When a few of the earliest fortune-hunters, Sutter included, tried to use Indian labor to cover more ground than a single man could work, the rest put a stop to it immediately. A man who discovered gold might be allowed two plots, but for the most part one individual could stake one claim, though banding together to work contiguous claims was permitted. The owner held title only so long as he worked the claim. In the early days, when the pickings were still good, a claim could be as small as ten feet square, though they grew larger as the gold played out.

A prospector squatting in a mountain stream would wash out a pan full of gold dust, the word would spread, and other miners would swarm to the spot. Tents would sprout, then a store would open, wooden shanties would follow, and soon a full-fledged community – called "Grizzly Flats" or "Grass Valley" – would come into being, growing rapidly until the gold played out, then disappearing, abandoned like the ships in San Francisco Bay. If San Francisco was a bawdy paradise, California mining towns were mean little hells, fueled by greed and desperation.

For, while some grew rich, most grew disillusioned. And when they realized that their high hopes for improved personal fortunes were doomed, Westerners looked for someone to blame. They blamed the foreigners: Indians, South

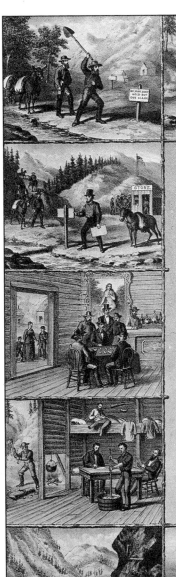

A MAN SPAKE THESE WORDS, AND SAID: I am a miner who wandered from "Away Down East," and came to sojourn in a strange land and "See the Elephant." And behold I saw him, and bear witness that, from the key of his trunk to the end of his tail, his whole body has passed before me; and I followed him until his huge feet stood still before a clapboard shanty; then, with his trunk extended, he pointed to a candle-card tacked upon a shingle, as though he would say **"READ!"** and I read the

PIONEERS' TEN COMMANDMENTS.

I.

Thou shalt have no other claim than one.

II.

Thou shalt not make unto thyself any false claim, nor any likeness to a mean man by jumping one. Whatever thou findest, on the top above, or on the rock beneath, or in a crevice underneath the rock, and when they decide against thee, thou shalt take thy pick, thy pan, thy shovel, and thy blankets, with all that thou hast, and go prospecting to seek good diggings; but thou shalt find none. Then, when thou hast returned, in sorrow shalt thou find that thine old claim is worked out, and yet no pile made thee to hide in the ground or in an old boot beneath thy bunk, or in buckskin or bottle underneath thy cabin; but has paid all that was in thy purse away, worn out thy boots and thy garments, so that there is nothing good about them but the pockets, and thy patience is likened unto thy garments; and at last thou shalt hire thy body out to make thy board and save thy bacon.

III.

Thou shalt not go prospecting before thy claim gives out. Neither shalt thou take thy money, nor thy gold dust, nor thy good name, to the gaming table in vain; for monte, twenty-one, roulette, faro, lansquenet and poker will prove to thee that the more thou puttest down the less thou shalt take up; and when thou thinkest of thy wife and children, thou shalt not hold thyself guiltless, but—insane.

IV.

Thou shalt not remember what thy friends do at home on the Sabbath day, lest the remembrance may not compare favorably with what thou doest here. Six days thou mayest dig or pick all that thy body can stand under, but the other day is Sunday; yet thou washest all thy dirty shirts, darnest all thy stockings, tap thy boots, mend thy clothing, chop thy whole week's fire-wood, make up and bake thy bread and boil thy pork and beans that thou wait not when thou returnest from thy long-tom weary. For in six days' labor only thou canst not work enough to wear out thy body in two years; but if thou workest hard on Sunday also, thou canst do it in six months; and thou and thy son and thy daughter, thy male and thy female friend, thy morals and thy conscience be none the less better for it, but reproach thee shouldst thou ever return to thy mother's fireside; and thou strive to justify thyself because the trader and the blacksmith, the carpenter and the merchant, the tailors, Jews and Buccaneers defy God and civilization by keeping not the Sabbath day, nor wish for a day of rest, such as memory of youth and and home made hallowed.

V.

Thou shalt not think more of all thy gold, nor how thou canst make it fastest, than how thou wilt enjoy it after thou hast ridden rough-shod over thy good old parents' precepts and examples, that thou mayest have nothing to reproach and sting thee when thou art left alone in the land where thy father's blessing and thy mother's love hath sent thee.

VI.

Thou shalt not kill thy body by working in the rain, even though thou shalt make enough to buy physic and attendance with. Neither shalt thou kill thy neighbor's body in a duel, for by keeping cool thou canst save his life and thy conscience. Neither shalt thou destroy thyself by getting "*tight*," nor "*slewed*," nor "*high*," nor "*corned*," nor "*half-seas over*," nor "*three sheets in the wind*," by drinking smoothly down "*brandy slings*," "*gin cock-tails*," "*whisky punches*," "*rum toddies*" nor "*egg nogs*." Neither shalt thou suck "*mint-juleps*" nor "*sherry cobblers*" through a straw, nor gurgle from a bottle the raw material, nor take it neat from a decanter, for while thou art swallowing down thy purse and thy coat from off thy back, thou art burning the coat from off thy stomach; and if thou couldst see the houses and lands, and gold dust, and home comforts already lying there—a huge pile—thou shouldst feel a choking in thy throat; and when to that thou add'st thy crooked walking and hiccupping; of lodging in the gutter, of broiling in the sun, of prospect holes half full of water, and of shafts and ditches from which thou hast emerged like a drowning rat, thou wilt feel disgusted with thyself, and inquire, "*Is thy servant a dog that he doeth these things?*" Verily, I will say, farewell old bottle; I will kiss thy gurgling lips no more; and thou, slings, cock-tails, punches, smashes, cobblers, nogs, toddies, sangarees and juleps, forever, farewell. Thy remembrance shames me; henceforth I will cut thy acquaintance; and headaches, tremblings, heart-burnings, blue-devils, and all the unholy catalogue of evils which follow in thy train. My wife's smiles and my children's merry-hearted laugh shall charm and reward me for having the manly firmness and courage to say: "*No! I wish thee an eternal farewell!!*"

VII.

Thou shalt not grow discouraged, nor think of going home before thou hast made thy "*pile*," because thou hast not "*struck a lead*" nor found a rich "*crevice*" nor sunk a hole upon a "*pocket*," lest in going home thou leave four dollars a day and go to work ashamed at fifty cents a day, and serve thee right; for thou knowest by staying here thou mightest strike a lead and fifty dollars a day, and keep thy manly self-respect, and then go home with enough to make thyself and others happy.

VIII.

Thou shalt not steal a pick, or a pan, or a shovel, from thy fellow miner, nor take away his tools without his leave; nor borrow those he cannot spare; nor return them broken; nor trouble him to fetch them back again; nor talk with him while his water rent is running on; nor remove his stake to enlarge thy claim; nor undermine his claim in following a lead; nor pan out gold from his riffle-box; nor wash the tailings from the mouth of his sluices. Neither shalt thou pick out specimens from the company's pan to put in thy mouth or in thy purse; nor cheat thy partner of his share; nor steal from thy cabin-mate his gold dust to add to thine, for he will be sure to discover what thou hast done, and will straightway call his fellow miners together, and if the law hinder them not they will hang thee, or give thee fifty lashes, or shave thy head and brand thee like a horse thief with "R" upon thy cheek, to be known and of all men Californians in particular.

IX.

Thou shalt not tell any false tales about "*good diggings in the mountains*" to thy neighbor, that thou mayest benefit a friend who hath mules, and provisions, and tools, and blankets he cannot sell; lest in deceiving thy neighbor when he returns through the snow, with naught but his riffle, he present thee with the contents thereof, and like a dog thou shalt fall down and die.

X.

Thou shalt not commit unsuitable matrimony, nor covet "*single blessedness*," nor forget absent maidens, nor neglect thy first love; but thou shalt consider how faithfully and patiently she waiteth thy return; yea, and coveteth each epistle that thou sendeth with kisses of kindly welcome until she hath thyself. Neither shalt thou covet thy neighbor's wife, nor trifle with the affections of his daughter; yet, if thy heart be free, and thou love and covet each other, thou shalt "*pop the question*" like a man, lest another more manly than thou art should step in before thee, and thou lovest her in vain, and, in the anguish of thy heart's disappointment, thou shalt quote the language of the great, and say, "*sick is life*," and thy future lot be that of a poor, lonely, despised and comfortless bachelor.

A new commandment give I unto you. If thou hast a wife and little ones, that thou lovest dearer than thy life, that thou keep them continually before you to cheer and urge thee onward until thou canst say, "*I have enough; God bless them; I will return.*" Then as thou journiest towards thy much loved home, with open arms, shall they come forth to welcome thee, and falling on thy neck, weep tears of unutterable joy that thou art come; then in the fullness of thy heart's gratitude thou shalt kneel before thy Heavenly Father together, to thank Him for thy safe return. Amen. So mote it be.

Among the "Miners' Pioneer Ten Commandments" were "Thou shalt have no other claim than one," and "Thou shalt not grow discouraged."

Steamer day in San Francisco. On the first and the fifteenth of each month, San Franciscans celebrated steamer day – the day on which mail ships arrived and departed from the harbor.

Americans, Frenchmen, and especially the Mexicans and Chinese. The first three were subjected to various restrictions, including mob violence. The Chinese, many of whom had fled a series of famines in China during the 1840s, clung to the centuries-old culture they brought with them, which included wearing traditional dress and gathering into clannish fraternal organizations called tongs. Which made them excellent scapegoats, as the infant California legislature proved in 1850, when it passed a series of special taxes aimed primarily at the Chinese and forbade them by law from working any mining district before the Americans had abandoned it. The Mexicans, citizens of a country that had just lost a war to the Americans, fared even worse. The persecution became so harsh that by 1854 they had ceased their annual migration from Sonora.

The truth of the matter, of course, was that most fortunes didn't lie around on the ground, waiting for someone to pick them up. In 1852, when gold production soared to an annual high of $81 million, most of the surface – or "placer" – gold was gone and large scale mechanized mining companies had replaced many of the individual prospectors. In the first seven years, the California gold rush's mother lode would produce about $350 million worth of gold, a much smaller yield than future strikes in Nevada, the Dakotas, and the Colorado Rockies.

The big mining companies would ultimately prove themselves more rapacious than all the '49ers put together. They would expose whole stream beds, even divert entire rivers out of their original channels in order to mine the gold. With their new hydraulic mining techniques, they would blast apart mountains and leave huge, gaping holes, artificial canyons 500 feet deep, as testimony to their hunger for profit.

The irony is, however, that so few of the great American fortunes launched by the gold rush came from the mining of gold. Collis Huntington and Mark Hopkins made their money cornering the market in shovels and blasting powder, taking most of what the '49ers did not throw away at the gaming table, in the saloon, or on loose women. Teamed with a prospector turned shopkeeper named Charles Crocker and a mining camp grocer called Leland Stanford, they would establish themselves as California's Big Four, the first of the great Western

A view of San Francisco by Tobin. Some of the buildings erected in San Francisco in the 1850s were prefabricated back in the East and then shipped around South America and north to San Francisco Harbor, where they were unloaded and rapidly thrown together.

railroad barons, flinging tracks half way across a continent.

John Studebaker launched his family's modest wagon works in Indiana on a decade of expansion with $8,000 he saved making wheelbarrows for miners in Placerville, transforming Studebaker into one of America's largest and best-known carriage makers. Levi Strauss, a silk-hatted Bavarian, changed the way Westerners dressed when he patented the use of copper rivets to reinforce the seams of the trousers he started making for miners from single bolts of canvas tenting, calling them "jeans." For five years, Philip D. Armour dug ditches, until he saved enough to open a butcher shop in Placerville, returning to Milwaukee after the rush to create America's foremost slaughterhouse and meat packing company. And Wells Fargo, founded by two Easterners who visited the West only once, built the quintessential company of the American West from a few mule trains carrying supplies to miners.

It lasted at best but a decade, the California Gold Rush, but it became the model for all the gold rushes that followed. For, despite the fact that few of the '49ers got rich, despite the fact that many of them returned home without even their dreams left, no one paid any attention. By mid-century California's population had swollen to a quarter million greedy souls. While that may appear a small number compared to the twenty-five million living elsewhere in the country, it was quite large enough to give Easterners an acute personal interest in the West. Chances were that a family member or friend had headed for the coast, hoping to strike it rich.

And it was precisely here that the history of the West took a turn from the yeoman farmer as the ideological centerpiece of Western migration. For the prospector, the '49er, is at heart not a farmer, but a businessman. His business is not agriculture, but mining – and mining is an industry that had a greater impact on Western history than any other. In a matter of a few short years mining had developed from an individual shovel-and-pan enterprise into a consolidated, concentrated heavy industry, and in doing so it propelled the West to the forefront of 19th-century industrialization. Afterward, the centerpiece of Western migration would be the extractive capitalist, whose credo became that of the majority of Westerners ever since – to quote Patricia Limerick – "get in, get rich, get out."

The passion of the Western adventure was no longer dressed in the genteel, 18th-century garb of the independent property-holder. The yeoman farmer, who was looking for a dignified plot of land, had been supplanted by the '49er, seeking an overnight fortune. Land hunger had become lust for profit.

Above: the California stagecoach leaving the International Hotel in Virginia City.

Below: a view of Sansome Street in San Francisco. By 1854, the placer gold on which the city's boom had

been based became scarce. A depression swept through the city. In 1855, two of the major banks in the city collapsed.

Above: emigrants taking the
northern overland route to
California, with Indian guides
to help them.

Below: To the Black Hills or
Bust!: *a pair of miners strike
out for Dakota Territory.*
Right: *a Leadville prospector.*

6

INDIANS

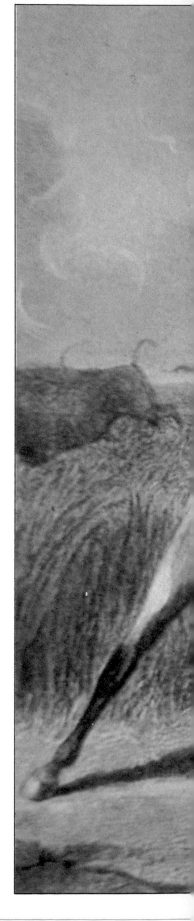

Before and during the California Gold Rush, western migration tended to travel around the concentrations of Indians on the Plains. But with California and the Pacific Northwest firmly anchored to the United States, its restless citizens began to traverse the country's center, some – as always – to settle along the way. And once again, the cycle of White/Indian violence escalated. Since the disputes were primarily racial, all solutions to the problem were temporary, and wars broke out over seemingly quite trivial matters.

But anchoring the Far West to the United States had an effect far greater than yet again pitting pioneer against Native American. It helped, too, to pit North against South, in a bloody civil war that also had race as its central issue. Like the various Indian treaties, the Compromise of 1850 through which California entered the nation, was a temporary solution. And,

as with the Indians a decade later, war came more and more to appear the only means for decisive resolution of problems.

If the West destabilized the country's traditional regional balance, whose collapse led to Civil War, the War Between the States in turn destabilized the West, encouraging various Indian tribes to strike while the whites were distracted by their determination to kill each other. The Civil War also validated the use of force to solve at last the Indian "problem," which by and large meant the existence of viable and active societies occupying land the Americans wanted.

In 1866, General William Tecumseh Sherman,

Engraving, after a drawing by Darley, of an Indian hunting with bow and arrow on *horseback. More than thirty tribes lived between the Mississippi and the Rockies.*

fresh from final victory in the Civil War, came west to command the army's Division of the Missouri. He proposed to bring to the Plains Indians what he had brought to the American South: total war, conducted not only between soldiers, but waged with equal ferocity against the civilian population. Yet, as he took up his new command, he reported to the 39th Congress on a note sympathetic to his adversary: "The poor Indian finds himself hemmed in."

The laconic general was right, of course. White civilization inexorably moved inland from both coasts, east and west, so that by the end of the Civil War, whites in the West outnumbered Indians by a factor of ten. Here and there, some whites thought the dispossession of the Indian was a tragic wrong, but they were outnumbered by those who found it inevitable and desirable. An ever growing number of the latter advocated, in varying degrees, the extermination of the Indians. Officially, the policy of the United States government was "concentration," the "removal" of Indian tribes to lands "reserved" for them, thereby making room for white settlement. In theory, reservation Indians were wards of the state, which promised to provide food, clothing and shelter. In practice, the reservation system was inept at best, corrupt at worst, and generally without heart. Many reservation Indians starved, fell prey to disease, or simply withered with despair.

Even if one ignores the inherent racism behind the policy of concentration and grants some degree of paternalistic good intention to its proponents, the cultural heritage of both whites and Indians made it impossible in practice. The whites had come to think of Indian land as "empty," land that could be "developed" and "improved," land that was theirs for the taking. The Indians' very way of life required a certain range of land for hunting and gathering, a range that could not be accommodated on a reservation.

On the relatively rare occasions when treaties were concluded in good faith, they were often signed without comprehension by so-called chiefs who, in the loose and organic government of most tribes, had little political authority. Add to this the race-hatred of the pioneer and the fact that, for the Plains tribes especially, warfare was an integral part of existence – a feature of the culture, which carried religious as well as sporting significance – and White/Indian hostility seems unavoidable.

That the western tribes – particularly those of the Plains – were loosely organized, warred with one another more frequently than against whites, were vastly outnumbered, and were technologically far less advanced, makes their defeat appear a foregone conclusion. Yet the military force the United States fielded against them was woefully inadequate. Before

BUFFALO BILL'S GREAT ACHIEVEMENT!

BEADLE'S Dime New York Library

Copyrighted, 1891, by BEADLE AND ADAMS.   ENTERED AS SECOND CLASS MATTER AT THE NEW YORK, N. Y., POST OFFICE.   November 18, 1891.

No.682.   Published Every Wednesday.   Beadle & Adams, Publishers, 98 WILLIAM STREET, NEW YORK.   Ten Cents a Copy. $5.00 a Year.   Vol. LIII.

BUFFALO BILL'S SECRET SERVICE TRAIL

BY MAJOR DANGERFIELD BURR U.S.A.

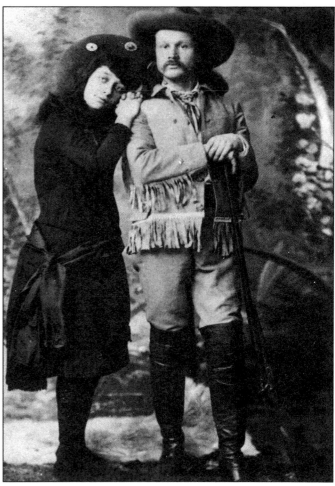

Left: William F. "Buffalo Bill" Cody (1846-1917) was one real-life Western hero of whom stories were told in dime novels published back East. Others were Kit Carson, Wild Bill Hickok, and George Armstrong Custer.

Above: Buffalo Bill's Secret Service Trail, *a Beadle's* Dime Library *publication. Erastus Flavel Beadle was the dominant figure in dime-novel publishing until 1889, when he retired after having amassed a fortune.*

Top right: Buffalo Bill Cody with a female friend, speculation holds that it might be Calamity Jane. Many dime novels portrayed Western women both as sturdy riders and as the pure keepers of moral standards.

the Civil War, campaigning was conducted mostly by local militias. After the war, the regular army took over for the most part, but it was an army that had been rapidly demobilized – almost a million men were discharged between 1865 and 1866. By the 1870s, the height of the Indian wars, troop strength was set at 25,000 men and 2,000 officers; effective numbers were probably under 20,000.

This meager force was distributed among some two hundred posts, one hundred of them thinly planted in the West. An officer of the all-black 24th Infantry complained in testimony before Congress that the largest company he could muster consisted of seven men.

The pay was miserable, promotion took years (General O.O. Howard protested that most of his captains were too old "for duty involving marching on foot or even drill requiring continuous movement"), desertion ran as high as thirty percent, and training was so inadequate that the troopers of the Second Cavalry at Fort Phil Kearny, along the Bozeman Trail, could not mount their horses unaided.

In contrast, the Plains Indians were born and bred to horsemanship and the arts of war. Moreover, they enjoyed the advantages of an indigenous people

Sport on the Plains, *an 1874 engraving. By the middle of the nineteenth century there were about fifty million buffalo in the West. When professional white hunters joined the business of buffalo-skin trading, each killed as many as 150 buffalo a day.*

An 1840s lithograph of an Indian buffalo hunt. Indians developed a thriving trade in buffalo skins at white military outposts, also selling buffalo dung for use as fuel.

Above: Red Cloud (1822-1909), Chief of the Sioux, waged a fierce war against white invaders on the northern plains, plaguing settlers and cuting off mail routes during the hostilities.

Above left: Buffalo hunters on the prairie in a lithograph by Currier and Ives. Between 1872 and 1874, more than 3.5 million plains buffalo were killed, most by white hunters.

Left: Life on the Prairie, *buffalo hunters in a Currier and Ives print.*

The Pursuit, a lithograph depicting the deadly combat between hunters – one white, one Indian. Indian braves treated their horses as extensions of themselves and were magnificent horseman, capable of all manner of riding styles and tricks which helped them in the hunt for buffalo.

repelling "foreign" invaders. They knew the country, and they knew how to use it as a weapon in a kind of guerrilla warfare for which the U.S. Army was wholly unprepared.

The first major western Indian wars were fought in the Northwest. In California, conflict developed when Indians got in the way of gold prospectors. The so-called Digger Indians, whose territory lay squarely in gold country, were subsistence farmers on whom whites looked with contempt. By the end of the gold era – the early 1860s – white aggression and white disease had wiped out two-thirds of them.

Certainly by the 1850s, violence had become second nature to whites and Indians alike whenever they confronted each other. Settlers clamored for army intervention and then protested when General John E. Wool, commander of the army's Department of the Pacific, failed to pursue a course of total annihilation. Indeed, the army often had to shelter persecuted Indians in local forts. Nevertheless, a pattern of raids on Indian villages followed by retaliatory attacks on white settlements developed. While most of General Wool's regulars fought the Wallawallas in the so-called Yakima War, an eighty-man garrison under Captain Andrew Jackson Smith

at Fort Lane, in southern Oregon's Rogue River country, managed to hold off a massive attack on May 28, 1856, by local Indians until reinforcements arrived. The augmented force so routed the Rogue River warriors that they immediately surrendered and despairingly submitted to life on a reservation.

Meanwhile, east of the Cascade Mountains, Isaac Stevens, territorial governor of Washington, hastily concluded treaties that bound the Indians to relinquish vast tracts of land. A band of young warriors, outraged by the capitulation of their elders, killed six white settlers in September 1855 and issued a warning that the same fate would befall other whites who ventured east of the Cascades. In October, a small force of army regulars reconnoitered the area and, true to their promise, the Indians attacked. Militiamen aggravated an already explosive situation by murdering the important Wallawalla chief Peo-Peo-Mox-Mox during a peace conference. Pursued by Wool's regulars, the Wallawallas and Yakimas retreated well east of the Cascades by 1857; there Kamiakin, a Yakima chief, worked to foment a general uprising against settlers and gold hunters east of the Columbia River.

Lieutenant Colonel Edward J. Steptoe rode out of

Fort Walla Walla in May 1858 with 164 regulars, intending to impress the Palouse, Spokane, and Coeur d'Alene Indians with the might of the U.S. Army. His command was ambushed by hundreds of mounted warriors, who did not attack at first, demanding instead that Steptoe and his men leave their country. Only when the column retreated did the Indians attack. Steptoe managed to stave off annihilation and, under cover of darkness, crept through the Indian lines, back to the safety of Fort Walla Walla.

The humiliation of this defeat triggered a vigorous punitive campaign. In two battles, Spokane Plain (September 1, 1858) and Four Lakes (September 5), Colonel George Wright defeated a force of six hundred warriors. Deeming this insufficient chastisement, Wright executed braves he accused of directing the attack against Steptoe. Chief Kamiakin had escaped to British Canada, but his brother-in-law, Owhi, was taken captive during a peace conference. Wright forced Owhi to summon his son, the war leader Qualchin, to another conference. When the young man arrived, Wright had him seized and summarily hanged – in the presence of his father. Owhi himself was shot and killed when he tried to escape. Now

thoroughly dispirited, the tribes of the Columbia River Basin submitted to dispossession and reservation life, as prescribed by Governor Stevens's treaties.

Whereas conflict in the Pacific Northwest was relatively short lived, the Southwest had a centuries-old history of White/Indian warfare. When the United States took possession of the territory encompassed by present-day New Mexico and Arizona during the Mexican War, General Stephen Watts Kearny promised that his government would "keep off the Indians." At first, it actually seemed a promise that could be kept.

Indian raids against the Mexicans had become so intense that the Mexican government established a bounty on Apache scalps. Since no one could really distinguish an Apache scalp from that of any other Indian, all Indians, friendly or hostile, were subject to attack. The Apache chief Mangas Coloradas – Red Sleeves – greeted the Americans as potential allies in the war against the hated Mexicans. General Kearny declined Mangas Coloradas's offer to invade Chihuahua, Sonora, and Durango, but U.S.-Apache relations remained relatively cordial from the late 1840s through 1861.

A lithograph of a pioneer wagon train being attacked by Indians.

An 1899 painting by Russell of a battle in the Indian wars. In 1867 Congress established a peace commission to negotiate with the Indians.

In February of that year, a rancher named John Ward accused Cochise, chief of the Chiricahua Apaches, of leading a raid and making off with the son of his common-law wife, Jesusa Martinez. Actually, she had been captured years before by Pinal Apaches and, during her captivity, had borne a son named Felix. Late in 1860, a Pinal band raided Ward's place and recaptured the child, rustling some cattle as well. Ward, who had been drunk during the raid, complained to the commander of Fort Buchanan, Arizona, who, a full three months later, dispatched Second Lieutenant George N. Bascom with sixty men to recover the cattle and the boy, and to capture Cochise, who had nothing to do with the raid.

Bascom found the young chief and demanded the return of the boy and the cattle. Cochise protested his innocence, drew his knife, slit the canvas of the conference tent, and escaped. One of the warriors who followed Cochise out the hole was killed, and six others were held hostage. Cochise raided the local Butterfield freight station, killing one employee and capturing another. He also attacked a passing wagon train, taking two Americans and eight Mexicans captive. The Mexicans he tied to wagon wheels and burned alive. The Americans – three, including the Butterfield man – he offered to exchange for the captives Bascom held.

Bascom refused and managed to summon reinforcements, who hunted for Cochise, but found only the mutilated corpses of the three American captives. In retaliation, Bascom executed his own prisoners. Cochise responded with a vow to exterminate all Americans in Arizona.

It was typical: a drunken rancher's false accusation gave rise to a quarter-century of bloody war.

Linguistically and culturally related to the Apaches were the equally formidable Navajo, feared by whites and other Indians alike throughout New Mexico and Arizona. Although Lieutenant Colonel Alexander Doniphan concluded a treaty with them in 1846, during the Mexican War, between that time and 1849, when another treaty was signed, the U.S. Army launched five expeditions against raiding Navajo bands. Finally, in 1851, Lieutenant Colonel Edwin V. Sumner assumed command of the Ninth Military Department and built a chain of forts throughout Navajo country.

Sumner had earned the sobriquet "Bull-head" when a musket ball struck him in the head and bounced off, and he spent a career living up to his nickname in his punitive dealings with Indians. Despite the peace efforts of two territorial governors, Sumner applied unrelenting pressure that resulted in counter-raid following raid and generally escalated tensions on the frontier.

Once again, it started with a petty dispute. On a spring day in 1858, some Navajos argued with soldiers from Fort Defiance who had been grazing their horses on land claimed by the Apache chief Manuelito. A few months later, Manuelito defiantly set his stock to graze on the land. Major Thomas H. Brooks, commander of Fort Defiance at the time, ordered his men to slaughter sixty of Manuelito's animals as a warning to clear off the disputed land. On July 7, Navajos let fly arrows into a soldiers' camp; on the 12th, a Navajo warrior murdered Brooks's black servant, Jim. The major demanded that the Navajos produce the murderer and, when they failed to do so, launched an expedition to Canyon de Chelly, Arizona, where soldiers burned fields of corn and a peach orchard, killed six Indians and appropriated six thousand sheep. The army conducted a raid on

Bottom left: a photograph, taken in the 1880s by Solomon D. Butcher, of a watermelon party at a sod house in Nebraska.

Below: an 1890 photograph of frontier farmers meeting on the Nebraska prairie near Lexington.

the village of another Navajo leader, Zarcillos Largos, wounding him at least three times and capturing forty warriors. The Navajos retaliated, and even attacked Fort Defiance. However, after the arrival of army reinforcements they sued for peace.

The terms dictated were harsh, and the treaty typically temporary. Peace lasted less than a year. By the beginning of 1860, Navajo raids were an almost daily occurrence – so fierce that Fort Defiance was abandoned in May of that year.

When the army decided to concentrate its undermanned forces against the Comanches and Kiowas raiding U.S. mail routes in Texas, the outraged territorial governor of New Mexico called for a volunteer militia force. By the time it had been raised, the army was able to release for New Mexico service 500 regulars, who, combined with an equal number of militiamen, burned Indian crops and destroyed cattle, thereby bringing about yet another treaty with the Navajos.

This agreement, too, was doomed, for the Civil War drew off the army garrisons of New Mexico and Arizona, laying the territory open to virtually unopposed Indian attack.

It was, however, the vast Plains that served as the setting for the most spectacular, tragic and protracted of the American Indian wars. On the Southern Plains, the Kiowas and Comanches had for decades been plundering Mexicans and Americans alike. The United States attempted to include them in a grand 1851 treaty with several Plains tribes – Sioux, Cheyenne, Arapaho, Crow, Gros Ventre, Assiniboin, Arikara, Shoshone and Pawnee – but the Kiowa and Comanche tribes refused. Later, representatives from these two tribes did sign a treaty agreeing to withdraw to assigned territory, but the raiding continued virtually unabated.

Several series of forts were built in the 1850s, but they were spread so thinly and manned so inadequately that they had little effect, and various volunteer groups, most notably the Texas Rangers, were formed in an effort to accomplish what the regulars could not.

The so-called Mormon War of 1857 badly strained the regular army's manpower. Much of the Second Cavalry left Texas for Utah, leaving the state exposed to Nokoni Comanche raids. Two hundred and fifteen Texas Rangers under Captain Rip Ford ventured across the Red River to "punish" the Comanches on their home ground. While Ford successfully engaged

Teamsters setting up camp for the night, from a mid-nineteenth-century wash drawing. Prospects of a new life out West retained its lure for pioneers– despite the incredible difficulties involved in getting there and the constant danger of bad weather and Indian attack.

warriors of the Kotsoteka Comanche tribe, killing seventy-six of them, including Chief Iron Jacket, he was forced to withdraw after his victory because he was short of supplies.

In the fall of 1858, regular troops under Major Earl Van Dorn joined the Texas Comanche campaign. On October 1, 1858, Van Dorn moved against a Comanche village of 120 lodges presided over by Chief Buffalo Hump, killing fifty-six warriors and two women and burning the lodges. The major was severely wounded, but recovered sufficiently to defeat another Comanche band at the Battle of Cripple Creek during the spring of 1869.

Despite such apparently decisive victories, raiding continued, and a Texas vigilante group was organized, which began terrorizing any Indians they encountered. Federal officials acted to move the reservation Comanches to Indian Territory – present-day Oklahoma – but the vigilantes were not appeased. On May 23, 1859, 250 volunteers led by John Robert

Baylor entered the soon-to-be-vacated Texas reservation, demanding that all Indians guilty of crimes be turned over to them. U.S Army regulars watched as a fight developed between Baylor's men and the Indians. The governor of Texas called out the militia against the Baylor band, but had to withdraw them when they threatened to join in the slaughter.

By 1860, approximately 850 regulars were broadcast across the Texas plains, charged with finding and killing Comanches. Oddly enough, when soldiers were withdrawn from Texas at the outbreak of the Civil War, Indian hostilities largely ceased – exactly the opposite of what had happened in New Mexico and Arizona, where withdrawal of the garrisons effectively yielded the territory for the duration of the war.

As bad as conditions were in the Far Southwest and the Southern Plains, the fiercest and most protracted warfare occurred on the Central and Northern Plains. It started, as usual, with a trivial

Left: an 1880s photograph of homesteaders leaving the Northern Pacific depot at Mandan, North Dakota, in ox carts loaded with supplies. During the 1880s these settlers transformed the Dakotas into rich farmland.

Below: pioneers crossing the plains before the construction of the Pacific Railroad. Railroad companies later encouraged settlement in the West by selling at low prices land from their government-granted rights-of-way.

A frontier woman, photographed circa 1880, collects buffalo chips for fuel. White settlers on the prairie were quick to learn from the Indians that buffalo dung made good fuel, and little else was available, as is evidenced by the treeless landscape.

incident. On August 18, 1854, a Brul Sioux named High Forehead shot an arrow into the flank of an ox belonging to a wagon train passing through Wyoming's North Platte Valley. The Mormon owner of the animal complained to the commandant of nearby Fort Laramie, who dispatched Lieutenant John L. Grattan with thirty infantrymen and two small cannon to the camp of Chief Brave Bear.

After High Forehead refused to surrender to Grattan, the lieutenant opened fire on the camp, mortally wounding Brave Bear. The Bruls retaliated by killing Grattan and all of his command, save one trooper who, though wounded, survived long enough to return to Fort Laramie and relate what had happened.

General William S. Harney – soon to earn the epithet of "Butcher" – led 600 men out of Fort Kearny, Nebraska, to punish the Brul Sioux. For some reason, the Indians did not resist the assault. On September 3, 1855, Harney's infantry attacked from the south

while his dragoons moved in from the north. Of 250 Indians in the settlement, eighty-five perished and seventy women and children were taken captive. Although Harney continued into the very heart of Sioux country, the sacred Black Hills of the Dakota Territory, no Indians offered to fight. Harney concluded a peace treaty with the Brul that endured for some years.

Meanwhile, that relentless and ruthless Indian fighter, Bull-head Sumner, was sweeping through Kansas and Nebraska. His largest single encounter was with a band of Cheyennes along the Solomon River. The warriors faced the cavalrymen with more than their accustomed confidence, for they had washed their hands in waters that, according to their medicine man, would protect them from white man's bullets. About to attack, Bull-head gave the order: "Sling – carbine. Draw – saber. Gallop – march! Charge!" And the Indians panicked. The magic of the waters was powerless against sabers. They were cut down, routed, and pursued for miles. In the end, the Cheyenne sued for peace.

The advent of the Civil War introduced a new element of instability to already volatile Indian relations. The Civil War itself in the West was not the same epic struggle that raged in the East: no major, decisive battles were fought; no great strategic ends were achieved. But in some places, most notably the Far Southwest, the withdrawal of federal troops to fight elsewhere unleashed a torrent of Indian raids, and in many other places, the massed presence of troops provided sufficient excuse for local settlers to bring the war to the Indians. Many soldiers and settlers believed – or convinced themselves – that the Indians had sided with the Confederacy.

In the Southwest, Colonel Edward R.S. Canby hastily organized two regiments of New Mexico volunteers. Lieutenant Colonel Manuel Chaves was given command of 210 men at Fort Fauntleroy, Ojo del Oso, New Mexico. In September 1861, Chaves's garrison was distributing rations, including liquor, to the local Navajos. A carnival atmosphere prevailed and, with the liquor, came gambling. Chief Manuelito squared off against an army lieutenant in a heavily wagered horse race. The Indian lost control of his pony – apparently the rein and bridle had been slashed – and lost. Not only did the "judges" – all army men – refuse to rerun the contest, they taunted the Navajos with a victory parade and arrogantly shut the doors of the fort upon them.

A typical, rough-and-ready frontier town in the West, boasting the characteristically wide main street lined with wooden buildings that housed general stores, a post office, and sometimes a saloon. Unusually, this particular example also has an Academy of Music ....

When one angry Indian attempted to force his way in, a sentinel shot him dead. At this point, Chaves turned his troops loose on the unarmed Indians gathered outside the fort. Thirty or forty Navajos were killed, including many women and children, some of whom were mutilated. Those who escaped embarked on a campaign of raiding. Fearing now that the outraged Navajos would unite with local Confederates, Canby dispatched the legendary trapper-scout Kit Carson, who was serving as commander of the First Regiment of New Mexico volunteers, to move harshly against the Indians.

After a series of early defeats at the hands of the Confederates, the Union army began to win in the Southwest. By the end of 1862, the Rebels had been pushed out of Arizona and New Mexico, so that, once again, the army of the West could turn its full attention to fighting Indians. Brigadier General James Henry Carleton, whose "California Column" had triumphed over the Confederates in New Mexico and Arizona, now addressed his efforts to the raiding Mescalero Apaches and Navajos.

Ever since the "Bascom Affair" – the capture and execution of Cochise's relatives on unfounded charges of theft and kidnapping – settlements and trade routes between El Paso and Tucson had felt the wrath not only of Cochise's band of Apaches, but those led by his ally, Mangas Coloradas. On July 15, 1862, 119 infantry troops and seven cavalrymen equipped with two howitzers were ambushed by Cochise and seven hundred warriors at Apache Pass. Partly due to the howitzers and to the new breach-loading carbines they carried – much faster than the old muzzle-loaders the Indians had encountered before – the small band of soldiers held off the Apaches until a shot from the rifle of Private John Teal found its mark in the breast of Mangas Coloradas himself.

Disheartened, the Indians broke off the attack. The chief recovered, but on January 17, 1863, he agreed to meet with an officer attached to Brigadier General Joseph R. West's command. Despite his flag of truce, Mangas Coloradas was seized and delivered to West's camp, where he was murdered, apparently on West's orders.

In 1862, Carleton replaced E.R.S. Canby as commander of the Department of New Mexico and in September called upon Kit Carson to pursue Mescalero Apaches and hold no "council ... with the Indians, nor any talks. The men are to be slain whenever and wherever they can be found. The women and children may be taken as prisoners, but, of course, they are not to be killed."

A complex man who respected the Indians, Carson did not quite obey Carleton's orders. Pursue the Mescalero he did, but he also arranged for five chiefs to visit Carleton at Santa Fe for peace talks. Two of the chiefs were killed, quite gratuitously, by a detachment of soldiers under Captain James "Paddy" Graydon, who liquored them up, invaded their camp, and cold-bloodedly shot them down.

The other three chiefs did reach Carleton, who informed them that their people had no choice other than marching off to a barren reservation at the Bosque Redondo on the Pecos River, New Mexico. The Bosque was such a dreadful place that many Mescaleros ran off to Mexico rather than submit to life there. Others, broken by Carleton's relentless campaigning against them, submitted.

The Navajos, too, were wearying of battle. Carleton told a delegation of eighteen important chiefs that the Navajos would have to join the Apaches at the Bosque Redondo. He set a deadline of July 20, 1863, after which "every Navajo that is seen will be considered as hostile and treated accordingly ... after that day the door now open will be closed." The influential chief Barboncito replied: "I will not go to the Bosque. I will never leave my country, not even if it means that I will be killed."

When the deadline passed, Kit Carson set out with 736 men and officers to wage war against the Navajo. Loss of life in battle was minimal, but destruction of fields and orchards was devastating. Within a month, many of the Navajos began trailing into the Bosque. Soon, the reservation was overcrowded, dysentery reached epidemic proportions, and rations failed to materialize.

The U.S. Indian policy of "concentration" had given birth to one of the world's first "concentration camps," with all its attendant horrors.

The Bosque Redondo and similar reservations would breed not only disease and despair, but discontent and rebellion. The case of the Bosque, however, was so deplorable that a June 1, 1864, treaty returned the Indians to their homeland, declaring it their "reservation."

Indian conflict was not confined to the southwest and southern plains during the Civil War. The Santee Sioux of Minnesota initially accepted the policy of concentration that the Apache and Navajo had so vigorously resisted. But forced confinement to a narrow strip of land along the upper Minnesota River soon changed their minds. On August 17, 1862, four Santee Sioux men were journeying home after a disappointing hunting trip. One of the hunters dared another to kill a white man. By the end of the day, five settlers had been slain.

Resentment of the whites was such that these murders touched off a general and immediate uprising among the Santee. On August 18, some four hundred settlers were massacred. Forty-six Minnesota militiamen blundered into the rampage;

half their number survived to return to Fort Ridgely, joining some three hundred refugees and a small volunteer garrison of 155. On August 20 and 22, the Santee chief Little Crow led 800 warriors against the fort. Howitzers loaded with deadly grapeshot saved the day, but on August 23, 350 Sioux fell upon New Ulm, Minnesota.

Forewarned, townsmen and soldiers were prepared to resist and forced the Indians to withdraw after a day long battle. The cost, however, had been heavy: a hundred dead and wounded, 190 buildings burned. In a single, deadly week of August 1862, eight hundred Minnesota settlers died.

A relief column of 1,600 men led by Henry Hastings Sibley entered the Minnesota River valley and defeated some seven hundred Sioux at Wood Lake on September 23. Within a week, two thousand Sioux surrendered to Sibley, who hastily convened a military tribunal to try individuals accused of participating in the raid on New Ulm. Over three hundred were sentenced to death; the remaining 1,700 were transferred to Fort Snelling (present-day Minneapolis) and suffered abuse and beatings at the hands of whites who harassed their march.

In the meantime, President Abraham Lincoln, doubting the absolute justice of Sibley's tribunal, personally reviewed the death sentences. He allowed thirty-nine of the sentences to stand – still a sufficient number to make the hangings at Mankato the largest mass execution in American history.

The defeat of Little Crow hardly brought peace to the Plains. Rather, it marked the beginning of eight years of warfare with the Sioux, though the theater of combat now shifted from Minnesota to Dakota Territory. There, Generals H.H. Sibley and Alfred Sully repeatedly engaged the Santee and Teton Sioux as well as the Cheyenne.

In Colorado, Governor John Evans called on Colonel John M. Chivington to drive the Cheyenne and Arapaho from their mineral-rich hunting grounds. Chivington, a former Methodist minister, was a rabid Indian hater, who declared in an 1864 Denver speech that all Indians should be killed and scalped, including babies. "Nits make lice!" he observed.

When a militant faction of the Cheyennes, a group of young warriors who formed the Hotamitanio, or Dog Soldier Society, harassed local settlers, Chivington had his excuse to go to war with the tribe. He and the governor formed the Third Colorado Cavalry and began a series of ruthless punitive raids. Black Kettle, an older chief opposed to the Dog Soldiers, sought an audience with the governor to negotiate a peace.

Evans and Chivington told a large group of Cheyennes and Arapahos that, to secure peace, they

A pioneer family poses in front of its sod house in Custer County, Nebraska, circa 1890. Built from tough buffalo grass plowed into strips of sod, the farmer would use an axe or spade to divide the strips into two- or three-foot pieces. With the help of his neighbors, he would then lay the chunks of sod like brickwork into two rows, making walls that were up to thirty-six inches thick.

A Concord stage coach guarded by Negro soldiers, photographed circa 1869. The Concord coach, manufactured in New Hampshire by Abbott, Downing and Company, became a familiar sight in the Western landscape.

had first to surrender their arms. The Indians retired to Sand Creek to ponder this demand. At the end of November 1864, Chivington deployed his Third Colorado – about seven hundred men and four howitzers – around the peaceful Indian camp. When some of Chivington's officers protested that they were about to commit murder, Chivington replied: "I have come to kill Indians, and believe it is right and honorable to use any means under God's heaven to kill Indians." And he opened fire on Black Kettle and his people.

Two hundred were killed, two-thirds of them women and children. Nine chiefs were also slain, though Black Kettle escaped. The massacre galvanized the Indians' will to fight. Sioux, Arapaho, and Cheyenne joined forces in conducting savage raids during January and February of 1865.

Somehow, in all of this, Black Kettle still hoped for peace, but most of his people had deserted him. They moved north, to the Powder, Tongue, and Yellowstone rivers, gathering more allies for a quick strike against military targets in Colorado. On July 26, as many as three thousand warriors attacked a cavalry detachment at Upper Platte Bridge. General Patrick E. Connor responded by sending three thousand regulars into the Powder River country, where he destroyed one Arapaho village and repeatedly engaged the Sioux. In all, the $20 million campaign accomplished little; indeed, it prompted Congress to reduce the size of the army, so that it became little more than an understaffed police force.

The end of the Civil War failed to bring a rush of reinforcements to the West. It did, however, free two able and aggressive commanders for service on the frontier: William Tecumseh Sherman and his right-hand man, Philip H. Sheridan.

While Sherman's inclination was always to act vigorously, he knew that he could do little with a small, poorly trained army. In order to secure a year

Execution of the Thirty-Eight Sioux Indians, at Mankato, Minnesota, on December 26, 1862. When the Federal Government delayed its annual payment to the Sioux, warriors left their reservation and swept through the countryside, burning homesteads and murdering more than 450 white settlers. The militia was eventually called in to regain control, and some of the Indian perpetrators were executed.

An 1884 engraving of a woman barring the door of her house against an Indian attack. Settlers on the plains lived in constant fear of such attacks. But by the 1880s that fear was largely unjustified as most of the Plains Indians had been sent to reservations.

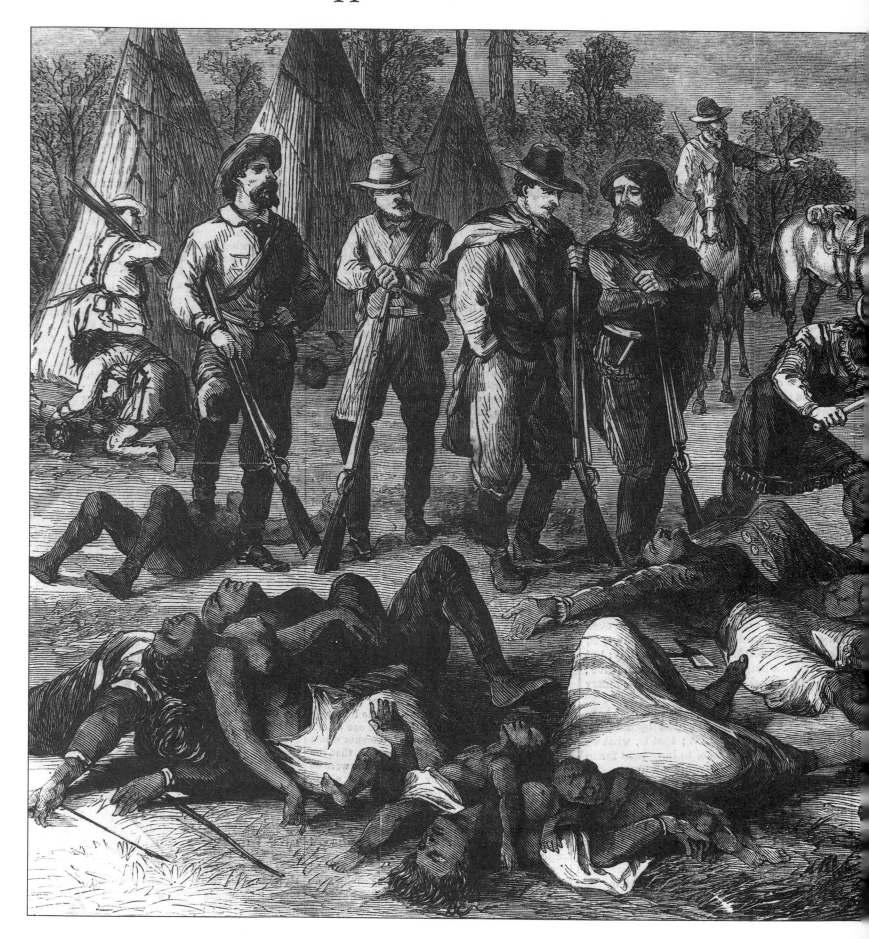

or two of relative peace on the Plains – time enough to whip his forces into shape – he negotiated treaties with the Kiowa, Comanche, Kiowa-Apache, Cheyenne and Arapaho tribes in the Southern Plains, the seven tribes of the Teton Sioux, and the Yanktonai Sioux in the Northern Plains.

That peace came to an end first in the north. Although the Teton Sioux had agreed to allow free passage along the Bozeman Trail, Chief Red Cloud was concerned that this would open his country to invasion. He went to Fort Laramie to negotiate with the peace commissioners headquartered there. While he was at the fort, he saw an infantry column commanded by Colonel Henry B. Carrington and learned that Carrington's mission was to build forts along the Bozeman. Knowing that forts presaged settlement, Red Cloud announced that he would not allow whites to use the trail.

In the face of Red Cloud's hostility, Carrington set about building Forts Reno and Phil Kearny in Wyoming and C.F. Smith in Montana. It would have been far wiser to spend the valuable time training his raw recruits, for Red Cloud did not wait for the completion of the forts before he began attacking them.

Carrington's officers resented what they perceived as their commander's cowardly indecision. Finally, Captain William J. Fetterman, tired of huddling in a stockade fort, boasted that with eighty men he could ride through the entire Sioux nation. When, on December 6, 1866, Red Cloud's warriors attacked a wagon train hauling wood near the Bozeman Trail, Carrington gave Fetterman a chance to prove himself, dispatching him and another officer with a small complement of troops to attack the warriors. The exercise proved to be a disaster, as the inexperienced soldiers panicked and stampeded out of control. The hasty retreat was humiliating.

On December 21, when the Indians again attacked the wood train, Carrington once more sent Fetterman to relieve the besieged party. This time, the captain hand picked his men, forty-nine seasoned infantrymen and twenty-seven mounted troops – just about the eighty he had said he needed to go up against the entire Sioux nation. What no one realized was that Red Cloud had massed between 1,500 and 2,000 warriors in ambush within a valley beyond Lodge Trail Ridge. A young Oglala Sioux warrior named Crazy Horse led a small decoy party that

An 1868 engraving of a massacre of Indian women and children in Idaho. Reports sent back to the Federal Government from the army in the West rarely included the numbers of women and children killed during battles.

lured Fetterman into the trap. The captain and his entire command were killed.

It was a terrible blow to the army. Yet the Sioux were unable to capitalize on their triumph. On August 1, 1867, they attacked a party of hay cutters near Fort C.F. Smith in the so-called Hayfield Fight. On August 2, they attacked woodcutters near Fort Phil Kearny in the Wagon Box Fight (so named because the soldiers took refuge behind a makeshift corral of wagon bodies, or "boxes"). In both engagements, the troops were equipped with new breach-loading rifles rather than the cumbersome muzzle loaders Fetterman's men employed. The Indians were stunned by the rapidity of the soldiers' fire and, in both cases, withdrew. But they did not make peace, settling instead into a program of hit-and-run harassment.

To the south, on the Central Plains, Major General Winfield Scott Hancock attempted a more decisive campaign, mounting a major offensive against the Cheyennes and Kiowas below the Arkansas River. He tried intimidation first, summoning Cheyenne chiefs to Fort Larned, Kansas, in the summer of 1867, where he lectured them on the might of the United States Army. The next day, Hancock and a detachment of soldiers marched to a combined Cheyenne and Sioux village to deliver the same lecture. Mindful of the Sand Creek massacre, the women and children of the village headed for the hills when they saw the soldiers approaching. Hancock ordered his principal field officer, Lieutenant Colonel George Armstrong Custer, to surround the village, lest the men also escape. Yet by morning the lodges were deserted.

"This looks like the commencement of war," Hancock summarily declared. He sent Custer, his most audacious officer, to prosecute the war. At twenty-five, Custer had attained the brevet rank of major general in the Civil War. The flamboyant, yellow-haired "boy general" was, like many other officers, reduced in rank at the conclusion of the war, but he was determined now to fight Indians and fight them unrelentingly. He led his 7th Cavalry in hot pursuit of the fleeing Cheyenne and Sioux throughout an entire summer, as it turned out, as the Indians always eluded him and continued to terrorize Kansas. Finally, Custer and the 7th, exhausted, had to withdraw.

"Hancock's War," costly and futile, prompted gestures of peace in the form of two sets of treaties, at Medicine Lodge Creek, Kansas, in 1867 and at Fort Laramie the next year. The Medicine Lodge documents established Cheyenne, Arapaho, Kiowa, Comanche, and Kiowa-Apache reservations in Indian Territory (present-day Oklahoma), and the Fort Laramie agreements gave Chief Red Cloud most of what he had wanted, including the abandonment of

Crow Creek Indian Agency, Dakota, in 1866.

the Bozeman Trail. That, however, had become largely a moot point since the transcontinental railroad was rapidly pushing west and rendering the trail obsolete anyway.

As usual, the treaties did not bring peace. The Cheyenne still harbored a militant Dog Soldier faction, who would not submit to life on a reservation. Combining with Brul and Oglala Sioux, Northern Cheyennes and Arapahos, these young warriors raided western Kansas and eastern Colorado throughout 1868. The Kiowas and Comanches, having withdrawn to their prescribed reservation, found themselves in February 1868 without the rations promised them. They revolted against their Indian agent and began to raid Texas.

With the post-treaty Plains in general upheaval and many of the poorly run reservations actually in revolt, General Sheridan (who had replaced Hancock as commander of the region) embarked upon a program of winter campaigns, reasoning that, with food in short supply, the Indians were most vulnerable in winter. While Sheridan planned his campaign, he sent fifty hand picked plainsmen under the command of Major George A. Forsyth to patrol settlements and travel routes.

On September 17, 1868, this small company was attacked by six or seven hundred Dog Soldiers and Oglala Sioux in western Kansas. Forsyth's party took refuge on Beecher's Island in an all but dried-up fork of the Republican River. The soldiers' repeating carbines twice turned back the Indians' headlong charges. Then the Cheyennes suffered a

serious loss. One of their most respected war chiefs, Roman Nose, had declined to join the first two charges because he had broken his protective medicine by eating bread that had been touched with a metal fork – the eating utensil of the whites. When a third assault was proposed, he could no longer restrain himself. Joining in the charge, he was felled by a bullet in the chest. Despite their evident superiority of numbers, the death of Roman Nose so disheartened the Indians that they broke off the attack and settled into a siege. The break in the fighting gave Forsyth the opportunity to sneak two messengers through the Indians' lines and fetch reinforcements. By the time a relief column arrived, Forsyth's men were subsisting by eating the horses that had been killed in battle.

Sheridan's winter strategy called for one column to approach from Fort Bascom, New Mexico, another from Fort Lyon, Colorado, and a third from Fort Dodge, Kansas, with the object of converging on the Indians' winter camps along the Canadian and Washita rivers in Indian Territory. Custer's 7th Cavalry, out of Fort Dodge, found a Cheyenne camp on the Washita, surrounded it, and, as the village slept, charged into it, shooting down everyone in sight: women, children and the elderly, as well as warriors.

Almost immediately, the 7th fell under attack from nearby camps. Custer held his position, slaughtering nine hundred Indian ponies and setting the tepees ablaze. Although his men were exhausted and outnumbered, Custer proceeded downstream,

The Custer Massacre. When, in 1874, George Armstrong Custer (1839-1876) reported that gold was present in huge quantities in the Black Hills of Dakota Territory, prospectors flooded to land which belonged to the Sioux. By the spring of 1875, irate Indians had gathered a force of 2,500 warriors and, in June 1876, the Sioux and the army clashed at the infamous Battle of the Little Bighorn.

as if he intended to attack additional camps. At this, the Indians broke off their assault and repaired to the defense of their other camps. Custer and the 7th quietly slipped out of the Washita Valley.

The Washita fight and the Battle of Soldier Spring, fought on Christmas Day against Comanches on the north fork of the Red River, suggested to Sheridan that the winter strategy was indeed successful. However, the weather was as hard on soldiers as it was on Indians. Snow and cold made logistics so difficult that Custer was unable to mobilize again until March 1869.

He launched his 7th against the Cheyenne, who had moved into the Texas Panhandle. At Sweetwater Creek, Custer discovered two villages, but he declined to attack, because he knew that the Indians held two white women hostage. Instead, he called for a parley and, during the talks, seized four chiefs. One he sent back with surrender terms, demanding that the hostages be released or he would hang the other three. The Cheyennes complied and, even more, lost their heart for fighting. They surrendered and promised to return to their reservation.

The Dog Soldiers, led by Tall Bull, did not

capitulate so easily. They united with the Northern Cheyennes in Powder River country. There, on July 11, 1869, Major Eugene Carr's 5th Cavalry, numbering in its ranks a seasoned scout named William F. "Buffalo Bill" Cody, surprised the Dog Soldiers in their camp at Summit Springs, Colorado. The cavalry's victory was total, and Tall Bull himself was killed. This not only finished the Dog Soldiers, it sent the Northern Cheyennes to join their brethren in retiring to the reservation.

At what seemed to be the height of the army's effectiveness against the Indians, General Ulysses S. Grant succeeded Andrew Johnson as president of the United States. Even before he was inaugurated, Grant announced a new policy of peace with the Indians, of "conquest by kindness." Taking office, he appointed a number of Quakers to serve as Indian agents and run the reservations.

Well intentioned as this policy was, it hardly undid decades of abuse or the racism on which it was based. The Indians of the Kiowa-Comanche reservation in Indian Territory took advantage of their new Quaker agent, Lawrie Tatum, to stage hit-and-run raids throughout Texas and then retreat to the reservation, from which the army was debarred. In May 1871, Satanta, Satank, Big Tree, Eagle Heart, Big Bow, and about a hundred braves lay in ambush on Salt Creek Prairie, Texas. They let pass unmolested a small wagon train, for the medicine man had predicted a larger one would follow. Sure enough, a ten-wagon train followed later in the day. Only four of the train's twelve teamsters escaped massacre.

Ironically, the smaller train had carried a much bigger prize: General William Tecumseh Sherman, on a tour of inspection.

The general was shocked by what he saw at Tatum's reservation. Sherman summoned the most important Kiowa chiefs, including Satanta, to Fort Richardson, and when they arrived, he announced to them that they were under arrest for murder. Satanta pulled a pistol, but Sherman was prepared. At his signal, the shutters of the fort commander's residence flew open. A squadron of black cavalrymen trained their carbines on the Indians. Another Kiowa, Stumbling Bear, shot an arrow at Sherman, but an alert officer deflected his aim. Lone Wolf leveled his rifle, but the fort commandant wrestled him to the ground. Satanta, Satank, and Big Tree were shackled and carted off to stand trial.

Satank tore the flesh from his wrists and managed to slip out of his handcuffs. Using a penknife he had concealed, he stabbed one of his guards and was about to escape when a soldier in another wagon shot and killed him. Satanta and Big Tree were tried, convicted, and sentenced to death. Pressure from the new, peace-oriented administration resulted in

Above: the frozen body of Big Foot, leader of the Sioux, after the Battle of Wounded Knee, South Dakota. By the end of the 1890 massacre, nearly 300 Sioux were dead – men, women, and children. The U.S. Army lost twenty five.

Left: Red Cloud, Chief of the Oglala Sioux. Red Cloud's War began when the army decided to build forts along the Bozeman Trail.

Right: Red Cloud (center) and a delegation of Oglala Sioux with interpreter John Bridgeman. On a visit to Washington, D.C. in 1870, Red Cloud saw the strength of the U.S. Army and never again led his tribe to war.

commutation of the sentences to life imprisonment, and further humanitarian agitation led to the release of Satanta and Big Tree in 1873.

Though the gesture was intended to foster peace, it hardly addressed the Indians' plight. The reservations continued to degenerate, white settlement continued to encroach, and the buffalo, crucial to Plains Indian subsistence and culture, continued to dwindle under indiscriminate slaughter by the whites. By the summer of 1874, with Indians raiding the Texas Panhandle at will, the army was given permission to carry its offensive into the reservations themselves.

Sheridan and his lieutenants, General John Pope and General Christopher C. Augur, planned to converge on the Staked Plain region of the Panhandle, with columns closing in from Fort Sill in Indian Territory, from Texas, New Mexico and Kansas. The crack 4th Cavalry, under Colonel Ranald Mackenzie, swept through an important Kiowa-Comanche-Cheyenne village, destroying it along with 1,500 ponies, and so disheartening the inhabitants that most surrendered to the local agencies. Through the winter and spring, an infantry command under Colonel Nelson A. Miles pursued and defeated the Kwahadi Comanches, who retired to a reservation. Sheridan sought to forestall further rebellion by exiling seventy-four militant chiefs to San Marcos, a

former Spanish fortress in Saint Augustine, Florida. Satanta was again sent to the Texas state penitentiary, where he committed suicide by leaping from a window in 1878.

To the north, the reservations themselves became hotbeds of resistance. There also remained a stubborn core of Indians – the Oglala, Hunkpapa, Yankton, Teton, Santee and Miniconjou Sioux as well as some Northern Cheyennes – who remained violently opposed to reservation life. Two leaders, Sitting Bull of the Hunkpapas and Crazy Horse, an Oglala, were achieving legendary status and accumulating a large following. Montana, Wyoming and Nebraska were subjected to repeated raids and Sitting Bull menaced parties laying out the Northern Pacific Railroad in 1873.

Then, in 1874, a military expedition under Custer discovered gold in the Black Hills.

Soon, thousands of prospectors swarmed over this most sacred of Sioux lands. In 1875, the Sioux tribes were issued an ultimatum: abandon the Black Hills and report to a reservation by January 31, 1876, or be dealt with as hostiles. When the deadline came and went, Sheridan prepared two campaigns. The first, to be led by Custer, was aborted because of heavy snow. The second, under General George Crook out of Fort Fetterman, Wyoming, did get under way on March 1, 1876.

Nine hundred men fruitlessly scoured Powder River country for almost a month. At last, a trail was discovered, and Crook dispatched Colonel Joseph J. Reynolds to attack a village of 105 lodges. The Oglalas and Cheyennes not only defended their settlement, but counter-attacked so effectively that Reynolds had to withdraw. Crook's abortive winter campaign did little damage; indeed, it galvanized a large number of Indians into a formidable fighting force under Crazy Horse and Sitting Bull.

Late in the spring of 1876, Sheridan commenced another campaign of convergence. General Alfred Terry (whose command included Custer and his 7th Cavalry), Colonel John Gibbon, and General Crook were to join forces on the Yellowstone River. Crook's column fell under attack from Sitting Bull's Sioux and Cheyenne at the Rosebud Creek on June 17, suffered serious losses, and was forced to retreat. Following this battle, the Indians established a camp that soon attracted others, until it grew into a large village of seven thousand. Unaware of Crook's retreat, Terry's column united with that of Colonel Gibbon at the mouth of the Rosebud.

The officers of both commands met in the cabin of the Yellowstone steamer *Far West* to lay out the campaign strategy. They planned to converge on a Sioux encampment on a stream the Indians called the Greasy Grass and the whites called the Little Bighorn. Custer would come up the Rosebud, cross to the Little Bighorn, and proceed down its valley from the south as Terry and Gibbon marched up the Yellowstone and Bighorn to block the Indians from the north. Sitting Bull would be caught in a classic pincers movement.

Custer planned to attack on June 26, the day Gibbon and Terry were scheduled to reach their position at the mouth of the Little Bighorn, but on June 25, the scouts not only discovered a Sioux camp, but also warriors lurking nearby. Custer decided that waiting would only cause the Sioux to flee – and he was tired of chasing instead of fighting. He led his men across the divide between the Rosebud and the Little Bighorn and sent Captain Frederick W. Benteen with three troops, 125 men, to the south, in order to make sure that the Sioux had not, in fact, moved into the upper valley of the Little Bighorn. Approaching the Little Bighorn, Custer spotted about forty warriors and ordered Major Marcus A. Reno, with another three troops, to pursue them. With his remaining five troops, Custer planned to storm the village from the north.

Not only was Custer wholly unfamiliar with the country in which he was operating, he had no idea of the number of warriors he was going up against – at least 1,500, though some estimates have put the figure as high as 6,000. Custer commanded 600 men, and that number had been split up.

Reno's 112 troopers were quickly overwhelmed by Sioux. They took a stand, retreated, and took another stand. Soon, their number had been reduced by half. It had taken Custer longer than anticipated to ascend a bluff overlooking the Sioux village. By the time he reached that position, he saw Reno under attack, called for his trumpeter, Giovanni Martini, and handed him a note to deliver to Captain Benteen, ordering him to bring the ammunition packs and join the fight. Martini was the last surviving cavalryman to see George Armstrong Custer alive. Warriors led by a Hunkpapa chief named Gall surged across the Little Bighorn. As Gall pressed from the south, Crazy Horse pushed in from the north. Within an hour, Custer and his men were dead.

Having received Custer's note, Benteen united with what remained of Reno's command, and the combined force of 368 officers and men fought a day-long siege, which was renewed on the next day, June 26. As Terry and Gibbon approached from the north, the Sioux broke off their attack and moved their entire village to the south.

The Custer debacle moved Congress to increase the army's strength in the West by 2,500 and grant the military control of the Sioux agencies. But it also demoralized Crook and Terry, who spent the summer

MANUELITO   1027

of 1876 in desultory, cautious, and futile pursuit of Sioux. It wasn't until November that Ranald Mackenzie and the 4th Cavalry won a significant victory in the Bighorn Mountains against a Cheyenne band led by Dull Knife. This was followed in January by the spectacular Battle of Wolf Mountain, fought in a snowstorm between Brigadier General Nelson A. Miles's small command of five hundred infantrymen and Sioux and Cheyenne warriors led by Crazy Horse.

Miles was not only victorious, he pursued Crazy Horse throughout the entire winter until the spring of 1877, when the Cheyennes surrendered and Crazy Horse brought the Oglala Sioux to the Red Cloud Agency, where he, too, capitulated. Crazy Horse was restless on the reservation, and General Crook, fearing that he would incite a revolt, ordered his arrest. The venerable chief was stabbed to death in a scuffle involving soldiers and Indians. It is unclear whether he was mortally wounded by his own hand, the knife of another Indian, or a soldier's bayonet.

Sitting Bull and the Hunkpapas had fled to Canada, and in October 1877, General Terry called on him in hopes of persuading him to come back to a reservation. The chief contemptuously refused, but, he faced a winter of famine and the Canadian tribes made clear that they did not welcome his presence. Sitting Bull at last surrendered with two hundred of his people at Fort Buford, Dakota Territory, on July 19, 1881.

In the northwest, the Nez Percés were divided into "treaty" and "non-treaty" factions. An 1863 gold rush prompted a revision of an earlier treaty that had defined the boundaries of the Nez Percé reservation. The new treaty excluded the mineral-rich lands from the reservation.

Those Indians whose homes remained within the revised boundaries signed the new treaty; those who were dispossessed by it refused to sign. Prominent among the latter was the revered Chief Joseph, who repudiated the treaty and lived with his people in land now technically beyond the reservation. Chief Joseph's truculence caused no real problem until after his death in the 1870s, when Oregon settlers clamored for more land. General Oliver O. Howard was charged with persuading Joseph's son, Young Joseph, and another Nez Percé leader, Old Toohoolhoozote, to sell their land and retire to the reservation. When both refused, Howard gave them one month to move to the reservation or be driven there by force.

Realizing that war would be fruitless, Young Joseph led his people to the reservation. En route, some young, liquored-up warriors killed a number of whites. A hundred cavalrymen from Fort Lapwai were dispatched, but were defeated in the Battle of

White Bird Canyon on June 17, 1877. Howard responded by leading a force of four hundred infantry and cavalry in a three-week-long pursuit of the Nez Percés. On July 11, the Battle of Clearwater began.

After two days of fierce combat, the Indians were routed, but Howard's exhausted men could not pursue the scattering bands. It was not until August 9 that the Nez Percé were engaged again, when Colonel John Gibbon, leading a small command of regulars and volunteers, surprised a camp on the Big Hole River in Montana. Chief Looking Glass counter-attacked, inflicting heavy losses – though suffering worse losses himself. After Gibbon withdrew, Looking Glass's warriors terrorized visitors to the newly created Yellowstone National Park.

Howard gave chase, but the Nez Percés managed to evade him. They sought refuge with the Crow Indians, but soon discovered that many of the Crow were allies of the "Bluecoats." They decided to press northward into Canada, where Sitting Bull would greet them. On September 30, 1877, while they were camped just forty miles south of Canadian border, on the northern edge of the Bear Paw Mountains, Nelson A. Miles attacked with some 400 men.

After killing sixty cavalrymen, the Indians dug in to endure a siege, which lasted from September 30 to October 5. During this time, they held council. Joseph argued for surrender; Looking Glass and White Bird were for fighting. On October 5, Looking Glass was struck by a stray bullet and died. At last, Chief Joseph went to Miles and spoke:

"I am tired of fighting. Our chiefs are killed. Looking Glass is dead. Toohoolhoozote is dead. The old men are all dead. It is the young men who say yes or no. He who led on the young men [Joseph's brother, Ollokot] is dead. It is cold and we have no

Apache prisoners at Fort Bowie, Arizona. By the spring of 1875, following years of fierce fighting by Cochise and Chiricahua Apache, most members of the tribe were forced onto reservations, but some fled to Mexico.

Chief Joseph (Heinmot Tooyalaket) of the Nez Percé Indians successfully petitioned President Ulysses S. Grant to ban settlement of the Wallowa Valley by whites in 1873. When gold was discovered there, however, the agreement was canceled. Fierce fighting broke out, but the U.S. Army prevailed. The Nez Percés were forced onto reservations or were taken as prisoners to Fort Leavenworth, Kansas.

blankets. The little children are freezing to death. My people, some of them, have run away to the hills, and have no blankets, no food; no one knows where they are – perhaps freezing to death. I want to have time to look for my children and see how many of them I can find. Maybe I shall find them among the dead. Hear me, my chiefs! I am tired; my heart is sick and sad. From where the sun now stands I will fight no more forever."

The epic Nez Percé's resistance was at an end. For three months, eight hundred strong, they had traveled over 1,700 miles of extraordinarily rugged terrain, eluding the army at each turn. About 120 died on the trek. Supported by his adversaries, Miles and Howard, who had come to respect him deeply, Joseph spent many years fruitlessly petitioning the United States government for permission to return to the Wallowa Valley. He died on the Colville Reservation in 1904.

In the late 1870s, the pattern of white invasion and abuse of treaty-granted rights, Indian retaliation, and military engagement repeated itself insistently. In Idaho and Oregon, a Bannock chief named Buffalo Horn was stirring the Northern Paiutes and his own people to war after white settlers invaded the Camas Prairie. The right to dig for camas roots, a staple food, was guaranteed by treaty; now settlers' hogs were destroying the roots, and the settlers themselves were depleting the area of game.

On May 30, 1878, Buffalo Horn led a raid into southern Idaho. On June 8, a party of civilian volunteers killed the chief, whereupon his 200 warriors rode to Oregon in order to join forces with Paiutes led by a militant medicine man named Oytes and a chief called Egan. General Howard pursued the combined Bannock and Paiute force, repeatedly engaging them through most of the summer. At last he succeeded in driving them to separate reservations.

The discovery of rich silver veins in western Colorado and eastern Utah in the 1870s only made matters worse. Miners invaded the territory of the Utes, and the tribe's Indian agent, Nathan C. Meeker, aggravated the situation by insisting that the free-ranging Indians settle down to lives as sedentary farmers – a manner of existence quite alien to them. On September 10, 1879, a medicine man known as Johnson protested to Meeker that plowing the grazing land would starve their ponies. The agent arrogantly replied: "You have too many ponies. You had better kill some of them." Infuriated, Johnson threw Meeker out of his own front door. The agent telegraphed for help, and Major Thomas T. Thornburgh, with 175 infantry and cavalrymen, marched to Meeker's relief. The approach of the soldiers provoked an attack, and the Battle of Milk Creek commenced.

Thornburgh was among the first to fall, and his

command endured a week-long siege before two of the defenders were able to break through the Indian lines and summon reinforcements. By the time more soldiers arrived, Meeker had been killed, along with nine agency employees. Mrs. Meeker, her daughter, and another woman and her two children had been taken captive. Sherman and Sheridan counseled an all-out punitive campaign, but Secretary of the Interior Carl Schurz and others, citing the danger to the captive women, managed to negotiate a truce. By 1880, the Utes were living on reservations in eastern Utah and southwestern Colorado.

Even when the Indians tried to accommodate the whites, the situation got no better. In the Lost River Valley of northern California and southern Oregon, the Modocs, a tribe perhaps three hundred strong, was trying to live peaceably with local miners. The tribe settled near Tule Lake, on land most whites deemed valueless. Nevertheless, on November 29, 1872, forty cavalrymen entered the camp of Kintpuash – known to the whites as Captain Jack – under orders to disarm the Indians preparatory to removing them to a reservation. A scuffle between a trooper and an Indian resulted in an exchange of fire. The Modocs scattered unharmed; several soldiers were hit.

With fifty warriors, Captain Jack hid in the Lava Beds south of Tule Lake. On January 17, 1873, Lieutenant Colonel Frank Wheaton took almost four hundred men with him in search of the Modocs. He withdrew after nine troopers were killed and twenty-eight wounded – all this without a single soldier ever having caught sight of a Modoc warrior. Unable to remove the Modocs by force, General Edward R.S. Canby, commanding the Department of the Columbia, decided to try negotiation. With three others, all civilians, he began talks with Captain Jack, who asked only that he be given "this Lava Bed for a home. I can live here; take away your soldiers, and we can settle everything. Nobody will ever want these rocks; give me a home here."

Neither side would back down; both withdrew for the day. Captain Jack's warriors pressured him into assassinating Canby during a meeting held on Good Friday, April 11, 1873

Pursuing forces pounded the Lava Beds with mortar fire and combed the area with infantry. Still, Captain Jack and his men eluded capture. On April 26, they surprised a reconnoitering party, killing five officers, twenty men, and wounding another sixteen. An Indian called Scarfaced Charley called out: "All you fellows that ain't dead had better go home. We don't want to kill you all in one day." Despite such victories, the Modocs were being worn down. On June 1, Captain Jack and his family surrendered to a cavalry detachment. Along with three others, Captain Jack was hanged.

It was the Apaches, who for centuries had been fighting foreign invaders, beginning with the Spanish, who mounted perhaps the most effective, certainly one of the most famous, late-19th-century Indian resistance movements.

Though by the early 1870s most Apaches retired to reservations in Arizona and New Mexico, the Chiricahuas, led by Cochise, were a notable exception. General O.O. Howard met with Cochise, who agreed to take his people to Apache Pass and live peaceably there. Other Apache bands, which had preceded the Chiricahuas to the reservations, were becoming disgusted with life there and had begun raiding. Lieutenant Colonel George Crook engaged such bands at least twenty times, killing some two hundred warriors, so that by the end of March 1873, Apaches began surrendering and returning to the reservations.

Two years later, the government decided to concentrate the Apaches further. The four separate reservations that had been established were reduced to one – San Carlos, in Arizona, an inhospitable, disease-ridden place. Had Cochise not died the year before, the Chiricahuas might have rallied around him and resisted the removal. Instead, they split up, about half going to San Carlos and half scattering, mostly into Mexico. The Warm Springs Apaches did much the same – a portion submitting, and a portion fleeing.

But reservation misery bred two strong leaders, Victorio and Geronimo. On September 2, 1877, Victorio led more than three hundred Warm Springs and Chiricahua Apaches out of the reservation. They held out against pursuing soldiers for a month, but were compelled to surrender and were ultimately returned to San Carlos. While most of the three hundred, resigned to their fate, trudged back peacefully, Victorio took to the hills with a band of eighty warriors.

The band could find no place to settle and started raiding western Texas, southern New Mexico, Arizona, and the Mexican state of Chihuahua, even stealing forty-six horses from a U.S. cavalry camp. Mexican and American troops cooperated in pursuing Victorio – up to a point. Colonel Joaquin Terrazas ordered Colonel George P. Buell and his men out of Chihuahua just as they closed in on Victorio; the honor of destroying this formidable adversary would belong solely to Mexico.

The battle took place on October 15-16, 1880, at Tres Castillos. Seventy-seven Indians died, in addition to Victorio. Those who survived made their way back to New Mexico to unite with Geronimo in a last-ditch effort at resistance.

Meanwhile, an Apache prophet named Nakaidoklini was preaching in the reservation about the imminent rebirth of Apache dominance. Officials

feared a rebellion, and on August 30, 1881, Colonel Eugene Carr arrested the prophet. About a hundred of Nakaidoklini's followers attacked Carr's camp, and in the struggle the prophet was killed. But his work had been done; by the end of September, Nachez – son of Cochise – Juh, Chato, and Geronimo, with seventy-four braves, were on their way to unite with the survivors of the Battle of Tres Castillos.

In 1882, a war party stormed back to San Carlos, killed the reservation police chief, and forced the leader of the Warm Springs Apaches, Loco, along with several hundred Indians, to return to Mexico with them. Later, another party killed the replacement police chief at San Carlos.

George Crook, given command of the Department of Arizona, pursued Apache raiders clear into Mexico. When he attacked what the Indians had assumed was a secret and, in any case, impregnable encampment at Chato on May 15, Geronimo and other leaders emerged to parley. The Apaches agreed to return to the reservation yet again – though Geronimo and the Chiricahuas took their time about it, arriving in March 1884.

But, as one might have guessed, the reservation did not remain quiet. Among Crook's many rules for the reservation was the prohibition of a traditional liquor called tiswin. The Indians defied the ban and, in May 1885, Geronimo, Nachez, Chihuahua, and the venerable chief Nana, together with 134 others, yet again headed for Mexico.

Crook gave chase, but the Apaches always eluded him, and they terrorized Arizona and New Mexico. By January 1886, however, the renegades were tiring. In Sonora, Mexico, at Canyon de los Embudos, on March 25, 1886, they surrendered to General Crook. On their way to Fort Bowie, Arizona, where the surrender terms would be formalized, Geronimo purchased liquor from a peddlar. Emboldened by drink, he bolted, along with twenty men and thirteen women.

A dispute between Crook and Sheridan put Nelson A. Miles in command of the campaign of pursuit. Miles sent Captain Henry W. Lawton to dog Geronimo throughout the summer of 1886. Lawton ran the chief and his small band to ground at the end of August. Geronimo surrendered, was exiled for a time to a Florida prison, and eventually returned to an Oklahoma reservation, where he died in 1909. The Apache resistance aside, for all practical purposes concentration of the Indian population had been

Kalkalshuatash, or Jason, a Nez Percé, in 1868. The last Indian treaty the United States Government signed was with the Nez Percé in 1868, granting them back part of the Wallowa Valley they had lost to white settlers.

achieved by the mid 1880s. One-hundred-and-eighty-seven reservations held 243,000 Indians. Even in captivity, however, many Indians refused to give up their identity.

Wovoka, a Paiute shaman's son, began to preach to the reservation Indians, like Nakaidoklini before him, of a new world in which only Indians dwelled and the buffalo were again plentiful. To bring about this rebirth, Wovoka counseled, all Indians must dance the Ghost Dance and must observe peaceful ways. The dance swept through the western reservations, alarming officials. On November 20, 1890, cavalry and infantry reinforcements arrived at the Pine Ridge and Rosebud reservations.

Their presence only incited further resistance, as some three thousand Sioux, led by Short Bull and Kicking Bear, gathered on a plateau on the Pine Ridge reservation called the Stronghold. When Sitting Bull, most influential among the reservation chiefs, began actively espousing the Ghost Dance religion himself, James McLaughlin, agent of the Standing Rock Reservation, proposed to have him quietly arrested. General Nelson A. Miles had another idea, however. He called upon Buffalo Bill Cody – in whose Wild West Show Sitting Bull had once performed – to remove the chief.

Appalled at the idea of importing a showman to conduct what should be a quiet, expeditious operation, McLaughlin did everything he could to keep Buffalo Bill away from Sitting Bull – including getting him drunk – while he worked to rescind the entertainer's authority. McLaughlin just succeeded, packed Cody back off to Chicago, and sent reservation policemen to arrest the old chief on December 15.

Despite good intentions, the arrest went badly, as Sitting Bull's adherents attempted to prevent his being taken away. Shots were fired, and the great chief was hit in the chest. As he died, his horse, which Buffalo Bill had given him when he was part of the Wild West Show, apparently stimulated by the noise of the crowd, performed his old circus tricks.

An Indian scout and troopers surrounded by Indians. In all, the U.S. signed 370 treaties with Indian tribes – the first being in 1778 with the Delawares, and the last, in 1868, with the Nez Percé – but treaties were broken as land-hungry whites pressed Congress to open more regions to settlement.

General Miles had one more important Ghost Dancer to neutralize. Big Foot led the Miniconjou Sioux, who lived on the Cheyenne River. In fact, the chief had given up the Ghost Dance religion, recognizing the futility of its message. But Miles did not know this; nor did he know that Chief Red Cloud, a Pine Ridge leader friendly to the whites, had asked Big Foot to come to the reservation in order to use his influence to convince the Stronghold party to surrender. Miles assumed that Big Foot was coming to Pine Ridge to join the resistance and incite a general uprising. He sent a large force to intercept him. A squadron of the 7th Cavalry found the chief and about 350 Miniconjous on December 28, 1890. They were camped near a creek called Wounded Knee.

By the morning of the 29th, about 500 soldiers had surrounded the camp, and four Hotchkiss guns were trained on its inhabitants. Colonel James W. Forsyth was under orders to disarm the Miniconjous

and take them to the railroad, where a train would remove them from the area. Resistance was not anticipated.

As the soldiers searched the camp for guns, an Indian named Yellow Bird began to dance, urging his people to fight. Another, Black Coyote, raised his Winchester above his head, shouting his refusal to surrender it. Troops spun him around. A rifle discharged – perhaps it was Black Coyote's, perhaps not; perhaps it was accidental, perhaps not.

Both sides began shooting, but the Indians had few arms. There was some hand-to-hand fighting, and then the Hotchkiss guns opened up on men, women and children. In less than an hour, Big Foot and at least 153, and maybe as many as 350, other Miniconjous lay dead.

Wounded Knee incited a few feeble uprisings, but meaningful Sioux resistance was finished. Formal surrender came on January 15, 1891. The Indian wars were over.

The U.S. Army near Fort Phil Kearney, Wyoming, in 1867. In May 1868, the Army abandoned its posts at forts Reno, Phil Kearney, and C.F. Smith, following the disaster of Fetterman's Massacre, during which Red Cloud's Sioux warriors killed eighty soldiers, and then burned the abandoned forts.

7

CATTLE

Like people, cattle migrated westward throughout the 1800s.

Until the end of the eighteenth century, livestock was being grazed in the Appalachian Piedmont. As population increased there, cattlemen moved their herds farther west, where the grass was sparser, but where more open land was available, which meant that larger, more profitable herds could be kept under unobstructed surveillance. By 1800, cattle were being grazed on the lower Mississippi, and twenty years later, the industry had penetrated as far as the Red River in Arkansas. Toward mid century, eastern cattle were interbred with western stock descended from the great herds started by the early Spanish missionaries. The heartiest result, and the breed most characteristic of the western cattle industry's boom years, was the Longhorn.

The Longhorn came to prominence when the Mexican War provided a bonanza of army beef contracts for Texas cattlemen. It was then that the cattle drive was born, as Texas ranchers drove some animals to markets in New Orleans and some up north, to fatten on public grazing lands before shipment east. The Civil War, which brought a Union blockade of Confederate Texas, halted shipment and drew men away for combat. The Longhorns were left to run wild on the Texas prairies, growing to herds of some five million head by war's end. When the Confederate sons of Texas returned home, these cattle were about the only assets remaining in the state.

The young men hired on as cowboys, rounding up the cattle, claiming them by branding, and trailing them to market. Since the war had depleted the North's supply of beef, a Longhorn worth four dollars

in Texas fetched forty or fifty up there. Moreover, as the army moved west to prosecute the Indian Wars, lucrative government beef contracts abounded, first for the soldiers, then for the Indians who had been pushed onto reservations.

Shortly after the war, Texas cattle were raised on ranches and shipped directly to market. By the 1870s, Texans began driving larger herds of yearlings and two-year-olds to northern ranges, where pasturage was richer and better suited to fattening. The Lone Star State remained the center of the cattle trade, but between 1870 and 1880 the number of beeves in Kansas increased from 374,000 to 1,534,000; in Nebraska from 80,000 to 1,174,000; in Colorado from 70,000 to 790,000; Montana, 37,000 to 428,000; Wyoming, 11,000 to 521,000; and Dakota territory, 12,000 to 141,000.

The industry had become big business, drawing large amounts of foreign capital, especially from Great Britain. But this "industry" was destined to be more than a business. Giant ranches – the XIT, for example, covered three million acres of Texas – were empires in the heartland of a democratic republic.

And the cowboy was the knight errant of these realms, satisfying not only the world's appetite for beef, but for legend, romance, and myth. As for the great stockmen and ranch owners, even in their own time they were called cattle *barons*. By the mid 1880s some thirty or forty men controlled twenty million

Round-up of cattle: cutting out a steer. When the time came for the round-up in the spring of 1887, cattle ranchers found they had incurred substantial losses during the previous winter. Drought in the summer of 1886 parched the grasslands and then winter froze the ground.

acres of the United States and owned about a third of the cattle in the West. They came from varied backgrounds. John Wesley Iliff, among the first to take ranching beyond Texas, was born in Ohio of wealthy parents. When his father offered him $7,500 to buy an Ohio farm, Iliff declined: "Give me $500 and let me go West," he said. He parleyed this modest investment into some 150 miles of range along Colorado's South Platte River, and eventually used his fortune to found a school of theology in Denver.

John Benjamin Kendrick was a cowboy employed by a successful Texas rancher in the 1870s. After he married the boss's daughter, he was able to buy land near the east slope of the Big Horn Mountains in Montana and Wyoming. In contrast to Iliff, who was a graduate of Wesleyan University, Kendrick had a seventh-grade education, but he became a millionaire nonetheless and went on to a brilliant political career as Wyoming governor and senator.

More famous than either Iliff or Kendrick was Abel Head "Shanghai" Smith, legendary for his hearty if crude manners: "uncouth as the cattle he drove." Restless as an apprentice in his uncle's Virginia general store, he stowed away on a schooner bound for Indianola, Texas, and found work on a ranch. The first spread he owned was a mere eleven acres, but eventually he acquired over a million. His enduring contribution to the cattle industry was the introduction of the sturdy, disease-resistant Brahma breed, which became the basis for numerous herds throughout the country.

George Littlefield was among the many young southerners broken in health and finance by the Civil War. While others in a similar condition became cowboys, working for a rancher, Littlefield borrowed a small amount of money and grew the investment into a major Texas ranch.

Alexander Hamilton Swan used foreign capital – $3,750,000 from a Scots concern – to found a 600,000-acre empire stretching from Nebraska to Wyoming. His outfit staged Wyoming's first rodeo. Swan's empire was buried in the great blizzard of 1886-87 – a calamity that wiped out many ranchers – and the cattleman suffered a breakdown, ending his days in an asylum.

But the most celebrated of all cattle barons was, without doubt, Charlie Goodnight. Born on a southern Illinois farm in 1836, he came to the Brazos River country of Texas with his family in 1845. Even then, the Longhorns were running wild, and Charlie naturally grew into the life of a cowboy. In 1856 he partnered with his stepbrother in looking after 430 cows of the C V Ranch. In lieu of cash, the boys were given every fourth calf that was born, and by 1860 they owned 180 head.

Above: Colorado cowboys lasso and brand calves. Each spring cowboys rounded up new calves and branded their ranch's symbol on their hides.

Top right: Texas beef being loaded into a Kansas-Pacific Railroad wagon at a cattle-shoot in Abilene, Kansas.

Right: In a Stampede, by Frederic Remington, shows cattle being run over the plains by steely-nerved cowboys.

Below: a dispute over a brand. "Creative" altering of brand marks was common practice.

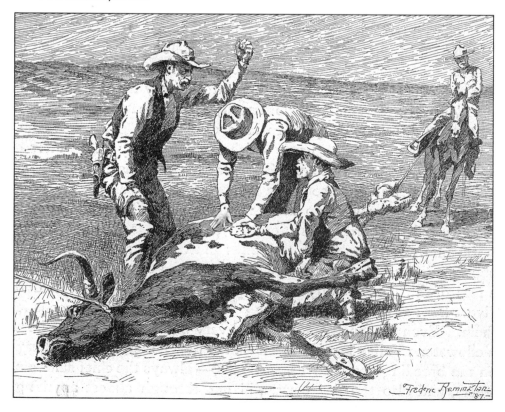

A faithful Texan, Goodnight joined the Confederate army during the Civil War, like many other young men, leaving his herd to fend for itself on the Texas grasslands. Mustered out of the army a year before war's end, he found that his small herd had increased to some five thousand head. Using the animals as collateral, Goodnight and his stepbrother borrowed enough money to buy out the cattleman they had worked for, thereby increasing their holdings to 8,000 animals.

In the cattle industry's boom years immediately following the war, most ranchmen were driving their beeves to Kansas railheads for shipment east. But Goodnight had a notion to pioneer a route to Colorado, where mining operations and Indian-fighting military outposts were creating an even more lucrative market for beef. He joined forces with veteran cattleman Oliver Loving, who was the first man to trail cattle to Colorado.

In 1866 the pair rounded up 2,000 market-ready head and, with eighteen riders, followed the Overland Mail route to the Concho River, where they watered the stock for the long, dry, punishing trip ahead. The herd moved a full eighty miles before reaching another watering place, by which point about three hundred cattle had been lost; another hundred were trampled to death in the stampede triggered by the sight of water. Nevertheless, Goodnight's feel for the market paid off, and the cattle were sold at a $12,000 profit.

Loving himself fell victim to another hazard of the trail a year later, when he was ambushed by Comanche warriors and shot in the arm and side. He escaped capture, traveling seven days without food, but he died of infection. Goodnight, however, continued to drive cattle over the trail he and his partner had pioneered – now called the Goodnight-Loving Trail – until 1870, when he decided he'd had enough of such difficult work.

Goodnight started a ranch near Pueblo, Colorado, married, settled down, and trailed up a ranch herd from Texas. Within three years he had became one of the wealthiest ranchers on the northern range. But, like everyone else in the capital-intensive cattle business, he depended heavily on bank credit, which, especially out West, came at a high premium.

With other Colorado ranchers, he formed the Stock Grower's Bank of Pueblo, a private lending institution, aiming to beat high interest rates. That very year, 1873, a financial panic swept the country, hitting the West especially hard. As Goodnight later said, it "wiped me off the face of the earth."

By 1876 he had recovered sufficiently to put together a herd of 1,600, which he trailed through the Texas Panhandle. Quite by accident, he discovered the Palo Duro Canyon, which widened into a vast pastureland, well watered, sheltered, and naturally

Above: Wyatt Earp, policeman and assistant marshal of Dodge City from 1876 to 1879. After the famous shoot-out at the O.K. Corral he had to move in order to avoid retribution.

Above right: dancer Lola Montez moved to San Francisco in 1853, where she became famous for her "La Tarantula," a dance during which she pretended to be attacked by and to free herself from spiders. However, the novelty of her performance soon wore off, and she never regained her fame.

Right: Lotta Crabtree began her life in the theater as a child performing in small-time shows at mining camps. She was "discovered" by Lola Montez in Grass Valley, California.

fenced in by high bluffs. He built corrals and a modest house and stocked the new ranch with what remained of his Colorado herd.

Next, he went in search of capital to rebuild his empire. He invited John and Cornelia Adair, a wealthy couple he had met in Denver, who had a yen for the ranching life, to settle on and invest in the Palo Duro ranch. Appropriating the young Irishman's initials – J A – for his brand, and with half a million dollars he borrowed from Adair, Goodnight bought up 24,000 acres of public land, making his purchases in a strategic pattern that allowed him to control much more acreage than he actually bought. Goodnight built a small village on his land and purchased 2,000 prized, blooded bulls, valued at $150,000. Within a short time he had grown his herd to 100,000. He was a cattle baron again.

If the big ranchers were barons, popular lore has cast the cowboys in the role of knights. Certainly, their calling required courage, honor, self-reliance, and physical prowess. Some historians, most Western writers, and virtually all Hollywood movies, have long pictured the cowboy, like the knight, as a lone rider, beholden to no one and noble in his freedom.

Viewed in a harsher light, however, cowboys were underpaid laborers doing a dirty and often lonely job. There is very little romance about what led most men to become cowboys. Many were discharged Confederate soldiers, bereft by the war of property and opportunity. Many were Mexicans and Indians, unable to find any other work. Blacks, many of them recently freed slaves, accounted for one in five cowboys. Black, white, brown, or red, cowboys could trace their pedigree not to the vaunted freedom of the plainsman, but to the virtual slavery of Spanish America.

When the herds of the Spanish missions had grown too large for the priests to handle alone, they trained mission Indians (by Spanish law free, but in point of fact indentured servants) to round up and tend the herds. They were called *vaqueros* – from *vaca*, the Spanish word for cow – and they roped steers with a braided rawhide rope called *la reata*, a lariat. Once the animal was caught in the loop, the *vaquero* wrapped the other end of the lariat around the saddle horn in order to jerk the roped steer to a halt. This was called *dar la vuelta* – making a turn – which Americans later transformed into "dally" roping. The *vaquero* rode a range overgrown with thorny chaparral, so he donned leather trousers called *chaparreras*, a word later shortened to "chaps" – and always pronounced "shaps," never chaps. Even *vaquero* was Americanized as "buckaroo."

The cowboy operated in two realms: the ranch and the trail. On the ranch, he rode over an assigned stretch of range, overseeing and tending to the cattle.

Left: the Dodge City Peace Commission: left to right, Charles Bassett, W. H. Harris, Wyatt Earp, Luke Short, L. McLean, Bat Masterson, and Neal Brown. Harris and Short owned Long Branch Saloon in Dodge City when the 1883 election put into office candidates who were intent on stamping out prostitution and vagrancy. Short enlisted these men to protect the Long Branch against the reform politicians …

Below: "Bucking the Tiger" in a gambling saloon in the Wyoming Territory.

Chores included rough and nasty veterinary work, such as treating open sores with a malodorous mixture of pitch and carbolic acid to kill deadly blowflies, and quick-thinking rescue efforts, such as pulling animals out of quicksand bogs. When a herd of Longhorns became excessively rambunctious, they had to be corralled and dehorned, by sawing or chopping, lest the animals injure one another – and the rancher's profits.

At branding time, calves were also castrated. While the animal was roped and down for one operation, it made sense to perform the other. Castration made the cattle more tractable and promoted fattening – but the cowboy had to do a conscientious post-operative follow-up on each animal in order to ward off blowflies. As if all these chores were not work enough, the range riders were also fire wardens. In the dry Southwest, brush fires were a constant danger. Not only might they consume hundreds of acres of valuable pasturage, they could easily stampede a herd.

The cowboy's biggest job was rounding up the cattle scattered across the range. Roundups generally took place twice a year, spring and fall, and were to the rancher what harvest was to the farmer. Mature steers were culled for shipment; yearlings and two-year-olds might be gathered for a long drive to another, richer range for fattening; calves had to be roped and branded to identify them as the property of a particular outfit.

The work required expert horsemanship, skillful roping, and steel nerves. To "bust a herd quitter," for example, required the cowboy to gallop after the errant steer, throw his rope around its horns, move up parallel with it, catch the rope under the animal's hind leg, then sharply turn his horse at an angle to the steer's path so that the rope suddenly tightened, turning the steer's head as it flipped him over by the hind leg. If all went well, the steer would end up on its back and turned around, so that it would rise and, greatly chastened, rejoin the herd.

Of course, a lot could go wrong: 800 pounds of beef on the hoof could pull a man off his horse, pull the horse down on the man, or pull the rope through a man's hand, sawing away a few fingers; or, if horse and rider survived, the steer could end up with a broken back – and the rancher would lose a substantial investment.

Much has been said and written about the bond between the cowboy and his horse. To be sure, the horse was a critical tool for handling stock. A good cow horse was trained to move among cattle, to dominate them without getting spooked or spooking them. Cutting horses were the most prized among the cowboy's stable. These animals had the special feel for working with stock that was necessary to

"cut out" – separate – cattle from the herd, as, for example, to cull a calf for branding. Astride a good cutting horse, the cowboy had only to gesture toward the calf to be cut, and the horse would give chase, overtake it, and prod it just enough to separate it from the herd without causing a stampede.

The truth is, though, that few cowboys got sentimental about their mounts. Fewer still owned their own horses. The animals belonged to the ranch, and in a typical fourteen-hour day the cowboy would exhaust at least two of them.

The cowboy's life was not lived entirely in the wide-open spaces. When he wasn't riding the range, a ranch hand lived in a slum dwelling called a bunkhouse. A crude frame structure, usually with a dirt floor, its rough walls sometimes papered with newsprint to conserve heat and to provide reading material, the bunkhouse was dark and fragrant of sweat, manure, leather, and lamp oil. Body lice were constant, if unwelcome, companions, and, as cowboy-historian Charlie Siringo observed, "clothes were

Above: Carson's Men, *a painting by Charles M. Russell. Kit Carson (1809-1868) was a noted mountain man, scout, soldier, and Indian agent.*

Top left: a cattle farm and stock rider in the far West. When the fur and gold that had lured Easterners to the West were gone, there remained a vast area of range.

Left: Cattle in a Kansas corn corral, an 1888 woodcut. At its height, between 1866 and 1886, ranching supplied 100 million cattle and one million sheep to the meatpackers back East.

hung on the floor, so they wouldn't fall down and get lost." Still, the bunkhouse was a place for companionship and recreation: playing cards, reading, playing the jew's harp, fiddle, guitar, or banjo, perhaps even singing a song or reciting a ballad that was an amalgam of sentimental literature, oral folk tradition, and off-the-cuff improvisation.

The fellowship of the bunkhouse was greatly valued, for much of the cowboy's work was tedious and solitary. Every hand had to take a turn "riding the line," for instance, which meant patrolling the perimeter of a particular range in order to keep stock from straying and to inspect and repair fences. The work entailed days or even weeks far from other human beings, holing up at day's end in a miserable and meager line camp – usually a lean-to shed or half dugout barely big enough for a man, furnished with nothing more than a straw-tick pallet and a fireplace.

Demanding as ranch work was, the trail drive presented challenges that seem epic by comparison. A herd of cattle, anywhere from a low of 500 head to

a high of 15,000, had to be moved from the home ranges in Texas to northern pasturage for maturing, or to railheads like Abilene, Ellsworth, and Dodge City, Kansas, Pueblo and Denver, Colorado, and Cheyenne, Wyoming, for shipment to market. Distances involved often approached a thousand miles over four principal trails: the Shawnee, from Brownsville, Texas, to Kansas City, Sedalia, and St. Louis, Missouri; the Chisholm, from various points in Texas to Abilene, Ellsworth, and Dodge City; the Western, from San Antonio, Texas, to Dodge City, and on to Fort Buford, at the fork of the Missouri and Yellowstone rivers in Dakota Territory; and the Goodnight-Loving, from the middle of Texas to Cheyenne.

The ordeals and hazards of the cattle drive almost beyond counting. There were storms, floods, and drought to contend with. Rustlers and hostile Indians were a danger – the former more so than the latter. Nor was there safety in numbers, for trail crews were not large; typically, one cowboy was hired for every

Above: Gambling tables and bar in Telluride, Colorado.

Left: cowboys relax at a game of Keno at a gambling house in Texas.

250 head of cattle – though some trail bosses and ranchers got away with one for every 400. If the average herd was 2,500 head, the average crew consisted of ten men, a wrangler or two, a trail boss, and a cook. A cowboy earned about $100 for three or four months' work, approximately the going rate for a common laborer of the period.

The first task of any drive was the roundup on the home range, which was followed by cutting out animals from the main herd to make up the trail herd. A trail herd being driven to northern ranges for maturing would consist of yearlings and two-year-olds; a herd being driven to market would be made up of cattle between five and seven years old. Putting together a trail herd was no small task. Depending on the size of the herd and the extent of the range, it could well take several weeks. The rancher used this time to make ready the necessary equipment for the drive, which included a covered wagon typically drawn by four mules. This celebrated "chuck wagon" carried food, bedding, and other supplies. It was a mobile kitchen, with a "chuck box" at the rear that folded down into a neat table for the preparation of meals.

Trail drive personnel included a trail boss – sometimes the ranch owner, sometimes a hired man

Driving cattle across the prairie. By the 1870s, the land that cowboys had freely covered with their herds was divided up into sections by barbed-wire fences marking out individual properties. Farmers had moved in to cultivate the region, putting an end to open ranges.

–a cook, at least one wrangler, and the cowboys. The trail boss had an awesome responsibility for life and property. He was, of necessity, an autocrat, whose word was law, though he worked right beside the cowboys. The cook was only somewhat less important. On him depended much of outfit's morale and physical well-being. The most junior position was that of wrangler. Usually a boy of fourteen or fifteen, the wrangler was a sort of apprentice cowboy assigned to care for the "saddle band," or *remuda*, or *caballada*, sometimes anglicized to "cavvy yard," "cavalry yard," or just plain "cavvy."

As for the cowboys, they were assigned specific positions relative to the herd. Leading the procession was the trail boss, who would often scout the trail a few miles ahead. Flanking the front were the point men; behind them, the swing riders; behind them, the flank riders; and, behind the herd, there were the cowboys riding drag.

It was best to get under way early in April, when there was sufficient growth of grass to support the animals. The first few days out were both crucial and tense. First, the cattle had to be "road broke," accustomed to the trail. Just how this was done could make the next three months unbearably miserable or relatively easy. The trail boss had to decide whether to begin by driving the animals

Lola Montez on her way to America. Born Marie Dolores Eliza Rosanna Gilbert, the Spanish dancer from Limerick, Ireland, traveled across Europe in the 1840s, becoming the lover of Franz Liszt, Alexandre Dumas, and King Ludwig I of Bavaria. In 1851, she moved to the East Coast of the United States.

A herd of Texas longhorn being driven to the cattle rendezvous at Dodge City to meet the train which would ship them back east to St. Louis. Abilene and Dodge City thrived as the towns where cowboys ended their work and began their much-needed vacations.

Bell Mare, *a painting by Frederic Remington. The cowboy had to be a careful planner; he had to pack everything he would need for the long ride to drive herds for miles across the range: bedding, clothing, food, firearms, and ammunition.*

Cattle and cowboys in Texas. Texas was the birthplace of the Western concept of ranching, and Texans excelled at the business. Between 1866 and 1880, five million cattle were sent to markets in the East from Texas ranches.

hours of riding to contain or round up the cattle.

If all went well these first days out, the drive settled into a hard routine of early rising, breakfast, relieving the night guard, and keeping an eye on the cattle as they grazed. By nine o'clock, the cowboys gradually drifted the herd up toward the north, stringing the animals out in a mile-long column. Meanwhile, the cook had washed his breakfast dishes, packed up his chuck-box kitchen, and set off ahead of the herd to a predetermined noon-time camp near a source of water for the cattle. There he started working on lunch.

At this stopping place, the cowboys let the herd spread out for grazing, seeing to it that the animals were also well watered. Once again, the cook washed up, packed up, and set out ahead of everyone else to the spot designated as the night campsite. There the animals were again allowed to graze and drink and were bedded down for the night.

Cowboys who were not part of the first-shift night guard could relax, enjoy the evening meal, a last cup of coffee, swap stories, and sleep. The night guards of the first shift circled quietly around the cattle, singing, perhaps, to settle them down. They were relieved at eleven by the second shift, which had the toughest job of the night, since cattle usually got up around midnight to stretch and walk about. Riders had to take care to keep them from straying too far. The last shift took over at two in the morning. The dreaded stampede was a particular hazard of the night. If the herd got spooked, all riders had to be roused, mount their horses, and gallop out in search of the "leaders." Once these animals were turned around, the stampede could be contained. The object was to create a "mill" – getting the leader to lead the herd in an ever-contracting circle, round and round, until all the animals were exhausted and ready to bed down again. Sometimes this meant a full night of hard riding.

While Indians occasionally harassed trail drives, such encounters were rarely fatal. Usually, all that was required was a tribute payment of a beef or two. If a stingy trail boss refused, the Indians might come back at night and deliberately stampede the herd.

Cattle raiders were a more serious threat. Their practice was to descend upon a herd, start shooting, stampede the animals, and appropriate the strays.

Finally, there were the Kansas farmers. Longhorn cattle carried Texas fever, a disease that did not harm the Longhorns themselves, but that was fatal to other stock, including that of the farmers of Kansas. Many drovers had run-ins with gun-slinging, self-appointed border guards.

Encounters between cattlemen and sodbusters and between cattlemen and sheepmen could also erupt into violence. Most familiar is the antipathy

hard, tiring them so that they would not be restive during the night, or pushing them gently, to avoid making them skittish.

A jumpy herd was a drover's nightmare. Such animals tended to stampede, usually at night when the least noise – the rustle of a cowhand's rain slicker or a distant peal of thunder – might spook them. An uncontrolled stampede meant loss of stock and risk to life and limb, and containing a stampede meant between sheepherders and cattlemen. It was not entirely groundless prejudice, for sheep and cattle could not coexist on the same range. Sheep grazed down to the roots, cutting them up with their sharp hooves and ruining the pasturage for cattle.

There was no dearth of ugly incidents. In Wyoming, for example, a vigilance gang of masked cattlemen used clubs, guns, and even dynamite to slaughter some 4,000 sheep. "Rimrocking" was a common occurrence. Flocks were led to a sheer cliff and driven off the edge. At times, isolated acts erupted into full-scale range wars, such as the Lincoln County War in New Mexico (1878-81) and the Johnson County War in Wyoming (1892), which were triggered by conflicting claims to public grazing lands.

The Johnson County War also involved a more-or-less organized program of cattle rustling, as cowboys turned homesteaders routinely appropriated the cattle of their former employers. Since rustling is very difficult to prove in court, the big ranchers formed the Wyoming Stock Growers' Association, compiled what today would be called a "hit list" of suspects, and dispatched forty-six Invaders or Regulators – as they called themselves – to seek out the condemned men.

Two, Nate Champion and Nick Ray at the KC Ranch, were killed before the Johnson County sheriff rounded up the Regulators. The intervention of federal troops was required to stave off a lynch mob, and the Regulators were tried. Through virtuoso legal maneuvering, all were acquitted, touching off a riot that required twelve troops of cavalry and a federal marshal's posse to put down.

If a drive weathered all the hazards of the trail, it reached a dusty hell hole called a cattle town. Here, cattle were transferred from trail to rail for shipment east, and cowboys could get a bath, a shave, a woman (300 prostitutes plied their trade in the small town of Wichita alone), and a drink (in many towns, saloons outnumbered all other buildings two to one). The cowpuncher could also gamble away three months' wages in a single night. And he could generally raise hell. It was the cattle towns, along with the mining towns, that bred the vintage western gunfighter.

The prototype cattle town was Abilene, Kansas, founded by Joseph Geiting McCoy in 1867. He rightly realized that the southern drover and northern buyer needed a neutral ground on which to meet. He went to Salina, Kansas, but failed to convince the citizenry to support his plan. Then he recalled a dreadful little collection of a dozen log huts – Abilene – he had seen from his train and decided to build it into a cattle town.

He enticed the railroad into laying the necessary sidings and the governor of Kansas into lifting a Kansas quarantine on Texas cattle. Within two months

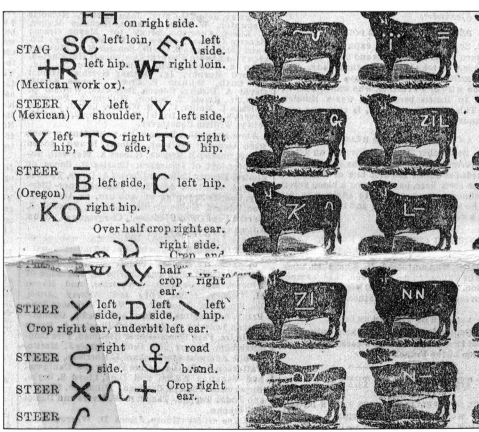

1887 THE PASSING OF THE WILD. 1897

Above: cowboys watering a herd of cattle. Arguments often erupted on the range over land and water rights, particularly between cattlemen and their old foes, sheep ranchers.

Top left: driving cattle in the Sawatch Mountains. America's first cattle were imported in 1611 into Jamestown, Virginia. From the grazing lands of the Southeast, they spread West to breed with herds of Spanish origin. Their progeny were better adapted to the arid conditions on the Plains.

Left: cowboy hieroglyphics, a form of shorthand for branding and identification used by the Wyoming Stock Growers Association.

of setting eyes on Abilene, McCoy was building stock pens, a scale capable of weighing a score of cattle at a time, a livery stable and other buildings, along with an eighty-room hotel to accommodate drovers and beef brokers. McCoy had arrived in Abilene in the spring; by August the cattle were arriving; on September 5, the first rail shipment was heading for Chicago; by November, one thousand carloads had left town.

Almost immediately after the founding of Abilene, cattle towns sprang up throughout Kansas and Missouri. The trade in range cattle grew and grew so that there seemed no stopping it. But contrary forces were gathering. First, there were the homesteaders, whose farm claims were steadily cutting up, dividing, and closing off the free range. With increased population came more rail lines, which meant that cattle did not need to be driven such long distances to railheads. The cattle towns, one after the other, began to grow into small, urban, agrarian centers with aspirations to respectability. Many of them summarily announced their unwillingness any longer to accommodate the rowdy, often violent, cattle trade, with its seasonal influx of trail-wild cowboys who kept in business the purveyors of liquor and flesh.

Then, in the winter of 1886-87, came a single and far more stunning blow.

The winter of 1885 had been a mild one, but the autumn that preceded it brought heavy rains, which, the cattlemen believed, "soaked the strength out of the grass." Moreover, it was the height of the cattle boom, and the range was being overgrazed. There were just too many animals and not enough good grass to go around. As a consequence, the stock was not healthy. When the winter of 1886-87 came, it visited upon the weakened cattle a series of blizzards that, in a single, terrible season, destroyed perhaps as much as ninety percent of the range animals.

This did not spell the end of the cattle industry, of course, but it did bring the range cattle business to an abrupt halt. After that memorable winter, those cattlemen who survived to pick up the pieces of their shattered empires would have to husband the animals with more discipline and care, breeding heartier stock, and fencing what was left of the open range.

For such work cowboys were still necessary, to be sure, but they were most accurately described as "ranch hands" now, rather than romantic trail riders on the long and hazardous haul, far from friends and family, free from friends and family, and untrammeled by the vagaries of civilization.

8
BANDITS, BADMEN AND ROBBER BARONS

There is a fine line between daring and desperation, and life in the West pushed many a man from one side of the law to the other. Popular fiction, films, and television have tried to persuade us that stagecoach and rail passengers were virtually guaranteed a robbery and that a stroller down the streets of Laredo (or Dodge City or Abilene or anywhere else) had to expect a gunfight.

While it is a fact that in 1860 Tucson's town cemetery had only two graves sheltering the remains of men who had died of natural causes, it is doubtful that nineteenth-century Western violence even approached our own century's urban mayhem. But almost every feature and activity of life in the American West did, indeed, breed its share of desperadoes. The Gold Rush that began in 1849 brought with it any number of thieves and swindlers, and gave rise to the vigilantes who took it upon themselves to deal swiftly and unambiguously with such miscreants. The influx of prospectors into California also displaced many Mexicans and native Californians, some of whom, as a result, became outlaws. The most famous of these – and the West's first legendary desperado – was Joaquin Murieta.

He was born in Sonora, a violent Mexican state seemingly in continual revolt. He married the daughter of a mule skinner who worked in the Sonora mines, and in 1848 the couple migrated to

American California. Murieta worked on a ranch near Stockton until 1850, when he was arrested on suspicion of robbery. Jailed briefly, he was acquitted, and moved to the California town of Sonora, named for its large population of Murieta's fellow countrymen. He built a cabin and staked a prospecting claim, but from this point on, the stories vary.

The most popular tale holds that a gang of Anglo miners raped Murieta's wife, rustled his cattle, murdered his brother, and whipped Joaquin himself off his claim. To avenge these injuries and insults, Murieta waged guerrilla war against the local miners, not only killing Anglos, but robbing them and distributing the spoils to the poor.

There is no doubt that the gold fields were plagued by crime, but it is by no means certain that the Ghost of Sonora, as Joaquin Murieta was called, was the only criminal. However, in 1853, the state legislature hastily established the California Rangers and ordered them to arrest five local men who happened to have the first name of Joaquin. Led by Harry Love, twenty Rangers spent two months looking for Murieta. In

A lone bank robber in Grover, Colorado, demanding cash from the teller. Although many bandits operated alone, those most feared were the ones who rode in gangs: the Jameses, the Youngers, the Daltons (cousins of the Youngers), the Doolins, and Butch Cassidy's Wild Bunch.

Jesse James, leader of the James Gang, operated in Missouri from 1866 to 1882. Jesse and his brother, Frank, began their outlaw careers as Confederate guerrillas. The gang they later formed made twenty-six raids on banks and trains. Their names alone were enough to frighten financiers.

the Tulare Valley, they came across what seemed to them a bandit gang, efficiently decapitated the man they took to be the leader, pickled the head in a jar of spirits, and displayed it as that of the infamous Joaquin Murieta.

In fact, the raids attributed to Murieta stopped at this time, but a woman claiming to be the bandit's sister examined the contents of the Rangers' jar and declared that it most definitely did not hold the head of her brother. Late into the 1870s, Joaquin Murieta was reported alive and well and ranching in northern Sonora, Mexico.

The cattle industry was chronically harassed by rustlers. While their ranks produced no figure to equal Murieta's fame, the Lincoln County War (1878-81) in New Mexico, fought between rival ranching interests, did spawn one of the West's most famous bad men.

New Mexico cattleman John Chisum, and Lawrence G. Murphy, a powerful Santa Fe merchant and financier, squared off against one another to obtain lucrative U.S. government contracts for supplying soldiers and reservation Indians with beef. Chisum knew the cattle business, but Murphy had powerful political connections and, as major creditor to a large number of local ranchers, was able to establish a virtual monopoly on the contracts.

In 1875, a lawyer named Alexander McSween and an Englishman turned rancher named John Tunstall, joined forces with Chisum against Murphy. By this time, however, Murphy had sold out to James J. Dolan and James H. Riley, who soon found themselves losing contract to Chisum, McSween and Tunstall. As the latter's business grew, Chisum appropriated large amounts of government land, thereby angering some smaller ranchers. Others, however, were eager to side with Chisum *et al* as a way of breaking Dolan and Riley's economic stranglehold on New Mexico ranching.

Suddenly, on February 18, 1878, John Tunstall was murdered by Dolan supporters, and Lincoln County erupted into war. Dolan's political interests had thoroughly corrupted local law enforcement, so that Sheriff William Brady refused to arrest Tunstall's accused murderers, even though he had warrants. Instead, he nabbed two of Tunstall's employees, Fred Waite and a teenager whose real name was Henry McCarty but who called himself William Bonney and was even better known as Billy the Kid.

Despite his subsequent fame, Billy remains a figure of mystery. Some say he was born in New York City; others believe it was in rural Indiana. It is known that, during the Civil War, he moved with his parents and older brother to Kansas, where his father died. Billy's mother moved her family to New Mexico, where she remarried in 1873 and succumbed to tuberculosis the following year. In 1875, Billy was arrested for the first time, on a charge of stealing clothes from two Chinese laundrymen. Actually, it is doubtful that Billy was guilty, but his imprisonment did give him valuable practice in jail breaking.

For two years Billy worked as a laborer, teamster, and cowboy. Then, on August 17, 1877, when he was seventeen, he had an argument with F.P. Cahill in George Adkins's saloon, Fort Grant, Arizona. A brawny Irish blacksmith, Cahill knocked the slightly built teenager to the sawdust floor and slapped his face. Billy shot him, and Cahill died the next day.

Billy the Kid was indicted for murder and sent to jail to await trial. That's when he made his second prison break and returned to New Mexico, where he went to work for John Tunstall. Billy could brook Sheriff Brady's insult no more than he had tolerated the slap on the face from Cahill. A few weeks after Tunstall's murder, Billy joined a posse of "Regulators"

The arrest of outlaw Bill White in a crowded saloon. Many Western lawmen of the late nineteenth century did not draw a strict line between their jobs and their personal grievances. They sometimes got carried away with their guns, as well. Lawman "Wild Bill" Hickok, for example, fired into a group of quarreling drunks in Abilene in 1871 and accidentally killed a policeman.

led by Dick Brewer, Tunstall's foreman, in pursuit of the Englishman's killers.

They captured two of the chief suspects, Frank Baker and William Morton. When the pair made a break for it, Billy and the other Regulators opened fire. Both men were killed, and Billy claimed credit. Now it was time to take care of Brady. With four others, the Kid set up an ambush behind a low adobe wall in the town of Lincoln. Brady walked by about mid morning with his deputy and three others. The Kid and his accomplices opened up, fatally wounding sheriff and deputy.

Between April and July of 1878, Billy continued to fight the Lincoln County War, which reached its crescendo in the so-called Five Day Battle of July 15-19. The Kid was holed up with ten other men in McSween's adobe house doing battle with Dolan's adherents, who kept the McSween place under siege for four days. On the fourth day, troops from nearby

Fort Stanton arrived, and the house was put to the torch. All who attempted escape, including McSween himself, were killed – except for Billy the Kid, who somehow ran through a storm of bullets unscathed. He turned himself in on the promise of amnesty, but as his trial approached, Billy bolted, got together a gang of cattle thieves, and ranged across the Southwest as far as the Texas Panhandle, getting into one shooting scrape after another.

If Billy could not resist getting into trouble, he also had nerves of steel. When he was tipped off that a gambler named Joe Grant was planning to kill him, Billy went to meet the man in Bob Hargrove's saloon, Fort Sumner, New Mexico. On the night of January 10, 1880, he walked up to Grant and asked to see the gambler's ivory-handled revolver. Grant handed it over, and Billy noted that the chamber contained only three rounds. Billy deftly turned the cylinder so that the next shot would hit on an empty chamber,

Cole Younger. He and his brothers, Bob and Jim, took a break from banditry in 1874 and moved to Dallas, where, eight years before, Cole had met and wooed the eighteen-year-old Myra Belle Shirley, who had Cole's daughter. Belle later married Sam Starr and established a ring of robbers near Fort Smith.

Bob Younger joined the James gang at the age of eighteen and participated in the robbery of the Kansas City Fair in 1872 and in several subsequent raids.

and returned the piece to Grant. Later that night, Grant insulted Billy, stuck the gun in his face, pulled the trigger – and clicked on the empty chamber. Billy the Kid drew his own weapon and shot Grant in the head.

After this, Billy was involved in a series of shooting scrapes with lawmen until December 19, 1880, when the Kid and five others were confronted at Fort Sumner by Sheriff Pat Garrett and a posse. All but one, including Billy, hightailed it. But Garrett dogged them, running them to ground in a rock house at Stinking Springs on December 23. After a lengthy siege, Billy surrendered, was tried, convicted, and condemned to death.

They held him in the Lincoln County Courthouse

to await hanging. About six o'clock on the evening of April 28, 1881, Billy asked one of his guards, J.W. Bell, to let him use the outhouse. On the way back upstairs to his cell, Billy slipped his small hands out of the handcuffs that bound them, raced past Bell (despite being manacled with leg irons), and broke open a weapons locker. (Some accounts report that a weapon had been planted in the outhouse.) When the Kid ordered Bell to put up his hands, the guard panicked and ran. Billy shot him, and Bell staggered

Jim Younger. He and his brother Cole became outlaws as Confederate guerrillas. In 1876, Jim, Cole, and their other brother Bob joined Jesse and Frank James on a raid on the First National Bank in Northfield, Minnesota. Frank, Bob, Jim, and Cole were wounded in the bungled robbery, and a few days later they were captured near Madelia, Minnesota. You can see the patch where Jim was shot in the lip.

off into the arms of Godfrey Gauss. Dying, Bell told Gauss to warn another guard, Bob Olinger, that Billy the Kid was out. Bell knew Billy would be gunning for Olinger, who had taunted him during his incarceration and had just that morning threatened him with a shotgun.

The Kid now armed himself with that very weapon and, still manacled with leg irons, hobbled out into the street. He called out to Olinger, who was running toward him. The kid said "Hello" – and discharged one barrel – "Bob" – and fired off the other. "You won't follow me anymore with that gun," Billy said, tossing the shotgun down beside the corpse. Leg irons and all, he casually rode away.

Garret did not give up on Billy. On Wednesday evening, July 14, 1881, Billy left his hideout at a sheep ranch and came to Fort Sumner, possibly to see his sweetheart, Celsa Gutierrez, who was also Garrett's sister-in-law. Another version of the story has him visiting Paulita Maxwell. In either case, it is probable that Paulita's brother, Pete Maxwell, had told Garrett that Billy was nearby. Francisco Lobato a sheepherding friend of Billy's, recalled that on the night of July 15, he and Billy went to the fort together:

"We were hungry and stopped at Jesus Silva's to eat. Billy wanted some beefsteak and asked Silva if he had any fresh meat. Silva replied that he had none but had helped Pete Maxwell kill a yearling that morning. He told the Kid he could get all he wanted if he went over to Maxwell's for it."

As luck, fate, or chance would have it, Garrett and two others rode into Fort Sumner at precisely this time. Garrett called on Maxwell and went into his bedroom while the other two men waited outside. Billy, unaware that Garrett was in Maxwell's house, approached them. *"Quien es?"* he asked twice.

The Kid stepped past the silent men and into Maxwell's room.

"Pedro, quien es son estos hombres afuera?"

"That's him," Pete Maxwell said to Garrett, and the sheriff fired at the dimly visible silhouette. Garrett later wrote that Billy the Kid was armed with a double-action ·41. More likely, however, he was carrying only a butcher's knife. The sheriff shot him dead.

The cattle trade also spawned cattle towns, which were beset by more than their share of rowdiness and outright lawlessness. A great deal of money changed hands in these towns, as drovers cut deals with beef brokers and paid the cowboys their wages – wages that, in turn, were liberally spent in places like Abilene's "Devil's Addition," haunt of the town's "soiled doves," "calico queens," or "nymphs du prairie," center of gambling, drinking, and fisticuffs.

The local newspaper protested that, in Abilene, "Murder, lust, highway robbery and whores run the city day and night." Yet, for the first three years of its existence, Abilene employed not a single law enforcement official. After several candidates turned down the job of city marshal, Thomas J. "Bear River Tom" Smith, a burly, handsome former New York City policeman, stepped forward.

Bear River Tom quickly made a name for himself as the marshal who enforced the law without a gun. Firearms were prohibited within Abilene's city limits, and when a man named Big Hank came into town with a sixgun in his belt, Smith quietly ordered him to comply with the law. Big Hank refused. Smith threw a left cross to his jaw, took the gun, and sent Big Hank out of town. It was a scene repeated numberless times. Bear River Tom was not destined,

Jesse (left) and Frank (right) James with their mother, Zerelda Samuel. Mrs. Samuel professed her sons' innocence time and again. During a raid by Pinkerton Detectives on her farm in January 1875, she was shot in the right arm and later had to have it amputated.

however, to hold his job long. On October 23, 1870, the marshal was called on to arrest Andrew McConnell for the murder of his neighbor. Smith took his deputy and rode out to McConnell's homestead dugout. Since the job was outside Abilene proper, Tom armed himself.

Marshal and deputy confronted McConnell and another man, Moses Miles. Bear River Tom began to read the warrant. Without warning, McConnell shot him in the right lung. The marshal managed to squeeze off a shot himself, slightly wounding McConnell, and the two injured men began wrestling. Miles exchanged fire with the deputy, who wounded Miles, but then fled. Miles turned on Smith, beat him to the ground with his gun, dragged him into the open, and chopped off his head with a wood axe.

(Both Miles and McConnell were captured within three days, tried, convicted, and given long prison terms.)

Abilene had lost a good man, and the question arose: who would be fool enough to replace him as marshal of what was popularly called "the meanest hole in the state"?

James Butler Hickok earned his more familiar nickname when, during the Civil War, he single-handedly backed down a lynch mob. A lady who saw it all shouted, "Good for you, Wild Bill!" and the name stuck.

Born on May 27, 1837, in Troy Grove, Illinois, Hickok earned a reputation as the best man, with gun or fists, in the state. Employed as a teamster by the age of eighteen, he had a fight with one Charlie

Bob Ford infiltrated the James gang in 1881, when Jesse moved to St. Joseph, Missouri. On April 3, 1882, Bob visited Jesse in his home. Walking into the living room from the kitchen, Jesse stepped onto the seat of a chair to straighten a picture on the wall. Bob Ford saw his chance and shot Jesse in the head, killing him instantly.

names, including "Duck Bill" – a reference to his protruding lips – and "hermaphrodite," a cruder anatomical aspersion. Finally, on July 12, McCanles came gunning for Wild Bill.

McCanles called to Hickok inside the freight station: "Come out and fight fair." When he threatened to drag Hickok out, Wild Bill at last responded. "There will be one less son-of-a-bitch when you try that," he said.

McCanles stepped inside. Hickok shot him dead.

Then it all got even uglier. McCanles's twelve-year-old son, a cousin named Woods, and a ranch hand came running toward the station. The boy cradled his father's lifeless body in his arms as Woods opened the door to the station kitchen. Hickok sent two slugs into him, then turned around and opened up on the ranch hand. Both were wounded and fled, with the station master and a stable hand in pursuit. The station master caught up with Woods and hacked him to death with a garden hoe. The stable hand finished off the other man with a shotgun blast.

Hickok fought in the Civil War, then set up as a professional gambler in Springfield, Missouri. While there, he had another gunfight over a woman. Hickok and Dave Tutt arranged a showdown for six p.m., July 22, 1865.

The two men faced off and halted at about seventy-five yards. Tutt drew and fired and missed. Hickok calmly drew his gun, steadied it with both hands, squeezed off a shot, and ended Tutt's life. Hickok was acquitted after a brief trial.

That duel is about as close to the classic Western movie gunfight as real shootouts ever got. Quick-draw contests simply never happened. For one thing, the revolvers were so unreliable that a shootist felt himself lucky if his piece didn't misfire. If he actually hit his mark, so much the better. Most Western shooting scrapes were from ambush or at point-blank range. If possible, one tried to shoot one's man in the back. And if one had a choice, one used a shotgun rather than a sixgun.

After the Springfield contest, Hickok moved to Fort Riley, Kansas, where he scouted for Custer's 7th Cavalry, ran unsuccessfully for sheriff of Ellsworth County, and became a deputy U.S. marshal. He distinguished himself as a scout and, in 1869, succeeded in getting elected to the office of Ellis County sheriff. His first official act was to gun down a 7th Cavalry trooper for resisting arrest. Next month, he put down a saloon riot by means of a well-placed bullet through the skull of the rowdiest rioter. The following summer, however, Wild Bill was himself in the center of a barroom brawl with 7th Cavalry men. When five troopers set on him, Bill shot two, killing one. He unceremoniously resigned his office,

Hudson, mauling him so badly that he thought he had killed him. Young Hickok fled to St. Louis, thence to "Bleeding Kansas," as the pre-Civil War border state was called, where he enlisted in the Free-State Militia. In 1858 he was elected constable of Monticello township, worked other odd jobs, and became a wagon master for the freighting firm of Russell, Majors & Waddell.

While leading a train through Raton Pass along the Santa Fe Trail, Hickok was attacked by a bear, which severely injured him. The firm sent him to Santa Fe and Kansas City for medical treatment and then assigned him to a light-duty post at Rock Creek Station, Nebraska. There, Hickok made an enemy of a local rancher, Dave McCanles, whose mistress he fancied. McCanles taunted Hickok by calling him

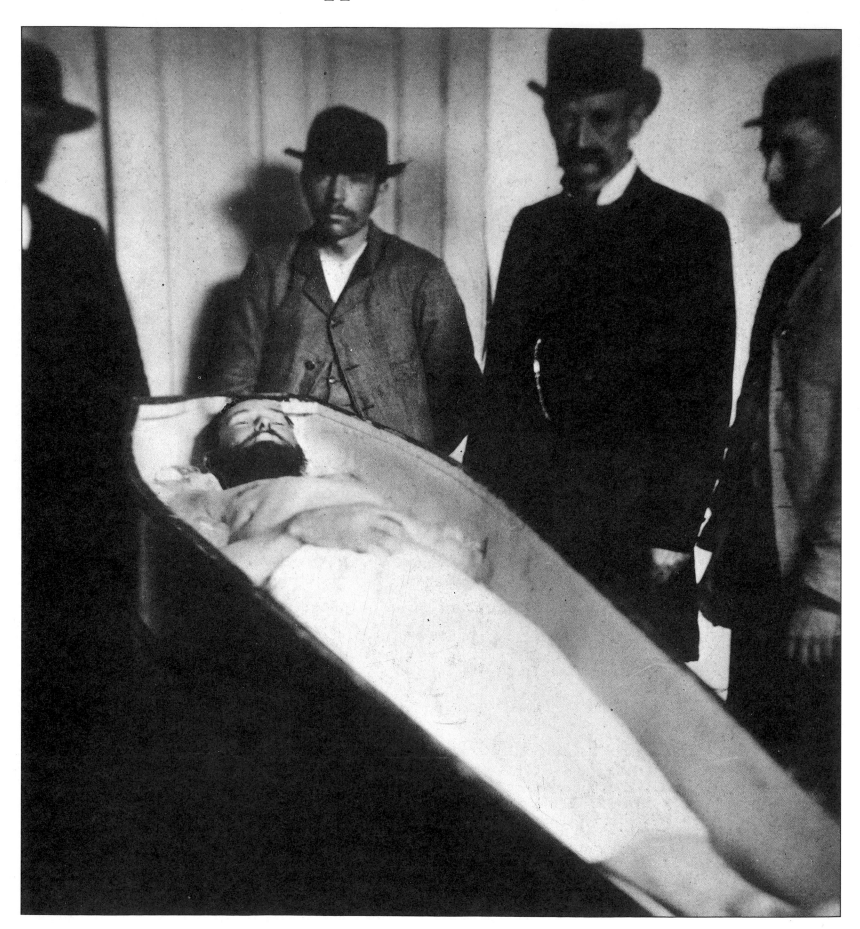

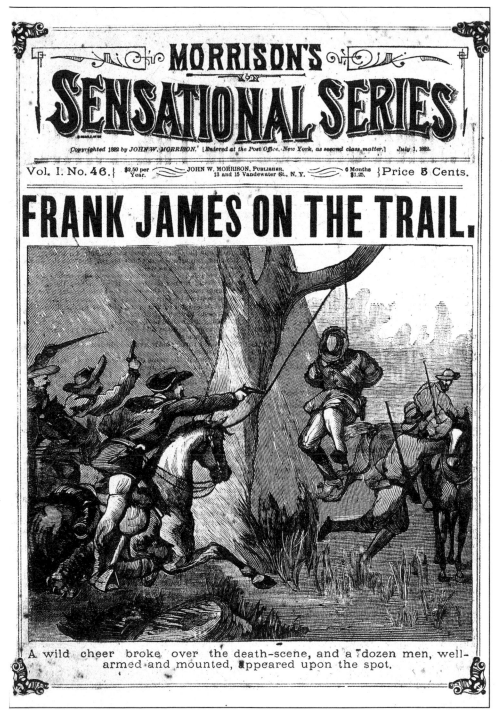

MORRISON'S SENSATIONAL SERIES

Copyrighted 1882 by JOHN W. MORRISON. [Entered at the Post Office, New York, as second class matter.] July 1, 1882.

Vol. I. No. 46.} $2.50 per Year. ⟶ JOHN W. MORRISON, Publisher, 13 and 15 Vandewater St., N.Y. ⟶ 6 Months $1.25. {Price 5 Cents.

FRANK JAMES ON THE TRAIL.

A wild cheer broke over the death-scene, and a dozen men, well-armed and mounted, appeared upon the spot.

Morrison's Sensational Series published the James' exploits, garnering a lot of sympathy for its members.

Jesse James in his coffin. Frank James was acquitted of his crimes and lived to the age of seventy-two, conducting tours of his birthplace and philosophizing on outlawry.

skipped town, and next turned up briefly in an Wild West show playing Niagara Falls, New York.

Shortly after he returned to Kansas, Hickok hired on as Abilene's marshal. Like Bear River Tom's, his tenure was destined to be brief. A few months after he was hired, outraged citizens sent Bill to the Bull's Head Saloon to see to the removal of a sign featuring a realistic depiction of that which makes a bull a bull. The job was done, but saloon owner Phil Coe took an intense dislike to Wild Bill. On October 5, 1871, he led about fifty Texas cowboys on a wild spree through

Abilene's streets. Hickok sent for his deputy, Mike Williams, who, however, had just received a telegram summoning him to the bedside of his ailing wife in Kansas City. He had to take the 9:45 p.m. train.

At nine, a shot rang out. Hickok went to investigate and found Coe at the center of a bunch of rowdies. Coe told the marshal he was just shooting at a dog. Something in Wild Bill snapped. He went for his gun, but Coe fired first, his bullet hitting the marshal's coattails. Hickok leveled, squeezed the trigger, and hit Coe in the gut. "I've shot too low," someone heard the marshal say.

Just then, Mike Williams came running through the crowd. Bill instinctively spun around and fired, hitting the deputy twice in the head.

After this, even violent Abilene had had enough of Wild Bill Hickok. He was relieved as marshal and, in going, made the gallant gesture of paying for Williams's funeral expenses. He seems not to have had qualms about the business of killing generally, however: "I never think much about it. I don't believe in ghosts, and I don't keep the lights burning all night to keep them away. That's because I'm not a murderer. It is the other man or me in a fight, and I don't stop to think – is it a sin to do this thing? And after it is over, what's the use of disturbing the mind?"

Hickok left Abilene and returned to the East, where he appeared in Buffalo Bill's celebrated Wild West Show.

There, too, Hickok could hardly contain his propensity for violence. He flattened a New York City hack driver for asking what Hickok considered to be an outrageous fare, shot out the first spotlight that threw its glare on him, demanded aloud real whiskey when some fool presented him with cold tea – theatrical hooch – on stage, and beat up half a dozen oil-field roughnecks in a local bar on a brief Pennsylvania stopover. Everybody, including Cody, breathed a sigh of relief when Wild Bill left a message for Buffalo Bill with a stagehand ("Tell that long-haired son-of-a-bitch I have no more use for him and his damned show business") and took off for the real West.

Suffering from venereal disease, he began to lose his eyesight and seems to have hit bottom in Cheyenne, Wyoming, where he was arrested on several occasions as a vagrant. In 1876, he married Agnes Lake, a circus owner, but two weeks after the wedding, he announced his departure for the gold fields near Deadwood, Dakota Territory.

The only prospecting he did there was in the town's gambling establishments. On August 2, he was in Deadwood Saloon No. 10, losing his shirt in an afternoon poker game. A drifter named Jack McCall drew his old Colt .45 and walked up behind

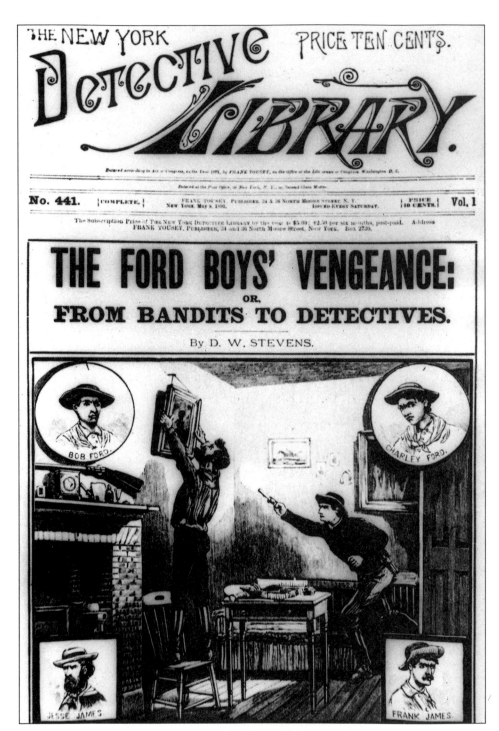

The Ford Boys' Vengeance: From Bandits to Detectives *popularized the story of Bob Ford, killer of Jesse James. Ford was convicted of the murder and was sentenced to death, but the Governor of Missouri pardoned him.*

Hickok. Wild Bill was holding his first winning hand of the afternoon – a queen and two pairs, aces and eights – when McCall shot him.

"Take that!" said the drifter.

Wild Bill slumped to the floor, dead, still gripping his cards.

The cattle towns had plenty of thieves, murderers, and plain-and-fancy hell raisers. But an astounding number of them were not simply criminals. Many, perhaps most, worked both sides of the law: Buffalo Bill Brooks, lawman and rustler; Mysterious Dave

Mather, horse thief, stagecoach and train robber, deputy marshal of Dodge City, and deputy sheriff of Ford County, Kansas; the Masterson brothers, Bat, Ed, and Jim, each of whom wore a badge and committed crimes. Men who used guns in the West are best described neither as lawmen nor badmen, but, more generically, as gunmen.

Perhaps the most famous were the Earps: James, Morgan, Virgil, Warren, Wyatt. The latter was born on March 19, 1848, in Monmouth, Illinois. He was variously a farmer, railroad section hand, buffalo

Above: dapper Bat Masterson, who took on the mighty job of cleaning up the streets of Dodge City, Kansas.

Above left: Ben Thompson, a marshal in Austin, Texas, in the early 1880s. A merciless gunman and no real lover of the law, Thompson killed a total of thirty-two men.

hunter, horse thief, bunco artist, prospector, saloon keeper, gambler – and law officer. In 1875, as a policeman in Wichita, he nearly shot himself while making an arrest, and he often "forgot" to turn over fines he had collected from the town's complement of soiled doves. Arrested for fighting, he was discharged from the force and became a policeman in Dodge City, later moving up to deputy marshal. He left Dodge for Las Vegas, New Mexico, in 1879, briefly stopping in Mobeetie, Texas, where he engaged in a bunco scheme with Mysterious Dave Mather.

Later in the year, Wyatt and his four brothers moved to Tombstone, Arizona, where they befriended a tubercular dentist named John Henry "Doc" Holliday.

The Earp brothers tried desperately to become solid citizens, going so far as to join the Republican party. Virgil became town marshal in 1880, Wyatt failed to win election to the office of sheriff of Cochise County, and James became a bartender. But their rise to respectability was menaced by a developing feud with N.H. "Old Man" Clanton and his sons, Ike, Phin, and Billy, all cattle rustlers by profession. When a stagecoach was robbed and two men killed, Wyatt saw a chance to attain the coveted sheriff's office. He would capture the robbers – and he knew just who could reveal their whereabouts. Earp offered Ike Clanton all the reward money in exchange for the information; all Wyatt wanted was the credit for the capture. Ike agreed, but the deal fell apart when the gang was shot and killed by others.

Now the deal was a threat to Earp and the Clantons – if word of it got out – and throughout the summer of 1881, threats and counter-threats flew between the Earps and the Clantons. When the Earps' friend Doc Holliday was arrested in June on suspicion of having participated in the stagecoach robbery, the Earps' reputation suffered. The charges were dropped, but the Clantons circulated a rumor that the Earps had been involved in the robbery. In retaliation, a friend of Wyatt accused Ike Clanton of having ratted on his friends, the slain stagecoach robbers. Ike now accused Wyatt Earp of having betrayed their bargain, and on the night of October 25, 1881, Ike boasted that he would make the Earps pay for all they had done.

On the twenty-sixth, Virgil Earp arrested Ike, but he was quickly released. On the same day, Wyatt had words with Ike's friend, a rancher named Tom McLaury, and cracked him over the head with the butt of his revolver. Then Wyatt antagonized McLaury's brother, Frank, when he ordered the man to remove his horse from the boardwalk.

"Take your hands off my horse!" Frank growled.

"Keep him off the sidewalk," Earp warned. "It's against the city ordinance."

One hour later, Marshal Virgil Earp recruited his brothers Wyatt and Morgan as well as Doc Holliday to help arrest the Clantons and McLaurys. Sheriff John Behan tried to intervene, but Holliday and the Earp brothers ignored him and approached Ike and Billy Clanton, the McLaury brothers, and a rustler called Billy the Kid, all of whom were standing outside the O.K. Corral.

"You sons of bitches," Wyatt said, "you've been looking for a fight and now you can have it!"

"Throw up your hands!" shouted Marshal Virgil Earp.

Above: Charles E. Bolton (1830 - 1917), known as "Black Bart," was a notorious stagecoach robber in California. Originally from New York, this Civil-War veteran turned drifter robbed twenty-seven stagecoaches between 1875 and 1882. During his last robbery, he dropped a handkerchief, whose laundry mark led lawmen to the San Francisco resident Charles E. Bolton.

Above right: He Danced For All He Was Worth – the Wancho Gang, notorious train robbers, relaxing at the expense of a grocery clerk near New Braunfels, Texas.

Morgan shot Billy Clanton. Wyatt opened up on Frank McLaury. Ike Clanton, unarmed, ran to Wyatt, grabbed his left arm, and begged him to stop shooting.

"The fighting has now commenced. Go to fighting or get away," Wyatt said.

Ike and Claiborne ducked into a nearby photo studio, and the gunplay continued. When it was all over, Billy Clanton and both McLaurys lay dead or dying. Virgil, Morgan, and Doc Holliday were all wounded. Wyatt was untouched.

The Earps were exonerated at a hearing, which determined that they had been acting in their capacity as "peace officers." But the battle was by no means over.

Virgil Earp lost his job as Tombstone's marshal, and Wyatt's aspirations to the office of sheriff were dashed. Then came the vengeance shootings. On December 28, 1881, at 11:30 p.m., Virgil was ambushed as he left the Oriental Saloon. Buckshot badly injured his arm, and, because the doctor was forced to remove four inches of bone, he never regained full use of it. On March 18, 1882, Morgan Earp was playing billiards

in Hatch's Billiard Parlor. At 10:50 p.m., as Morgan was chalking up, several men crept to the rear door of the building and fired two shots. One of the slugs ripped through the right side of Morgan's stomach, shattered his spine, and exited, slightly wounding a bystander. Morgan was carried to an adjacent room and laid out on a sofa, surrounded by his brothers Wyatt, Virgil, James, and Warren. "This is the last game of pool I'll ever play," Morgan groaned, and he died. Most attributed Morgan's assassination to Clanton sympathizers Frank Stilwell, Pete Spence, a gambler named Freis, Florentino Cruz, and Indian Charley.

Wyatt wanted his own revenge, and enlisted the aid of Doc Holliday in killing Stilwell. Wyatt, Holliday, and Warren Earp next killed Florentino Cruz. Wyatt also dispatched Curly Bill Brocius, known to have rustled cattle in company with the McLaury brothers. Wyatt Earp skillfully avoided arrest for all of this work. He died in Los Angeles from natural causes in 1929, aged 81.

If the Earps were eyed with suspicion by their

A fearsome crew of gunmen. From left to right: Pawnee Bill (Major Gordon Lillie), Captain Lute North, Deadwood Dick (Robert Clark), Dr. W.F. Carver, Idaho Bill (B.R. Pearson), and Diamond Dick.

contemporaries, later popular fiction and, even more, Western movies have tended to cast them in a positive, even heroic light. The case of Frank and Jesse James is different. Thieves and murderers, they were celebrated in their own time as latter-day Robin Hoods – though there is absolutely no evidence that they ever gave anything to anyone.

Frank was born in 1843 and Jesse four years later, sons of a Clay County, Missouri, Baptist preacher, who left Frank and Jesse when they were seven and three in order to work the gold fields of California. He died there, and Zerelda, his widow, instantly remarried. Almost as instantly, she divorced – for the stepfather was mean to her boys. In 1855 she married a quiet and passive physician. But the boys' coming of age was hardly tranquil. In Civil War-era Missouri, they quickly came to know violence. The brothers joined the notorious Confederate guerrilla band led by William Quantrill and Bloody Bill Anderson. It was a schooling for terrorists.

Jesse and Frank joined forces with the Youngers – Cole (also a Quantrill alumnus), James, Bob, and

John. They pulled off their first robbery on February 13, 1866 – though it is not absolutely certain that this first job included Frank, nor Jesse, who may have been recovering from a lung wound received while he was riding with Quantrill. In fact, since the gang always wore masks, it is impossible to tell for certain just who participated in what robberies. On this occasion, a dozen men rode into Liberty, Missouri. Two entered the Clay County Savings Bank, drew revolvers, locked the cashier and his son in the vault, and made off with $60,000. Outside the bank, accomplices panicked and fired, killing college student George Wymore.

Perhaps the money lasted them a while; for it wasn't until two years later that the gang struck again, hitting the Southern Bank of Kentucky in Russellville. This time, the cashier was not so compliant, but a few "warning" shots convinced him to turn over the loot. However, the shots also alerted Nimrod Long, the bank's president, who was at home, eating lunch. He came running, burst through his bank's door, and was grazed on the

As robberies became more frequent, banks took steps to put an end to banditry. They offered rewards for the killing of robbers, hired their own guards, and employed Pinkerton Detectives to track down the outlaws. The Pinkerton Detective Agency, founded by the Scottish immigrant Allan Pinkerton in 1850, worked not only for banks and railroad companies but also for industries experiencing labor problems.

scalp by a bullet. The shot sent him crashing to the floor, and Jesse shouted to the rest of the gang that he had killed the president. The gang made off with about $12,000.

Next year, the gang was back in Missouri, where, on December 7, they calmly strode into the Gallatin bank and asked to speak to its owner, a Mr. John W. Sheets. This time, more than money was involved; Sheets had served with the Union during the late war, and the boys held a grudge. They began to talk "business" with Sheets. Without pausing in the conversation, one of the James brothers pulled a gun and shot the man twice. A clerk was also fired on and hit, and the boys also stopped long enough to gather a sackful of cash.

They hid out at their stepfather's farm – the Samuels farmstead – in Clay County. On December

15, four men, hankering after a $3,000 reward, laid siege to the house. Deputy Sheriff John Thomason was not about to allow civilians to claim all the glory – let alone the reward – and stormed the farmhouse with a posse. Frank and Jesse galloped out of the barn. Shots were furiously exchanged, and the posse gave chase. The deputy leaped off his horse, intending to use his mount to steady his aim across the saddle. But the horse bolted before he could get off a shot and, riderless, pulled up parallel with the fleeing brothers, one of whom shot the animal dead.

Another Kentucky job followed on April 29, 1872, but that netted a paltry $600. More pathetic was the September 26 robbery of Ben Wallace, a ticket seller at the Kansas County Fair. As Jesse attempted to relieve Wallace of his tin cash box, the ticket seller wrestled with him. Jesse – this "Robin Hood of the West" – drew his revolver, fired, and the wild shot hit a little girl in the leg. The bandits quickly rode off.

By the next year, the gang was after bigger game: trains. Their train holdups became epidemic, and the frustrated railroads hired Pinkerton detectives to hunt the group down. After a Pinkerton operative named John W. Wicher turned up dead – shot in the head and heart – near the Samuels farmstead on March 10, 1874, the detective agency retaliated on January 5 the next year by tossing a railroad flare into the Samuels farmhouse. Not only did it burn the house down, it blew away (or necessitated the amputation of) the arm of the James boys' mother. This incident turned public opinion against the railroads and in favor of the boys, very nearly moving the Missouri state legislature to grant the James gang amnesty.

But the James's next job took them far from Missouri. Eight of the gang rode to Northfield, Minnesota, on September 7, 1876, intending to rob the First National Bank there. Three gang members waited just outside town, two others were deployed outside the bank, and three entered the building, announced a robbery, and demanded the money. Cashier Joseph L. Heywood refused. One of the gang slit his throat and shot him. A teller ran outside for help, but was felled by a bullet in the shoulder.

Then the robbery began to fall apart, as townsmen, alerted by the shouts and shots, began firing on the outlaws, killing Clell Miller and William Stiles and gravely wounding Bob Younger. The remainder of the gang fought its way out of town, killing a local named Nicholas Gustavson. Jesse proposed that they abandon or "finish off" the wounded Bob Younger, who was slowing down the getaway. But Cole refused to leave his brother, and Frank and Jesse left the two of them. In a matter of days, gang member Charlie Pitts was killed by a posse, and Bob, Cole, and Jim Younger were captured. But it seemed

$5,000 REWARD

DEAD Bank Robbers Wanted

$5,000 Cash will be paid for each bank robber killed while robbing a Texas bank

THE Texas Bankers Association offers a standing reward of $5,000 for each dead Bank Robber, killed while in the act of robbing a member bank in Texas. No limit as to place of killing — in the banking house, as the robber or robbers leave the bank, as they climb into their car, ten or twenty miles down the road as they flee, or while resisting a posse giving chase. This reward applies to night attacks as well as to daylight holdups.

The Association will not give one cent for live robbers. They rarely are identified, more rarely convicted, and most rarely kept in the penitentiary when sent there — all of which operations are troublesome and costly.

But the Association is prepared to pay for any number of dead Bank Robbers, killed while robbing its member banks, at $5,000 a piece.

$5,000 in cash will be paid for the killing of any robber while robbing

THIS BANK

$5,000 for each Dead Robber — not one cent for a hundred live ones!

The Wild Bunch. Seated at the far left is the Sundance Kid (Harry Longbaugh) and at the far right is Butch Cassidy (Robert LeRoy Parker). Cassidy's gang was the last of the Western outlaw bands. After having this photograph taken in Fort Worth in 1901, the gang sent a print to the Winnemucca, Nevada, bank they had robbed in September 1900.

Jesse and Frank had vanished.

They lay low for three years in Nashville, Tennessee, then reemerged in 1879 to rob a train at Glendale Station, Missouri. On July 15, 1881, they robbed a Rock Island train at Winston, Missouri, killing a conductor and a passenger. While they made off with a large amount of cash from the express car, the Winston robbery was to prove the James's undoing. Now the state offered a widely publicized $5,000 reward, which some found impossible to resist.

Jesse was living in St. Joseph, Missouri, under the name of Thomas Howard. On April 3, 1882, he was standing on a chair in his house, adjusting a crooked picture. Robert Ford, a new member of the gang – who had joined up with the object of claiming the reward – walked into the room and shot Jesse in the back. "The dirty little coward," went the lyric to an immediately popular ballad, "That shot Mr. Howard / And laid poor Jesse in his grave." A few months later, Frank James turned himself in. Twice tried for robbery, he was twice acquitted for lack of evidence. It seemed that no Missourian was willing to convict the outlaw, and he died quietly in 1915. In the West, killers and thieves became heroes. From John Wesley Hardin (a homicidal youngster who once shot a man sleeping in the next room for snoring too loudly) to Bat Masterson (who died in the 1920s, at his sports-

Pinkerton's National Detective Agency.

FOUNDED BY ALLAN PINKERTON, 1850.

OFFICES.

ROBT. A. PINKERTON, New York. } Principals.
WM. A. PINKERTON, Chicago. }

GEO. D. BANGS, General Manager, New York.
ALLAN PINKERTON, Assistant General Manager, New York.

JOHN CORNISH, Gen'l Sup't., Eastern Division, New York.
EDWARD S. GAYLOR, Gen'l Sup't., Middle Division, Chicago.
JAMES McPARLAND, Gen'l Sup't., Western Division, Denver.

Attorneys:— GUTHRIE, CRAVATH & HENDERSON, New York.

TELEPHONE CONNECTION.

REPRESENTING THE AMERICAN BANKERS' ASSOCIATION.

DENVER, OPERA HOUSE BLOCK, J. C. FRASER, Sup't.
NEW YORK, 57 BROADWAY
BOSTON, 30 COURT STREET
PHILADELPHIA, 441 CHESTNUT STREET
MONTREAL, MERCHANTS BANK BUILDING
CHICAGO, 201 FIFTH AVENUE
ST. PAUL, GERMANIA BANK BUILDING
ST. LOUIS, WAINWRIGHT BUILDING
KANSAS CITY, 622 MAIN STREET
PORTLAND, ORE., MARQUAM BLOCK
SEATTLE, WASH., BAILEY BLOCK
SAN FRANCISCO, CROCKER BUILDING

$4,000.00 REWARD.

CIRCULAR No. 2.

DENVER, Colo., January 24th, 1902.

THE FIRST NATIONAL BANK OF WINNEMUCCA, Nevada, a member of THE AMERICAN BANKERS' ASSOCIATION, was robbed of $32,640 at the noon hour, September 19th, 1900, by three men who entered the bank and "held up" the cashier and four other persons. Two of the robbers carried revolvers and a third a Winchester rifle. They compelled the five persons to go into the inner office of the bank while the robbery was committed.

At least $31,000 was in $20 gold coin ; $1,200 in $5 and $10 gold coin ; the balance in currency, including one $50 bill.

Since the issuance of our first circular, dated Denver, Colo., May 15th, 1901, it has been positively determined that two of the men who committed this robbery were :

1. **GEORGE PARKER**, alias "BUTCH" CASSIDY, alias GEORGE CASSIDY, alias INGERFIELD.
2. **HARRY LONGBAUGH**, alias "KID" LONGBAUGH, alias HARRY ALONZO, alias "THE SUNDANCE KID,"

PARKER and LONGBAUGH are members of the HARVEY LOGAN alias "KID" CURRY band of bank and train (express) "hold up" robbers.

For the arrest, detention and surrender to an authorized officer of the State of Nevada of each or any one of the men who robbed the FIRST NATIONAL BANK OF WINNEMUCCA, the following rewards are offered :

BY THE FIRST NATIONAL BANK OF WINNEMUCCA: $1,000 for each robber.

Also 25 per cent., in proportionate shares, on all money recovered.

BY THE AMERICAN BANKERS' ASSOCIATION: $1,000 for each robber.

This reward to be paid on proper identification of either PARKER or LONGBAUGH.

Persons furnishing information leading to the arrest of either or all of the robbers will be entitled to share in the reward.

The outlaws, whose photographs, descriptions, and histories appear on this circular MAY ATTEMPT TO CIRCULATE or be in possession of the following described NEW INCOMPLETE BANK NOTES of the NATIONAL BANK OF MONTANA and THE AMERICAN NATIONAL BANK, both of HELENA, MONT., which were stolen by members of the HARVEY LOGAN, alias "KID" CURRY BAND, from the GREAT NORTHERN (RAILWAY) EXPRESS No. 3, near Wagner, Mont., July 3rd, 1901, by "hold-up" methods.

$40,000. INCOMPLETE NEW BANK NOTES of the NATIONAL BANK OF MONTANA (Helena, Montana), $24,000 of which was in ten dollar bills and $16,000 of which was in twenty dollar bills.

Serial Number 1201 to 2000 inclusive;
Government Number—Y 934349 to 935148 inclusive;
Charter Number 5671.

$500. INCOMPLETE BANK NOTES of AMERICAN NATIONAL BANK (Helena, Montana), $300 of which was in ten dollar bills and $200 of which was in twenty dollar bills.

Serial Number 3423 to 3432 inclusive;
Government Number V-662761 to V-662770 inclusive;
Charter Number 4396.

THESE INCOMPLETE BANK NOTES LACKED THE SIGNATURES OF THE PRESIDENTS AND CASHIERS OF THE BANKS NAMED, AND MAY BE CIRCULATED WITHOUT SIGNATURES OR WITH FORGED SIGNATURES.

Chiefs of Police, Sheriffs, Marshals and Constables receiving copy of this circular should furnish a copy of the above described stolen currency to banks, bankers, money brokers, gambling houses, pool room keepers and keepers of disorderly houses, and request their co-operation in the arrest of any person or persons presenting any of these bills.

THE UNITED STATES TREASURY DEPARTMENT REFUSES TO REDEEM THESE STOLEN UNSIGNED OR IMPROPERLY SIGNED NOTES.

☞ Officers are warned to have sufficient assistance and be fully armed, when attempting to arrest either of these outlaws, as they are always heavily armed, and will make a determined resistance before submitting to arrest, not hesitating to kill, if necessary.

Foreign ministers and consuls receiving copy of this circular are respectfully
Postmasters receiving this circular are requested to place same in hands of reliable

Below appear the photographs, descriptions, and histories of GEORGE PARKER, alias "BUTCH" CASSIDY, alias GEORGE CASSIDY, alias INGERFIELD and HARRY LONGBAUGH alias HARRY ALONZO.

GEORGE PARKER.
First photograph taken July 15, 1894.

GEORGE PARKER.
Last photograph taken Nov. 21, 1900.

Name..George Parker, alias "Butch" Cassidy, alias George Cassidy, alias Ingerfield.
Nationality....................American
Occupation................Cowboy; rustler
Criminal Occupation......Bank robber and highwayman, cattle and horse thief
Age..36 yrs. (1901)..Height....5 feet 9 in
Weight..165 lbs.....Build....Medium
Complexion..Light..Color of Hair..Flaxen
Eyes....Blue......Mustache. Sandy, if any
Remarks:—Two cut scars back of head, small scar under left eye, small brown mole calf of leg. "Butch" Cassidy is known as a criminal principally in Wyoming, Utah, Idaho, Colorado and Nevada and has served time in Wyoming State penitentiary at Laramie for grand larceny, but was pardoned January 19th, 1896.

HARRY LONGBAUGH.
Photograph taken Nov. 21, 1900.

Name......Harry Longbaugh, alias "Kid" Longbaugh, alias Harry Alonzo alias Frank Jones, alias Frank Boyd, alias the "Sundance Kid"
Nationality........Swedish-American..Occupation............Cowboy; rustler
Criminal Occupation........Highwayman, bank burglar, cattle and horse thief
Age........35 years...........Height...........5 feet 10 in
Weight...165 to 175 lbs...........Build..............Good
Eyes......Blue or gray......Complexion..............Medium
Mustache or Beard................(if any), natural color brown, reddish tinge
Features......Grecian type..........Nose..........Rather long
Color of Hair.........Natural color brown, may be dyed ; combs it pompadour.
IS BOW-LEGGED AND HIS FEET FAR APART.
Remarks:—Harry Longbaugh served 18 months in jail at Sundance, Cook Co., Wyoming, when a boy, for horse stealing. In December, 1892, Harry Longbaugh, Bill Madden and Henry Bass "held up" a Great Northern train at Malta, Montana. Bass and Madden were tried for this crime, convicted and sentenced to 10 and 14 years respectively ; Longbaugh escaped and since has been a fugitive. June 28, 1897, under the name of Frank Jones, Longbaugh participated with Harvey Logan, alias Curry, Tom Day and Walter Putney, in the Belle Fourche, South Dakota, bank robbery. All were arrested, but Longbaugh and Harvey Logan escaped from jail at Deadwood, October 31, the same year. Longbaugh has not since been arrested.

We also publish below a photograph, history and description of CAMILLA HANKS, alias O. C. HANKS, alias CHARLEY JONES, alias "DEAF" CHARLEY, who may be found in the company of either PARKER, alias CASSIDY or LONGBAUGH, alias ALONZO, and for whom a proportionate amount of a $5,000.00 Reward is offered by the GREAT NORTHERN EXPRESS COMPANY upon arrest and conviction for participation in the Great Northern (Railway) Express robbery near Wagner, Mont., July 3rd, 1901.

CAMILLA HANKS.
Photograph taken 1892.

Name..O. C. Hanks, alias Camilla Hanks, alias Charley Jones, alias Deaf Charley
Nationality......American...........Occupation...................Cowboy
Criminal Occupation ....Train robber ; an ex-convict
Age..........38 years (1901)...........Height...............5 feet 10 in
Weight....156 lbs...........Build...............Good
Complexion....Sandy...............Color of Hair..................Auburn
Eyes........Blue...............Mustache or Beard......(if any), natural color sandy
Remarks:—Scar from burn, size 25c piece, on right forearm. Small scar right leg, above ankle. Mole near right nipple. Leans his head slightly to the left. Somewhat deaf. Raised at Yorktown, Texas, fugitive from there charged with rape ; also wanted in New Mexico on charge of murder. Arrested in Teton County, Montana, 1892, and sentenced to 10 years in the penitentiary at Deer Lodge, for holding up Northern Pacific train near Big Timber, Montana. Released April 30th, 1901.

HARVEY LOGAN, alias "KID" CURRY, referred to in our first circular issued from Denver on May 15, 1901, is now under arrest at Knoxville, Tenn., charged with shooting two police officers who were attempting his arrest.

BEN KILPATRICK, alias JOHN ARNOLD, alias "THE TALL TEXAN" of Concho County, Texas, another member of the Harvey Logan band of outlaws, was arrested at St. Louis, Mo., on November 5th, 1901, tried, convicted and sentenced to 15 years imprisonment for participation in the robbery of the GREAT NORTHERN EXPRESS COMPANY, near Wagner, Mont.

WILLIAM CARVER, alias "BILL" CARVER, of Sonora, Sutton County, Texas, another member of this band, was killed at Sonora, Texas, April 2nd, 1901, by Sheriff E. S. Brant, while resisting arrest on charge of murder.

IN CASE OF AN ARREST immediately notify PINKERTON'S NATIONAL DETECTIVE AGENCY at the nearest of the above listed offices.

Or

JOHN C. FRASER, Resident Sup't., DENVER, COLO.

Pinkerton's National Detective Agency,
Opera House Block, Denver, Colo.

requested to give this circular to the police of their city or district.
Police official, Marshal, Constable, Sheriff or Deputy, or a Peace officer.

---

writer's desk on a New York newspaper, of too many nights on the town), the Western gunslingers became folk legends, many of them – like Hickok – appearing as the upright-and-true protagonists of a dozen dime novels.

More was going on here than Ned Buntline's genius as a publicist and writer. The popularity of the West's violent individuals had to do with the audience's identification with them. If a cold-blooded murderer like Jesse James was mourned, and no jury of peers could be found to convict his brother, it had

less to do with who they were than what they represented. Perhaps in general the people of the West felt themselves less victimized by a small gang of thieves than by the powerful men in the West who owned the banks, the big businesses, and, especially, the railroads. These men would come to be known as robbers barons, and in stealing from them, men like Frank and Jesse James were – albeit symbolically – only recovering what was rightfully their – and the public's – own.

Since at least 1853, when Congress – on the heels

Pinkerton's National Detective Agency offered a $4,000 reward for the capture of the Wild Bunch. This circular printed the serial numbers of bank notes stolen by the gang during the Great Northern Railway Express robbery in July 1901.

The posse that tracked the Wild Bunch: George Hiatt, T.T. Kelliher, Joe Lefores, H. Davis, Si Funk, and Jeff Carr.

of the California Gold Rush – authorized detailed surveys of prospective rail routes to the Pacific, the nation was fitfully astir with schemes for a transcontinental railroad. Yet little actually happened, beyond the completion of the surveys, until Theodore Dehone Judah, a civil engineer, built a short line for the Sacramento Valley Railroad in 1854. He told the company's president, Colonel Charles Wilson, that this could well be the Pacific terminus of a transcontinental line.

But then the gold ran out, and the rail line went

no farther than twenty-two miles. Nevertheless, Judah was intoxicated by his own idea. He published pamphlets on the feasibility of a transcontinental railroad, he lobbied Congress, and he even conducted his own surveys. In 1860, after traipsing through the region north of Lake Tahoe in search of a pass across the mountains, he received a letter from a pharmacist and amateur surveyor named Daniel "Doc" Strong, who had read Judah's literature, and who had already charted an abandoned wagon route through a viable pass. In a back room of Strong's drug store, the two men drew up a survey of a transcontinental rail line and, then and there, incorporated a Pacific railroad association. That's when Judah hunted up his backers, chief among whom were Collis P. Huntington, Mark Hopkins, Leland Stanford, and Charles Crocker – all men who had made a living, one way and another, servicing the gold trade.

The story of building what came to be called the Union Pacific is, of course, an epic in itself, filled with heroism and ingenuity, as well as greed, error, and delay. But, whatever the problems, there was always a fortune in it. The financiers secured federal legislation granting liberal loans for every mile of track built. Moreover, huge tracts of public land were allotted to the railroad in alternating sections on either side of the right-of-way. Still, Judah's Big Four – Huntington, Hopkins, Stanford, and Crocker – wanted to halt west-to-east construction at the Nevada line until settlement of the area caught up with the tracks and insured maximum profitability. Disgusted with this timidity, Judah started off for Washington, D.C., to obtain new backers. He took the sea route, via the Isthmus of Panama, where he contracted yellow fever and died, aged thirty-seven.

But President Abraham Lincoln, in the midst of civil war, realized just how crucial it was to link the Northeast with the West. He authorized new loan money and bigger land grants. He also enlisted the aid of a man known as the King of Spades, Oakes Ames, who had built his family's shovel works into one of the largest and most successful industrial concerns in the United States. Ames and his brother, Oliver, invested in the railroad and thereby attracted others to do that same. They contributed not directly to the Union Pacific, but to a corporation the railroad's vice president, Thomas Durant, had created. Named after the company that had successfully financed the French railway system, Credit Mobilier worked like this: Credit Mobilier, run by the directors of the Union Pacific, was paid by the Union Pacific to build the Union Pacific; the directors (who were also the major investors) making a profit on the cost of construction as well as on the eventual benefits of construction.

It sounds crooked enough, but was, in fact, legal. However, it inevitably led to gross abuses and tremendously padded construction bills, with some sections of track being charged many times over.

While Credit Mobilier and other scandals threatened to derail the Union Pacific, the needs of the nation kept it on track. The Big Four – along with many other investors – made the West's greatest fortunes. Collis P. Huntington, who had started as an itinerant peddlar of watches and watch parts in the South, became the most important of the major investors. Legendary for his stinginess, he managed

the Central Pacific with such parsimonious skill that the line was quickly free of debts incurred during construction. Like Huntington, Mark Hopkins also carefully conserved the fortune the railroad earned him – his one extravagance being a magnificent Nob Hill mansion built to please his wife. Leland Stanford, in many ways the least talented of the Big Four, nevertheless exploited his fortune the most fully, investing in farming, horse breeding, art collecting, and European travel. He also became a mediocre U.S. senator and, after his son died of typhoid during

The posse that tracked the Wild Bunch boarding a Union Pacific train. They had been hired and were paid by the Railroad and were closing in on Cassidy when he and the Kid moved to Buenos Aires in 1901. Reports of the outlaws' deaths at the hands of the Bolivian Army were never substantiated.

a European trip, he founded Stanford University in the boy's memory. When construction efforts faltered in the Sierra Nevada Mountains, Charles Crocker saved the Central Pacific by promoting the use of Chinese laborers, who were numerous, hard working, and, in the racist view of Crocker and most everyone else at the time, expendable. Crocker also invested heavily in another successful railway venture, the Southern Pacific, bought up huge tracts of California real estate, ran ranches, and founded banks.

The works and lives of men such as these are the fruit of the freedom and challenge of the West, even as the tremendous power they achieved – dictating legislation, acting as landlord and creditor to thousands – did not sit well with those who most cherished the dream of western freedom. Ordinary folk were, indeed, more comfortable with a romanticized image of out-and-out lawbreakers, who shared the rapacity and daring of the millionaires, but who only wanted to rob you, after all, not own you lock, stock, and barrel.

9
WATER

Since the late 18th century, Westerners had relied heavily on the federal government to provide them with inexpensive land, transportation, and protection. In fact, federal largess had long been one of the West's major resources. And the tendency to look to Washington for help – directly in the form of cash, when necessary; indirectly in federally-mandated access to land, water, grass, and timber as a matter of course – in underwriting the region's economy was one Western habit that would live on long into the new century, despite all the *fin de siècle* talk among historians and American ideologues about the "closing" of the Frontier.

Not that any self-respecting Westerner would ever admit the central role the federal government played in his precarious existence. What had been a fortune-hunter's code for the pioneers became an entrepreneurial injunction for their robber baron descendants. Even as the giant freeway projects, the huge defense installations and the massive land reclamation programs of the 20th century replaced the railroad, mining, and lumber industries of the last half of the 19th century, Western businessmen still expected the government to help them build their fortunes while keeping its hands out of their private affairs.

The mining industry set the mood. Modern mining had been born in the played-out placer fields of the California Gold Rush, and was fed by fresh new finds along Cripple Creek in Colorado and near the junction of the Klondike and the Yukon in Alaska.

With the coming of electricity and its copper wiring, the profits from gold mining found a fresh new field for investment.

Armed now with new equipment, the steam shovel especially, a group of Cripple Creek entrepreneurs began to exploit vast, low-grade copper deposits in Bingham Canyon, south of the Great Salt Lake, and within thirty years had extracted some six billion pounds of the stuff. The techniques developed in Utah spread to Arizona and Montana. By 1903, mining interests were so powerful in the latter state that they could blackmail the Montana legislature into passing any law they wanted simply by closing mines, smelters, lumber camps and mills, and threatening to leave twenty thousand men out of work in the dead of winter.

Big Lumber, too, had a venerable pedigree in the Gold Rush. In the early 1840s, the huge forests of the Pacific Coast had hardly been touched. A few sawmills scattered along the sea from California to Washington produced enough lumber for local settlement, with a little left over for export. But with the coming of the '49ers, San Francisco and the mining boomtowns needed much more lumber than these two-man teams, working with an eight-foot whipsaw off a pit

An abandoned farmhouse in Texas. As many as half a million people left their farms in the Dust Bowl and headed for California and the Pacific Northwest. There was little to keep them on their land; what few crops they could raise brought low prices on the depressed market.

Above: the Dust Bowl, Guyman, Oklahoma. Dust storms brought all manner of respiratory illnesses to drought-stricken farm families. During the worst of the storms, people caught outside sometimes suffocated struggling to find their way back through the dust.

Imperial, California, in 1904. Water played an essential part in the growth of the West. Towns formed where no water existed only grew once aqueducts and dams brought water to parched areas.

and a platform, could produce. At first, the lumber was imported by ship from Maine, but before long entrepreneurs were staking out vast tracks along the coast and on up to Puget Sound, bringing in well-organized teams with steam-powered circular saws and the beasts they needed for transport.

In the 1880s, the circular saw had been replaced by the donkey engine, also steam powered, which ran a steel cable through a pulley near the top of the towering western trees and yanked mighty logs out of the woods in minutes. A high-yield operation with a sharp crew could produce 5,000 tons of logs in eight hours. Lumber ships the world over crowded into harbors such as Port Blakely and Port Gamble to pick up the sea of timber floating in Puget Sound.

By the turn of the century, railroads began replacing the ships as the transport of choice, and with their arrival came the timber barons of the Great Lakes, eager to exploit the seemingly endless

An Oklahoma dust storm in the 1930s, during which temperatures exceeded 100°
and clouds of dust swept the region. Farmers watched their soil simply blow away.

stretch of Douglas fir. Highly industrialized, these companies used the railroads to bring western timber to eastern markets, markets that had already consumed the great American forests written about with such awe by the original pioneers.

In fact, the peculiar nature of extractive industries had become part of the very essence of the American West, as the Southwest's oil boom amply illustrated. By 1900 inventors had discovered that oil, once used mostly for producing kerosene and for lubricating machines, could, in one of its distillations called gasoline, be used to propel the motors of the new, strange-looking horseless carriages. Some 8,000 of the vehicles pinged and banged their way along America's still dusty highways in the year a bull-

headed Texan named Pattillo Higgens finally proved that he was right, and conjured a tower of thick, dark liquid to spew heavenward through hundreds of feet of loose sand on a rise of land just outside a hick town in South Texas.

The great 1901 Spindletop gusher, just outside Beaumont, made oil the "black gold" not only of Texas, but of Oklahoma, southern California, and even Wyoming. The 20th-century prospectors who arrived in the western oil fields came not with picks and shovels on a covered wagon, but by railroad, armed with drills and pipe. To towns like Batson, Texas, and Cushing Field, Oklahoma, and even Los Angeles, California, they would come – a horde of would-be millionaires, confidence men, thugs, whores and gamblers enough to warm a '49ers heart. Within a few months of the first discovery at Spindletop, some 40,000 people descended on little Beaumont, Texas.

The stakes were more astronomical than any of the gold rushes. Within 40 miles of Ranger, Texas, wildcat mines pumped, in 1919, oil worth nine times all the gold mined in California in 1849. The boomtowns were as raucous and dangerous as any in the Old West, with saloons, dance halls and whorehouses sweeping into every oil town on the torrent of money that followed a strike, while the amenities of normal life – beds and food and water and laundries – seemed to vanish under the flood.

There was so much money that even the Indians benefited. The Osage had been forced out of Kansas in the 1870s onto barren land in Oklahoma, where they lived lives of grinding poverty till someone found oil there. As whites suddenly began competitive bidding for Indian oil leases, the once-proud Osage became – courtesy of Messieurs Frank Phillips and Harry Sinclair – the richest ethnic group per capita in the world. With an average annual family income of $65,000, a fortune for the time, the Osage went on a spending binge, buying among other goods Cadillacs and Pierce Arrows, which they drove till the cars gave out, then abandoned for new ones.

Schemes to separate the Osage from their money abounded, and though swindle and murder occurred with frightening frequency, the regular checks – fed by the new American cult of the automobile that was transforming the way westerners lived even as it reinforced the way they thought – kept coming, and the Osage at last were able to enjoy the good life, American style.

A reckless rush in East Texas in the 1930s finally led to overproduction, the price plummeted in a single year from $1.30 to five cents a barrel, and for every barrel shipped ten more oozed back into the Texas dirt. Geologists began to warn of depletion of

Above: a family of migrant agricultural workers. Once in the "promised land" of California, migrant workers often found conditions no better than those they had left.

Left: in the 1860s John Wesley Powell, as director of the U.S. Geological Survey, explored the West, later founding the Bureau of Ethnology at the Smithsonian Institution.

Below: Los Angeles in 1857. From the start, this city was plagued by water shortages. Until a solution was found, its growth was slow.

Above: California-bound cotton pickers in the 1930s. Known as "Okies" and "Dokies," these economic migrants become a symbol of the Depression to John Steinbeck in his novel The Grapes of Wrath.

Hollywoodland. The motion picture industry trickled out to California in the early 1900s. By 1912, more motion-picture companies were located in Los Angeles than anywhere else.

oil reserves, Texas imposed limits on production, and the other states followed suit. It took the Texas National Guard to enforce compliance with the new rules, but soon wildcatters grew choosier about picking sights, and roustabouts drifted to steadier jobs, while oil wells were tapped for a few barrels a day, a few days a month.

If extractive industries were the bedrock of the West's early 20th-century economy, its ideology was the overnight fortune – the by now centuries-old dream that the individual, if he was rugged enough and lucky, could indeed transform himself from beggar to baron. That ideology required a special sense of financing, one diametrically opposed to House-of-Morgan, merchant-banking, Eastern conservatism. One Amadeo Peter Giannini, raised on a fruit orchard outside San Jose, California, understood just how important money was to the

small investor, and he decided to make it available on terms peculiar to the West.

A towering and tyrannical man, Giannini founded the Bank of Italy in San Francisco in 1904. Unlike most of the other savings and loans in the capital of western finance, which provided loans at high interest rates to the wealthier ranchers, miners, and lumbermen, Giannini's bank encouraged small depositors and offered modest loans to individuals at reasonable rates. In the 'teens, Giannini initiated branch banks, which he called "money stores," and in which local managers and personnel provided easy access to money for local farmers and businessmen. By the late 1920s he had a hundred branches, and in 1930 he changed the operation's name to the Bank of America, destined to become the world's largest just after World War II.

Though Giannini avoided speculative land deals

*t: Sixth Street and
adway in Los Angeles,
a 1890. The city bounced
k to life towards the end of
nineteenth century after a
I and a drought in the
s nearly ruined its
my. The 1880s brought
n to the real estate
t. Consequently the
outlying towns of Pasadena,
Long Beach, and Glendale
grew rapidly, linked to Los
Angeles by streetcars.*

*Left: Los Angeles Civic
Center and City Hall, circa
1950. By 1940, Los Angeles
had become one of the nation's
largest cities. Today, in the
consolidated metropolitan
area, its population numbers
more than twelve and a half
million people.*

and oil booms, he did try to nurture new industries, among them motion pictures. At the turn of the century a few street-wise New Yorkers, most of them Jews – attracted to the little backwater suburb of Hollywood by its cheap real estate and its cloud-free sky – opened up their shops, selling dreams to the poor and lonely. Giannini lent money to the first nickelodeon in San Francisco in 1909, and would wind up sinking some $50 million into the films of Douglas Fairbanks, Charlie Chaplin, Harold Lloyd, and Walt Disney – all in a time, of course, before a moderately produced feature film alone cost $50 million.

It was fitting not only that the West should become the home of the greatest dream factory in the world, but also that Giannini should help finance it – because that was what he had been doing all along: financing the quotidian dreams of the West. For, make no mistake about it, though the western immigrants' dream of overnight success were for the vast majority only dreams, such dreams were essential to the region's existence.

They explain the continual pull of the West throughout the 20th century. In the 1920s, hundreds of thousands of young women between the ages of 19 and 25, responding to motion picture industry-sponsored, rags-to-riches Hollywood stories like Gloria Swanson's and Mary Pickford's, left the farms and small towns of the South and Midwest and headed West to become stars. The influx in no small measure explains the luscious scandals that titillated the nation, and led the Hollywood Chamber of Commerce to post signs in railway stations as far away as New Delhi, India, warning that there was

*Above: Los Angeles in 1925.
On November 5, 1913, water
spilled into the city through
an aqueduct built by the
Owens Valley Project. On its
completion Los Angeles was
ready to boom. Her water-
supply problems were history.*

*Left: Hollywood freeway
traffic. In 1923 there were
430,000 passenger cars in the
city; one to every three people.
By 1952 that ratio had risen
to one car for every two people.*

no work for females in the movies. Similarly, when the disastrous farming practices of the plains led to the collapse of hope in the 1930s Midwestern dust-bowl, Okies almost by instinct picked up and once again headed West. Even in the late 20th century millions of illegal aliens from Central and South America continued to chase the same dreams straight into the barrio and the irrigated field.

Hopes so high, dreams so strongly embraced, do not gently vanish in the face of harsh reality. They result instead in the search for racial scapegoats. From the officially sanctioned violence of the Texas Rangers toward Mexican-Americans to the anti-"foreign" Gold Rush laws, from legislation against the immigration of Chinese women to the Zoot Suit riots in Los Angeles and from the Japanese-American concentration camps of World War II to the illegal alien act of the Reagan administration, scapegoating was a hallmark of the West.

Closely allied to that tradition is the West's famed propensity toward vigilantism. One historian has estimated that, excluding lynch mobs, there were some 210 vigilante movements – organized, extra-legal groups meting out a violent "justice" – in the far West between 1849 and 1902. California – with San Francisco's Committee of One Hundred – provided the model. Montana, with its Johnson County War, offered the deadliest single episode. And Texas, being Texas, created the largest number of vigilante activities.

Occasionally, however, the targets of Western disillusionment were more plausible, and consequently the West also had a long tradition of political radicalism – stretching back to Andrew Jackson's time – that blamed big capital for its problems. Since the farmers were the first group of Westerners for whom the dream failed, they were the first to act.

The truth of the matter was that with the improved equipment of the late 19th century, the rapid development of rail transportation, and the revolution in communications, the farmer had become increasingly tied to and dependant upon a market economy and its swings of fortune. But the market was an abstraction, something Western farmers could not see.

What they could see was that, as their productivity increased, the prices for their commodities fell: the more they grew, the less they earned. As they became poorer, their expenses mounted, and as the gap between income and expenses increased, they found themselves forced to mortgage their land or borrow money to cover debts. For almost a century now they had been told that "rain followed the plow," that all they had to do was cultivate the land, no matter how barren, and God would see to it that the climate

Above: the Hoover Dam power plant on the Colorado River. The dam was originally called Hoover, then Boulder, and then in the late 1940s it reverted to Hoover again.

Left: the Grand Coulee Dam under construction on the Columbia River, the fourth largest river in North America.

Right: Shasta Dam on the Sacramento River, a 1945 Bureau of Reclamation project. In 1936, this dam, and three others under construction – Hoover, Bonneville, and Grand Coulee – were the largest concrete dams ever to be built. Shasta Dam stores river floodwaters that used to flow away into San Francisco Bay.

Left: Roosevelt Dam on Salt River, Arizona, was opened in 1911. By 1936, nineteen new dam projects were underway in the West. Today the only major river yet undammed is the Yellowstone River.

Above: Hopi Tribal Chairman Ivan Sidney (right) helps Robbie Honani (left) to place rocks staking his claim to land partitioned on the reservation at Seba Dalkai, Arizona, in July 1986.

cooperated. The goal in coming West, ever since Jefferson dared dream of a nation of yeoman farmers, had been self-sufficiency. Instead, they were going bankrupt, or – worse – becoming tenants.

They all agreed with the Iowa farmer who said, "We worked like fools all our lives, and we wound up with nothing," and they felt, as Populist Party leader Thomas Watson described it, "like victims of some horrid nightmare." Throughout the 1880s and the early 1890s, halls of government everywhere rang with the voice of the farmers' complaints. They proposed some of the most radical political and economic changes of the late 19th century: government ownership of the railroads and utilities, a graduated income tax, the secret ballot, women's suffrage, prohibition, and most of all the creation of inflation through manipulation of the money system, or as they called it "the free coinage of silver."

The unions and alliances of the farmers went by a number of different names, from the Grange in 1874 to the Farmers' and Laborers' Union in 1890, but it was in 1892 that they formed the most radical third party yet to appear on the American scene: the People's Party, which became better known as the Populist Party. Farmers had reached the lowest point in their history. Their national alliance dominated the huge Confederation of Industrial Organizations meeting that year in St. Louis, which was attended by delegates from a dozen assorted reform groups. The new party called for a national convention to nominate a candidate for president, which it did in

Above: in 1989 Leonard Haskie became iterim tribal chairman of the Navajo Indians when Peter MacDonald was charged with bribery and corruption.

Right: Peter MacDonald, leader of the Navajo, speaks at his inauguration at Window Rock, Arizona, after being elected to a fourth term as tribal chairman in 1987.

Above: Richard Milhous Nixon, a former Congressman and Senator from California, and Vice President in the Eisenhower Administration, won his bid for the presidency in 1968, and again in 1972.

kept reformers apart in the past, reviving the old agrarian alliance between the South and the West and creating a new one between farmers and labor. They were the first to insist that *laissez-faire* economics was not the final solution to all industrial problems, and that government had some responsibility for social well-being. And they scared the hell out of people, especially Eastern capitalists.

But not as much as the organizations of industrial workers. As the big ranches and the huge corporate mining concerns had taken control of the market, squeezing out ever greater profits for the rugged individuals running those concerns, working men struck the corrals and smelters of the American West. In the early '90s the Knights of Labor unionized cowboys. Later in the decade miners, led by a one-eyed giant named "Big" Bill Haywood, took on management at Coeur d'Alene Lake, Idaho, in a strike that resulted in violence, leaving five men dead, sixteen wounded, and which lead to the creation of the Western Federation of Miners.

Omaha, Nebraska, on the Fourth of July, 1892.

The Populists lost that election, and most of the elections in which they participated, but their main service was to usher in a long-delayed period of reform; reform that would be taken up in less radical fashion by the Progressives. They bridged the gap between parties, sections, races and classes that had

In 1905, Haywood took his miners into the Industrial Workers of the World, the powerful and determined "Wobblies." Seeking to establish "one big union" of industrial workers and appealing to laborers, such as lumberjacks and migrant workers,

Left: Ronald Reagan walking along the White House colonnade. Governor of California from 1967 to 1975, Reagan was previously a sportscaster and movie actor. In 1975 he announced his candidacy for the Republican presidential nomination, but lost to Gerald R. Ford. In 1979 he won his party's nomination and was elected President by a huge majority over Jimmy Carter.

Right: Earl Warren, a native of Los Angeles, served as Attorney General (1939-43) and Governor of California (1943-53) before President Dwight D. Eisenhower appointed him to the United States Supreme Court in 1953. He was Chief Justice until 1969, when he retired.

who were ignored by the major trade unions, the IWW preached the violent overthrow of the government and the destruction of the managerial élite. By the time *it* was destroyed in the first American "Red Scare" of the 1920s, the union numbered more than 100,000 among its ranks, including some 20,000 farm workers stretching from the wheat fields of the Midwest to the fruit orchards of California. The Wobblies engaged in battles of historic proportions at mines in Colorado, during which the state imposed marshal law, and in Montana, in an incident which became the basis for Dashiell Hammett's landmark tough-guy novel *Red Harvest*.

The fierce confrontation between entrenched capital and organized labor that raged from the late decades of the 19th century through the first two of the 20th was a national, even an international phenomenon. But just as the West's strong extractive industries had a lasting effect on the Western temperament, fostering a "get in, get rich, get out" mentality among its entrepreneurs, so too did the West's strong radical movement, manifesting itself in everything from the tenacity of California's Communist Party (which remained strong and active right up to the HUAC and McCarthy purges of the 1950s) to the Berkeley Free Speech Movement and to Ceser Chavez's migrant farm workers union. And not surprisingly, as Progressive politics took the air out of more robust reform movements, Westerners were disproportionately represented in the ranks of Progressive leaders, from Wisconsin's Robert La Follette to Idaho's William E. Borah to California's Hiram Johnson.

Focusing attention on issues such as federal assistance to the economy and the conservation of natural resources, the West became in the 20th century a leader of national politics. It was one of the West's great ideologues, Theodore Roosevelt – never tiring of recounting the importance his two youthful years on a Dakota ranch played in his life – who led the country into the Progressive Era at the turn of the century. A national political movement that transcended party but not class, born of the decay of Populism, the sensational writings of muckraking journalists, and the involvement of America's churches in social issues, Progressivism reacted to the growing power of organized labor, the revolutionary demands of America's intellectual radicals, and the changing racial and ethnic composition of America's cities with a moral "uplift" program of reform intended to check the excesses of capitalism while preserving it.

The so-called "Oregon System," which came to stand for Progressive experiments everywhere, was the brainchild of Portland's William S. U'Ren, a Republican. Like all Progressives, he spoke largely

Above: John Connally, Democratic Governor of Texas from 1963 to 1969.

Right: President Lyndon B. Johnson encourages his beagle to yelp for visitors.

Below: Barry Goldwater of Arizona was pitted against the incumbent, Lyndon B. Johnson, in the 1964 presidential election.

Left: Democratic Senator Gary Hart, native of Ottawa, Kansas, was elected Senator from Colorado in 1976. He entered the race for the presidency in 1984 and 1988, but a scandal over his alleged extramarital activity ended his chances of success.

Below: John Muir, the noted writer and naturalist from Scotland, attempted to influence Government policy on the West, believing that the land should be kept pristine and inviolate.

for upper- and middle-class reformers and developers, business and religious leaders, and the more successful newspapers, was interested in economic growth and clean government, and talked in lofty terms of "progress," "civic reform," and "modernization." Attacking politicians as such, especially those elected officials more interested in patronage than patriotism, in political power than honest government, in vote-getting than moral decay, the Progressives crusaded for "good government," called for the initiative and referendum, public control of the railroads and utilities, a certain amount of trust-busting, primary elections, the popular election of senators, female suffrage, and prohibition.

Long before the rest of the country, the West had given women the right to vote. And the initiative and referendum became a mainstay of Western government that to this day distinguishes the region, with its tax revolts, its extremely powerful environmental movement, and its recall of elected officials, such as Arizona Governor So-and-So.

The Progressives, however, did not speak for the urban poor, or racial and ethnic minorities or labor radicals, all of whom they tended to view as morally decadent at best, viciously criminal at worst. It was the Progressive who created the first great "Red Scare" to purge those intellectuals who took up the cause of the oppressed, and who used World War I as an excuse to attack ethnic cultures and homogenize America's white population. Hence the spectacle of William Borah achieving his national reputation as the state's prosecutor in the trial of Big Bill Haywood, the personification of radical western labor.

In fact, Borah represents the ambiguity at the heart of the Western personality: a virulent opponent of monopoly who consistently attempted to curb the excesses of big business, but who was also an adamant enemy of organized labor. As with Borah, so with the West. A coherent region of the United States, its ideology managed at the same time to encompass rugged individualism and centralized government, a free market economy and huge public works projects, giant extractive industries and a strong conservation movement, a Howard Hughes and a Henry Wallace.

Only the American West could produce a Lyndon Johnson, a senator from perhaps the most conservative state in the Union who, as president, launched the Great Society, one of the most liberal federal programs in American History. And only the American West could spawn a Ronald Reagan,

Right: Chinese workers on the Union Pacific Railroad. In the early twentieth century, the Chinese were the largest Oriental group in the West. In the 1860s and 1870s, thousands of Chinese came West to work on the railroads.

who in one lifetime managed to be a Hollywood movie star, the head of a major labor union, and a popular *laissez-fair* American president. And only a Westerner like Reagan could model his term in office on the presidency of the progressive Franklin Delano Roosevelt while trying to return the country to the heyday of Adam Smith.

What makes the American West a coherent region, however, is not its politics, its industries, or its populations, but its aridity. For it is around the question of water that all the strands of Western history come together in an intricate but understandable economic and social pattern. The men and women who trekked along the overland trail to California learned how precious a resource water could be, as they carefully portioned it out in order to make it through the Great American Desert. For them, the 850 million acres of arid public lands were something to escape, not conquer and farm. But, beginning in the 1870s, the desert took on a different hue for a few men of vision.

After all, a thousand years ago the Indians of the Southwest had brought water to the desert through long canals. In the 19th century, the Mormons, too, had reclaimed wasteland not only with irrigation ditches, but also with reservoirs for storing the run-off from melting spring snows. Now, the dream took shape. In 1873, Colorado Governor S.H. Elbert invited delegates from Kansas, Nebraska, Wyoming, Utah and New Mexico to an irrigation conference in Denver, which produced the nation's first reclamation proposal.

Others got the fever. In the 1890s, a New England journalist named William Ellsworth Smythe converted to reclamation and began to wax poetical about the power of dams, canals, ditches and sprinklers. He saw the arid West as a challenge that God had put before Americans, to urge them out of their isolated, individual enterprises into the community-wide cooperation needed to build and maintain the dams and ditches necessary to transform the desert into a garden.

Certainly, the Desert Land Act of 1877 seemed to support Smythe's emphasis on cooperation. Passed in order to encourage the private development of irrigation, it was based on Western water law spawned by the Gold Rush miners for operating placer claims – priority of appropriation. The result was that early filers claimed more than they could use, hoping to sell the surplus, and late filers claimed more than was left in order just to get some water when prior rights were satisfied. If every claimant asserted his rights, the West's few rivers would have been sucked dry, and at least one – the Umatilla in Oregon – suffered such a fate at three different spots during a drought year. Western farmers sat up nights

Above: Japanese-Americans in 1942 on a train bound for a relocation center. At the time of Japan's attack on Pearl Harbor, nearly 118,000

Japanese-Americans lived in the West. Panic-sticken politicians called for their internment in the interests of national security.

Below: Japanese-American girls from Los Angeles at Owens Valley Alien Reception Center, Manzanar, California, in March 1942.

with shotguns, watching their headgates, and Colorado sugar-beet growers made plans to drain the Arkansas River, despite the fact that it fed Kansas wheat crops.

When demands for federal intervention led Congress to authorize the United States Geological Survey to conduct an irrigation study of the West, John Wesley Powell's powerful voice was added to that of Smythe in urging growth managed by the government's manipulation of water, always ostensibly in favor of the small homesteader. Since efficient water management required healthy watersheds, reclamation fit right into Teddy Roosevelt and Gifford Pinchot's conservation plans. Hence the Newland Reclamation Act of 1902, which established that the federal government would build dams to irrigate arid land for small family farms whose settlers would repay Uncle Sam.

The modern West was born. Henry Kaiser dammed the Colorado and Columbia rivers. The Imperial Valley sprang into existence, producing fruit and vegetables year round. The Federal Reclamation Bureau grew into perhaps the most powerful agency in the West. Of course, the small farmers never repaid their debts, and most of the water eventually fed huge agribusinesses and sprawling suburbs. The early diversion of the Truckee River to Nevada farms and ranches caused the Pyramid Lake to wither away, and destroyed the

economy and spirit of the Paiute Indians. Men like Fred Eaton, J.B. Lippincott, and William Mulholland conspired to steal all the water from the Owens Valley to wet their interests in Los Angeles, and did so despite the best efforts of valley residents to hang on to their precious commodity. By the Great Depression, the federal pork barrel was rolling, and great dams went up everywhere as Reclamation Bureau commissioners like Michael Straus and Floyd Dominy played God to their constituents and

Above: Japanese-Americans line up in the mess hall at the Manzanar Reception Center – a wire-enclosed compound.

Below: a Chinese butcher and grocery shop in San Francisco's Chinatown, around 1900.

feathered their bureaucratic nests, competing with the Army Corps of Engineers for ever more grandiose projects. Even when the Teton Dam burst and it became clear that many of the others were eroding, the building went on.

For the dream – Eden from a desert – was intact. From 1900 to 1910, the West's population jumped by 66 percent, while the nation continued to grow by only 21 percent a year. A half-century later, from 1950 to 1960, the states west of the Rockies were still growing by the equivalent of the population of all of New York's five boroughs combined. The new Westerners, like the old Westerners, were a restless and mobile bunch, only now they worked on federal highway projects, or in federally-related industries like aerospace, instead of in the mines or as lumberjacks. For eight decades they swelled the suburbs around Los Angeles, Phoenix, and Dallas.

The truth was that for some time the West's population had been running ahead of Western resources. Take Spokane, Washington. In the 1960s, the farmland southwest of the city enjoyed a surplus

San Francisco's Chinatown became the cultural center for Chinese-Americans, housing the headquarters of such institutions as secret societies, family associations, and guilds, also known as tongs.

saline deposits in the Mexican desert. The huge Central Arizona Project, when finished, will divert 1.2 million acre-feet from the Colorado River down 400 miles of aqueducts and dams into Phoenix and Tucson.

At the same time, Western cities are tapping into table water at an alarming rate, and the great Ogallala aquifer that lies underneath virtually all of the Great Plains – the subject of many competing claims among the various states – will be depleted sometime within the next couple of decades. Its exhaustion will at least mean that the West won't have water to fight over any longer.

In 1957, Texas historian Walter Prescott Webb wrote an article in *Harpers* entitled "The American West, a Perpetual Mirage," in which he argued that the greatest folly the U.S. as a nation could engage in would be to break the Treasury trying to make the West look like Illinois. The magazine's editors were inundated by a flood of western hate mail attacking Webb as a colossal crepe hanger. But if anyone doubted that by then Webb's "folly" had become American policy, a simple drive from, say, downtown San Diego out into the desert in any year before 1990 would have sufficed to disabuse them.

Heading out, you would have passed pleasant suburbs with manicured lawns, a few trees, and affordable homes. Soon these would have turned abruptly into a dusty construction site surrounding the wooden skeletons of the latest development. No grass would be growing on the site, no trees would be in evidence, and just beyond the construction would lie the desert. If you drove far enough into the desert, you would find on the trip back a new construction site. The one you passed before would now be a pleasant suburb with manicured lawns, a few trees, and affordable homes ....

As Marc Reisner makes clear in his groundbreaking book, *Cadillac Desert*, the West's dream of reclaiming America's wastelands is not so much folly as a kind of hubris, the stuff of tragedy. The dream seems doomed to glorious failure. As the water runs out, more grandiose schemes are hatched to keep the play running. Southern California movers and shakers talk about raiding the Pacific Northwest for water. Certain Reclamation Bureau contingency plans investigate the feasibility of gargantuan projects to pipe water from the Canadian Rockies into the American Southwest. Rich Texans seriously consider building a canal to divert the Mississippi from its Louisiana delta to the caprock around Lubbock.

No matter, as Reisner points out, that all the West has managed to do is turn a Missouri-size section of the Great American desert green at tremendous cost, and to potentially-disastrous environmental effect.

What matters is the dream.

George Bush of Texas was elected President in 1988. As Vice President in the Reagan Administration, he was one of several Westerners selected for key positions. Others included Attorney General William French Smith, and Defense Secretary Caspar Weinburger of California.

of cheap hydroelectric power. The power companies struck a deal with area farmers to install deep-well, electric-powered irrigation systems and to sell the farmers all the power needed at a discount. Immediately aluminum refineries and other industries flocked to the region to take advantage of the cheap power, the water surplus disappeared, and the power companies turned to expensive, coal-fired plants and nuclear reactors.

As early as 1927, the subsiding water table in Arizona had caused 400-foot-deep fissures in the earth. With the coming of air-conditioning, the population boomed, and by 1983, there were more than 100 such cracks. To support the boom, the Colorado River has been dammed from tip to toe, and now ended in an unusable trickle amidst massive

10

MYTH

The myth of the American West was the outgrowth of a massive migration to, and colonization of, the lands west of the original, revolution-born United States. East of the Appalachian Mountains, America's "foundation" myth concerned the love of freedom and the fight against tyranny; its heroes were the Patriots and the Founding Fathers. Beyond those mountains, it centered on the pursuit of happiness and the civilizing of a savage land; its heroes were rugged individuals and the common man. And, like all foundation myths, the latter was an attempt to resolve the contradictions of the society it served, to obscure and justify as well as explain and celebrate the reality it attempted to portray.

The legendary part of the myth was the product of romantic dreamers, monumental liars, self-promoting showmen, and dime-novel hacks, all of whom "packaged" a West for middle-class, mostly Eastern consumption. This was the "Wild West," a fantastical place filled with brave and independent pioneers, carefree and fun-loving cowboys, strong and silent lawmen, hard-bitten and talented gunslingers, brave and pure horse-soldiers, treacherous and bloodthirsty Indians, demure and faithful wives, dedicated and beautiful school ma'ams, visionary and community-conscious businessmen, danger-loving scouts and dashing gamblers, and it continues to account for the widespread popular interest in the region.

But there was also another part of the myth, interwoven with the legendary accounts, now and then contradicting them, now and then supporting them or calling on them for support. This was the West of the "Frontier," of the ever advancing line of civilization into untamed, "virgin" territory, the

"Great Green Breast" of the New World, that suckled and transformed its new European children. This historical West was a product of greedy real-estate promoters, circulation-hungry newspapermen, ambitious politicians, and American ideologues, who needed it to populate a harsh land, flatter and distract the disgruntled public, justify racist and imperialist policies, and protect and promote the political and economic establishment.

Hence the West of the Frontier that had started out as the land of opportunity and freedom, turned into a violent and troubled region in need of taming, and finally developed into a progressive and broad-minded polity that supported traditional American values. It was no accident, therefore, that by the 1890s, with the defeat of the Native American resistance and the rise of capital-intensive extractive industry, American historians were talking about the "closing" of the Frontier. The Frontier had now undergone completely its historical transformation from a topographical to a metaphorical demarkation.

For in truth, American's western migration – since at least the discovery of gold – was not a matter of a steadily advancing border "line" of civilization across empty lands whose fauna happened to include Red Savages as well as Grizzly bears. The "frontier" skipped from Missouri to California, long avoiding the Indian-infested Western Great Plains and the forbidding wastelands of the Southwest's Great American Desert. By the time Americans, buoyed by

Souvenir hunters climb over a wrecked train. The first transcontinental railroad was completed on May 10, 1869, when the Union Pacific line was connected to the Central Pacific line at Promontory Point, Utah.

the "scientific" assurances that "rain followed the plow," started settling the vast interior of the continent, the Frontier had clearly become merely the most recent spot at which they were stealing land from the Indians.

The myth of the frontier had long been used to disguise the fact that western migration was really an occupation, and now that it was no longer needed, the metaphor itself was being discharged. It became Frederick Jackson Turner's Frontier "thesis," an historical theory that came to dominate the way Americans officially thought about themselves and their past for most of the current century. The closed Frontier became the American equivalent of the Greek Golden Age, that period of time when the American character was formed. Always in the past now, the institutionalized Frontier allowed the white denizens of the North American subcontinent to celebrate the virtues of that character while distancing themselves from its ... excesses. All despite the fact that, long after Professor Turner announced the closing of the Frontier, the similarities between the contemporary American West and that of the pioneers seemed much more significant than the differences. The cornerstone of the myth was laid by eastern seaboard land companies promoting western settlement, and it was built upon constantly by local boosters hoping to make a killing in real estate. From

Oklahoma land rush, September 16, 1893. Approval by Congress of the Dawes Severalty Act brought incredible numbers of land-hungry people to Indian territory. On one day alone, April 22, 1889, an estimated 50,000 to 60,000 people filed land claims. The towns of Guthrie, Norman, Oklahoma City, and Kingfisher were created almost overnight.

the very beginning, then, the West was seen as a vast region of inexhaustible living space just beyond the fringe of civilization. Out there in the wilderness there was enough land for everyone, with soil so rich and productive that a man (and his family) could make a good living, if he was daring enough to take a chance and hard-working enough to stake his claim and use it. Thus the image of the rugged individual masked the massive land speculation, fraud, and greed evident everywhere on the Frontier, and we have the spectacle of America's great man of letters, Ralph Waldo Emerson, writing home from an early trip beyond the Mississippi with some distaste about all the talk of quarter-sections while publicly extolling the birth of the New Man, who even called himself by new names – Hawkeyes, Buckeyes, Hoosiers.

Many of the earliest artists of the West were commercial – German lithographers producing panoramas for promotional purposes, the Romanticizing of the region already evident in their brooding Edens overlooking blossoming new towns with smoke – that 19th century synecdoche for Progress – artistically billowing from every smokestack and riverboat. Even the serious artists – Alfred Jacob Miller, Albert Bierstadt – in their painting expeditions of the West in the 1830s emphasized the romantic glory of nature, setting their figures against dramatic background panoramas or illuminating them by the light of a dreamy moon and flickering

Above: standing in line at the Land Office in Oklahoma. In drives between 1830 and 1846, the Creek, Cherokee, Choctaw, Chickasaw, and Seminole were marched along the "Trail of Tears" to what is today the eastern half of Oklahoma. The land was promised as theirs forever …

Top: swarms of grasshoppers stop a West-bound train on the Union Pacific Railroad.

campfire. George Catlin, Karl Bodmar, and Charles Bird King produced fine Indian portraits in meticulously accurate detail, but they had a sure eye for the exotic nature of the subject. And what artist – from Charles Wimar to Thomas Moran – could resist the aesthetic potential of the West's vast landscapes?

As white Americans flocked to this veritable Eden, whose beauty and opportunity were so well attested to by the cultured and the crass, they learned, too, about its heart of darkness. The demonizing of the Indian, of course, began much earlier in American history than the great Western migration. For a century, Indian captivity narratives had enjoyed

great popularity among those in the United States who could read. And while many of them may have been based on fact, they certainly never considered the Indians' perspective – their traditions and culture – but concentrated instead on the degradations enacted on white women. At the same time, and for similar reasons, fanciful biographical accounts of Indian-fighting Frontiersmen – the Daniel Boones and the Davey Crocketts – also attracted huge numbers of devotees.

Such popular propaganda fit nicely into the growing belief that Americans had a special moral endowment among the peoples of the earth that provided them with a manifest destiny to control first the West, then the world, and it should come as no surprise to hear a William Hart Benton calling for the genocide of the Native Americans. Quite simply,

the Indian had to become a devil, so that the settler could destroy him with apostolic zeal while believing all along in his own innocence.

This then was the deep structure of the Frontier myth: an Eden of God-given opportunity and immense natural beauty was occupied by a savage and evil race whose fate it was to be destroyed by the morally superior whites, duty-bound to seizing this paradise through a regenerative violence that would restore their innocence and launch a new progressive era in history. It was a belief shared at some level by almost every Westerner, and it informed every aspect of the region's story, from the desperate need to transform the desert into a garden to prove the validity of the myth, to the moral rectitude with which American imperialists like Teddy Roosevelt conducted foreign affairs.

Above: shooting buffalo on the Kansas-Pacific Railroad, an 1871 woodcut. During the 1860s, around thirteen million buffalo roamed the West, but over the next thirty years, professional buffalo hunters made them all but extinct.

Right: a Union Pacific train snowbound in a drift near Ogden, Utah. In 1893, the Great Northern Railroad was completed, and thousands of Easterners moved with relative ease to the West, weather permitting.

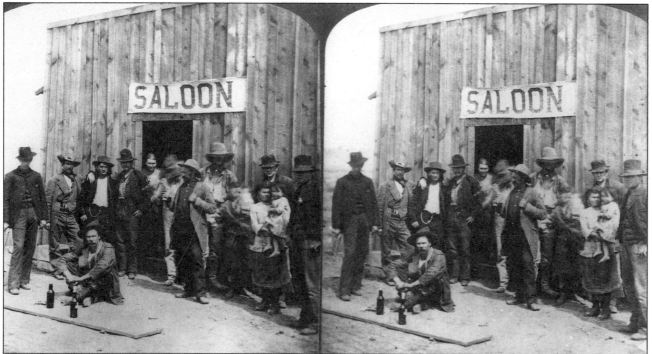

Above: railroad workers clear snow from the tracks. The major railroad of the Northwest was the St. Paul, Minneapolis, and Manitoba, built by Minnesotan John J. Hill. The line, renamed the Great Northern in 1889, ran from the Twin Cities to Winnipeg, Canada.

Left: saloon life in the West. A Western saloon contained rooms for sleeping and a drinking hall. Although cowboys and miners frequented saloons for relaxation, they could be deadly places. In emotional states heightened by alcohol, patrons often engaged in brawls and gunfights.

Buffalo Bill saves a female stagecoach passenger from Indians. His outdoor show went to Europe in 1887 and was performed in London for Queen Victoria.

If the morality play of the Frontier belonged to the West, the saga of the Old West belonged to the East. Boston swells and New York dandies, along with a few globe-trotting Britons, ventured out amongst the Sioux, buffalo guns in hand, the minute Lewis and Clark returned from beyond the Rockies, and they had been coming ever since. After the Civil War, their ranks were swelled by reporters and artists from the illustrated weeklies – *Harper's* and *Frank Leslie's*, the 19th century's television news teams. On their heels came the freelancers, the public relations hacks like Ned Buntline (who lived a life every bit as raucous and disreputable as any Western hardcase), romanticizing burnt-out cases and psychotic killers as heroes in their immensely popular dime-novels about Jesse James, Billy the Kid, Wild Bill Hickok, Calamity Jane and Buffalo Bill Cody.

If some didn't buy it – one European traveler wrote that cowboys impressed him as "brutal and cowardly" – there was always another Easterner like Frederic Remington, who painted historical Western scenes with great drama and an even greater sense of

freedom, or Owen Wister, who wrote perhaps the most popular Western novel ever, *The Virginian*, to put them straight with a new set of exaggerations. The eastern Dude himself would pass into Western mythology as an effete newcomer trying desperately to become one of the boys, failing to much amusement at first, but ultimately succeeding. But it was the Dudes who, in fact, created the "Wild West," and sold it to their pals back East.

And the greatest Dude of them all was Teddy Roosevelt, amateur rancher, future commander of the Rough Riders – a crew of Westerners that Roosevelt recruited to help invade Spanish Cuba. Roosevelt wrote a four-volume history called *The Winning of the West*, and – more importantly – he advertised its contents far and wide. In doing so, he promoted a new image of the Westerner all his own, a hard, enduring, brave and patriotic plainsman, making himself famous enough in the process to become President of the United States.

Westerners themselves were not unaware of the success the Wild West created by the Dudes enjoyed

Above: the railway station in Guthrie, Oklahoma. A few months after the land rush in 1889, Guthrie became the capital of the new Territory of Oklahoma. After it became a state, the capital was moved to Oklahoma City in 1910.

Right: the great Sioux Chief Sitting Bull and Buffalo Bill Cody. Sitting Bull had unified the Sioux against white invaders. In 1875, he had a vision of a massive Indian victory, and, shortly afterwards, General George Custer and his troops were annihilated at the Little Big Horn. But by 1885, Sitting Bull had joined Buffalo Bill Cody's Wild West Show, a sign of how much the Indian way of life had been destroyed.

Left: The Oklahoma Land Rush: Ejection of the "Boomers" based on a sketch by Frederic Remington.

with the American public, and a few were not beyond taking advantage of that creation, especially as some of their marginal professions – army scout and cowboy among them – disappeared or suffered economic declines. Some turned to Wild West shows, like Buffalo Bill Cody's, others took to a new kind of performance competition called the Rodeo, while still others drifted into the movies as stunt men and – very rarely – matinee idols.

The Wild West shows were staged spectaculars, including dramatic reenactments of robberies and Indian attacks, as well as stunt riding, roping, and shooting. In the closing decades of the 19th century they were incredibly popular in the eastern states and even in Europe, but by the early 20th century they fell into decline through a mixture of mismanagement and decreasing popularity.

Cody's show featured "authentic" Indians, including Sitting Bull, who made most of his money selling photographs of himself to members of the audience. Cody, a dipsomaniac and womanizer, was a former scout and famous Indian fighter, and he made and lost a fortune in his show business. By the time he died, he was fat and enfeebled, working for a pittance in a show that played off his name but was owned by someone else.

Rodeo fared better, perhaps because it was less a craven attempts to profit from the loss of the Western soul than a nostalgic perfecting of skills that would

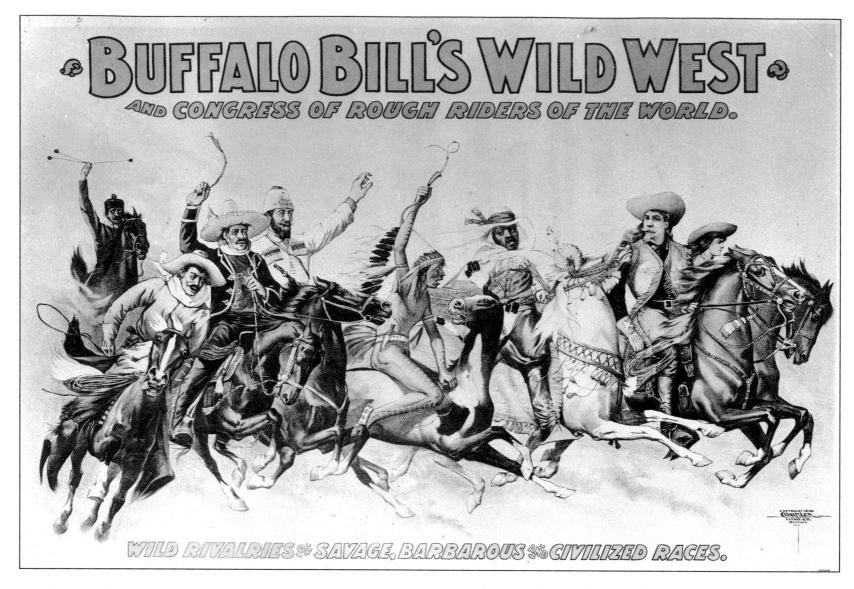

BUFFALO BILL'S WILD WEST
AND CONGRESS OF ROUGH RIDERS OF THE WORLD.

WILD RIVALRIES OF SAVAGE, BARBAROUS AND CIVILIZED RACES.

otherwise have vanished. The founders of rodeo wanted to keep the memory and part of the reality of the cowboy's profession alive by bringing him into the arena, and letting him perform what had once been his everyday tasks. From the first Frontier Days in Cheyenne, Wyoming, when the participants simply tamed wild horses and roped and branded cattle in more or less an exhibition of their past training, rodeo developed into a highly specialized sport, featuring riders specifically trained for its events who performed for glory and good prize money.

Though both the Wild West shows and the rodeo probably did serve to keep a nostalgic vision of the old West alive for a while, the one proved too hokey and the other too ephemeral to serve America's need for a viable Western myth. For that purpose, the movies proved much more serviceable. In fact, movies as a true narrative form and the "Hollywood" western were born in the same film, Edwin S. Porter's *The Great Train Robbery* of 1903 – made in New York.

The genre proved extremely popular, and after the industry moved to southern California in the 'teens, a number of ex-cowhands and old roustabouts begin looking for work as extras, and the rest is history. William S. Hart, Tom Mix, Hopalong Cassidy, Gene Autrey, Roy Rogers, Bob Steele, Gary Cooper, Jimmy Stuart and John Wayne become the cowboy heroes of generations of Americans. In the hands of directors like John Ford, Howard Hawks, Anthony Mann, Sam Peckinpah and Walter Hill, motion pictures more than any other medium perfected and perpetuated the myth of the American West. With a mixture of melodrama and hokum, movies today still manage to pass on the major legacy of western migration – the tradition of violent acts married to pure motives.

On the 12th of July, 1893, an obscure history professor from the University of Wisconsin rose to deliver a paper at the Art Institute of Chicago as part of that city's Columbia Exposition. In reaction to the

Poster advertising Buffalo Bill Cody's Wild West Show. Buffalo Bill first took his show on the road in 1883. For three hours, audiences thrilled to demonstrations of marksmanship and horsemanship. Cody began his life in the West as a rider for the Pony Express.

Above: Buffalo Bill Cody and his gun. Buffalo Bill first gripped the American imagination in a series of novels written by Edward Z.C. Judson, under the pen name Ned Buntline. The first novel, Buffalo Bill, the King of the Bordermen, *was serialized in the* New York Weekly *and later rewritten as a play.*

Above right: Gene Autry and his horse. When Hollywood adopted Gene Autry as its new star for Western movies, he did not know how to ride a horse. Doubles were used for most of the stunts.

New England-dominated academic history of his day, which blithely ignored any event that had occurred south or west of Harvard Square, Frederick Jackson Turner brought his remarks to a conclusion: "What the Mediterranean Sea was to the Greeks, breaking the bond of custom, offering new experiences, calling out new institutions and activities, that, and more, the ever retreating frontier has been to the United States." No one in the hot, stuffy auditorium stirred from their lethargy as he went on to say, "And now, four centuries from the discovery of America, at the end of a hundred years of life under the Constitution, the frontier has gone, and with its going has closed the first period of American history."

In the course of his speech, Turner had argued that the expansive character of American life would not end with the closing of the frontier, but that instead "American energy will continue to demand a wider field for its exercise." The closing of the

Frontier was not so much to be mourned as appreciated, for the subduing of the American wilderness had made its conquerors a superior people.

What Turner had done was to give articulation to the feelings underlying western expansion, for there was a considerable difference between a myth – that set of deeply held, often unspoken beliefs that allows a social group to make sense of its contradictory actions and assertions – and a the codifying of those beliefs into a coherent thesis. Turner may have thought he was simply advancing a reasonable hypothesis for testing by his fellow professional historians, but he was in fact providing the ideological ammunition needed by a nation that, just now completing its internal colonization, was about to follow its manifest destiny onto the world stage as an imperial power.

For the Frontier thesis was both true in the statistical sense – there had always, up until 1890, been a line recorded by successive generations of census takers beyond which the population shrunk to less than two people per square mile, but which the 1890 census declared was "so broken by isolated bodies of settlements that there can hardly be said to be a frontier line" – and wildly misleading in its claims for uniqueness.

Throughout the 19th century land-hungry white settlers from the British Empire had been sweeping across wildernesses wilder than the American West all over the world – in the South African veldt, the Canadian prairies and the Australian outback – provoking native resistances the suppression of which

Below: Captain Jack Crawford, the "Poet Scout," and Gertie Granville.

put to shame the sporadic colonizing of the French and the more localized internal colonization by the Russians and the Americans. Not in the existence of the frontier itself, nor in the harshness of the terrain, nor in the genocidal reaction to indigenous peoples (the Belgians slaughtered eleven million Congolese in scarcely a decade), did the American experience in its western lands differ from that of the rest of the world.

Instead, the United States distinguished itself in its political handling of the colonized lands and in its moral self-assurance. The first was an outgrowth of its revolutionary-spawned republicanism, which resulted in the "mother" country East of the Appalachians treating its western colonies not as colonies, but in the long run as full partners in a single nation. Alone among the expansive powers of the 19th century, the United States established an

Above: the Austin Brothers, Wild West Show performers. Around the turn of the century, several "Wild West" shows competed for audiences. Among them was "Pawnee Bill's Historic Wild West." The format survived until the late 1930s with Colonel Tim McCoy's "Real Wild West" and "Rough Riders of the World" as the last big show.

Above right: The Great West, an 1881 lithograph by Gaylord Watson.

orderly method of creating a single, coherent national polity. That, in combination with the Puritanical belief in the justness of its cause, created the sense of a special moral endowment different from the English and the Dutch, which Americans would call Manifest Destiny.

With its optimism and flattery, Turner's thesis seemed part and parcel of the ideology by which the new imperialists intermingled manifest destiny with Social Darwinism and racial arguments, to respond to pressures from industrial and agricultural groups for new overseas markets, by engaging in a much more activist foreign policy. A McKinley, and especially a Teddy Roosevelt, would willingly ignore the worries behind the rise of Populism to engage in gunboat diplomacy, arguing that the expansive character of American life and American energy demanded wider fields, while reassuring the voters

that, since the wilderness had made them superior people, American individualism would survive every trial. The spread of slums and the growing inequities of industrialism were nothing to pioneers who had reclaimed a continent from a savage race.

Not that any of this was evident the night Turner gave his speech. Indeed, there were no questions at all in the discussion session following, and except for a brief mention in a single Chicago newspaper the thesis was ignored. There was some notice given it along with a bit of faint praise when the State Historical Society of Wisconsin reprinted the speech six months later. However, not until Turner's friend, Woodrow Wilson – the president of Princeton who was himself destined for a higher calling – accepted the ideas, borrowed and adapted them for his own use, and pushed them on anyone who would listen did the theory began to receive the notice it deserved.

A town in the California gold region of Placerville-Hangtown, photographed around 1900. "Western" movies rarely portrayed the Western town as it really was: shabby and rather dirty.

Gradually, other academics and a few editors saw the revolutionary potential of the piece, one being the editor of *Atlantic Monthly*, who wrote about it. As the Turnerian view spread it changed utterly the teaching of history, as professor after professor, high school teacher after high school teacher, politician after politician took up and exaggerated the new theory. Before 1900, virtually no space was given to the West in the standard textbooks, but more than 90 percent of those published between the turn of the century and 1925 trumpeted the Frontier as the major force in America's development as a nation. Turner got a job at Harvard, and as his students scattered and the number of his disciples grew, his thesis became the Holy Writ of a new social gospel.

A reaction to the theory set in during the Great Depression, but it did not last long, as post-war America entered the longest wave of economic expansion in capitalist history, and pundits began talk of the American century. Turner's message seeped into the national conscious and became ideological fact. No history of the West could afford to ignore Turner's ideas. Then, beginning in the 1960s and gaining steam over the next three decades, a number of historians challenged, even rejected the theory. For some it obscured the evident continuities in the history of the region. For others, like Patricia Limerick, it contributed to that most dangerous of

American habits born in the West – believing in the essential innocence of Americans.

The emphasis on the frontier did, in fact, seem to obscure the colonial heritage of the West that remained a clear characteristic of the region. The West's dependance on the central government for its economic livelihood, indeed its tendency to view federal largess as something of a right, is a trapping of the colonial past. Like colonials everywhere, Westerners continued to imagine themselves free of the cultural and social restraints that made life in the East, the homeland, so constricting. Even the West's prototypical fortunes – extractive industry, the huge, plantation-like citrus farms – resembled the typical sources of colonial wealth.

For looking at the West as primarily a Frontier belies the fact that it was really a territory. And a territory was really Republican America's version of a colony. It was a change in political status to statehood that transformed a territory's colonial status, not the advancement of a theoretical line. It seems that Frederick Jackson Turner may have – like many pioneers before him – traded a point in time, statehood, for movement in space, the frontier, in an attempt to escape the burdens of the past and start anew.

Hardly surprising, since Turner was not only a great historian of the American West, but also a Westerner himself.

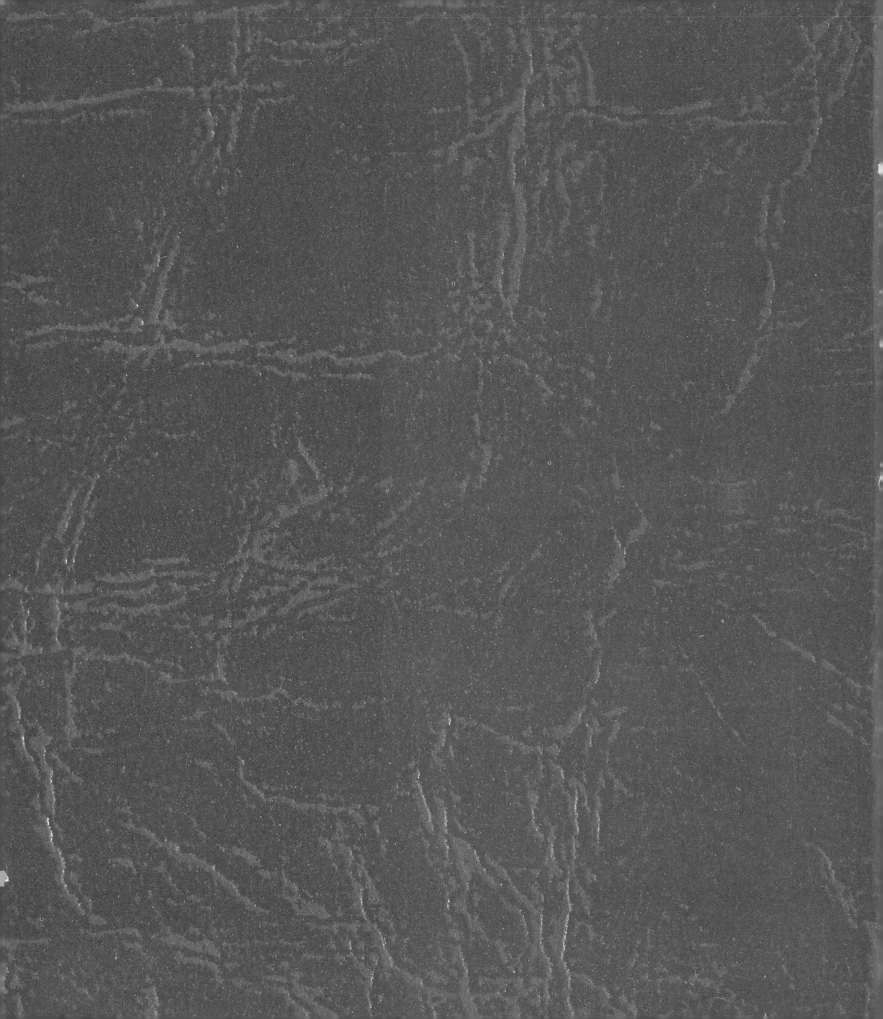